PAUL GOLDING

THE BATTLE FOR BRITAIN

DEAR JAMES
YOURS FOR BRITANNIA

ISBN 978-164945838-4

CONTENTS

This book is dedicated to my grandfathers, Edward and Roy, both of whom started off as fierce opponents of my political views but now support me wholeheartedly...

Introduction

Paul Anthony Golding was born in Sidcup, South East London, on Monday 25th January 1982.

The eldest son of Anthony and Christine Golding, the family were inner-city refugees from the multiculturalism and mass immigration overrunning South London in the 60s and 70s. Paul's parents grew up in the Camberwell district and witnessed first-hand the transformation of whole swathes of the Southbank by immigration.

Anthony's grandfather, Edward, was a war veteran (artillery regiment) who fought at the Battle of Dunkirk in 1940. He spent most of the war in a POW camp (Stalag XX1D) in Poland and then on the Rhine, having been left behind at Dunkirk to keep the Panzers at bay while the British Expeditionary Force escaped on the small boats back to Blighty. Anthony's father, also called Edward, spent the war as a young boy in Pembrokeshire, South West Wales, watching the occasional dog fight between the RAF and the Luftwaffe with his siblings.

Even to this day, the small cemetery at Monkton, just outside

Pembroke, is saturated with Golding headstones, including whole swathes of Paul's close paternal family. Paul's great-grandmother, Elizabeth, was the last person recorded to have been born on Caldey Island off the cost of Tenby, Pembrokeshire.

The whole Golding family are working class through and through and because of this, Paul's grandfather, also called Edward, leaned heavily towards the Labour Party and socialism, as many during that era did. In fact, the young Edward joined the British Communist Party in the early 1950s at a time when Stalin was still in power in the Soviet Union. Edward voted Labour his entire life, but ended up despising the likes of Tony Blair and the rest of the privileged, trendy 'New Labour' sell-outs.

In the 1950s, Edward was conscripted into the army during his National Service years and served in the 1st Airborne Brigade, Parachute Regiment. In 1956, he took part in the Suez Canal conflict and saw active combat, having been stationed at the nearby British Army bases in Famagusta, Cyprus.

Upon his return to the UK after his military service, Edward married a South London girl called Mary, who bore him three sons, the oldest of which was Anthony Golding, Paul's father.

The family lived for many years in rough areas of South London, the children growing up in the tense atmosphere that accompanied mass immigration and enforced multiculturalism at the start of the immigration invasion. Finally, when Anthony married a local girl called Christine, they decided to move to the suburbs of London to a town called Erith, which was completely untouched by mass immigration.

Anthony and Christine were married in Sidcup in 1980 at All Saints church and just two years later, their eldest son Paul was born in the nearby Queen Mary's Hospital.

Erith is the furthest small town on the outskirts of Greater London, in the South East corner of the conurbation. During the

1990s Erith was a peaceful English area, undisturbed by the social and ethnic transformation that was blighting the inner-city areas. Erith, and in particular the Slade Green area where Paul and the family grew up, were heavily working class. Unlike modern working class council estates however, Slade Green was completely free of social ills such as drugs, knives and antisocial behaviour. The youth of the area spent their time playing football, kerbsy, manhunt, cricket and other harmless street activities.

Paul spent his childhood in large groups of friends in youth clubs and engaging in these social activities. The appearance of the dreaded knife and hoodie cultures came later. Paul attended Bexleyheath Secondary School, but showed a complete lack of interest in academic study, instead preferring to spend time down the snooker hall or playing truant with friends.

Paul emerged from secondary school with no education whatsoever, on paper at least. As his parents will attest, Paul preferred to educate himself, devouring books by the dozen and soaking up knowledge like a sponge. He would later be described as a 'human photocopier' by BNP leader Nick Griffin. Paul engaged in relentless study of history and politics, a process lasting decades. By the time he was eighteen, he completely lacked any educational achievements whatsoever, but had read somewhere in the region of five-hundred books.

For some inexplicable reason, at the age of fifteen, Paul began to take great interest in the direction his country was heading in. Completely disinterested in employment, education or sports (except boxing), Paul was gravitating towards politics and began to study the myriad of problems that were transforming his country for the worse. Upon surveying the political landscape of the UK, the only political movement that came close to representing a genuine patriotic fight back against an establishment that was turning Britain into a Third World slum was the British National Party, led at that time by John Tyndall.

Upon leaving secondary education with nothing at all under his belt, Paul decided to join the BNP, although more due to a lack of options than by any genuine conviction that the BNP was the answer to the nation's prayers. The BNP at that time was riddled with genuine racists and extremists, but the only alternative to the BNP was the Conservative Party, which was no option at all having spent the last century - along with the Labour Party - betraying the British people at every opportunity, opening the floodgates to mass immigration and ramrodding us into the EU superstate.

The BNP at that time was going through a period of great tumult, with rival camps vying for control over the party's 2,000 members. One camp, led by party leader John Tyndall, represented the 'hardliners', determined to keep the BNP in the dark ages of racism, fascism and irrelevance. The other camp, led by Nick Griffin, was determined to 'modernise' the party, emulating the success of European patriot movements such as the Front National. To do this, they planned to move the party away from race-based politics and towards a form of civic nationalism that could appeal to a wider strata of society. The two camps were implacably hostile to each other.

After officially joining the BNP in 1999, Paul quickly attached himself to the 'modernisers' under Nick Griffin and campaigned hard for him to win a leadership election that had been called. A bitter internal struggle took place, but Griffin managed to comfortably win and set about revamping the party's image and policies. Had this new 'modernisation' process not been set in motion, Paul would not have joined the BNP, pure and simple. It was only with the hope that Britain's only patriotic party could be reorganised along the same moderate lines that gave the Front National so much success that he decided to join up.

Now safely ensconced as party leader, Griffin quickly took

Paul under his wing and appointed him 'Director of Publicity', giving him control over party publications and cyberspace. Paul quickly rose to become number three within the party and helped Griffin to modernise the BNP's toxic public image. In the year 2000, Paul helped organise and execute a local election campaign that came within a whisker of winning the BNP its first council seat, which, ironically, was in Paul's home area of Slade Green, in South East London. The BNP came second, with a huge share of the vote, knocking the Tories into third place!

Paul's contribution to the 'modernisation' process in the BNP cannot be overstated. For the first time, the party looked like a credible and professional political alternative. The party's leaflets and booklets, magazines and newspapers, looked slick and modern. The party had a professional website for the first time. Things that were viewed as the norm in other parties were now introduced to the BNP. The result of this transformation process, led by Nick Griffin, was to put the party on a gradual upward trajectory to the point where it would win seats in local government across the country and in the London Assembly and European Parliament eventually.

In 2002, primarily due to youthful burnout, Paul spun out of the BNP and spent several years finding work, recuperating and living what can only be described as a 'normal' life for a man in his twenties. During this period, he started to compete in Thai Boxing and MMA fights.

Several years later, Paul re-joined the BNP and started to get back involved, mainly at a local level. By this point, the BNP had dozens of local councillors elected all over the country. It had become a serious force in British politics and was starting to panic the establishment.

Paul and party leader Nick Griffin began to converse again and within no time, Paul was taken under the wing of a marketing specialist that had been bought into the BNP to overhaul its chaotic administration and fundraising affairs, called Jim Dowson.

Jim was having great success dragging the BNP into the 21st century and very quickly put in place an efficient and professional administration machine that led to rapid growth. Jim wanted someone who could work under him to operate the marketing arm of the BNP and, without hesitation, chose Paul. Over the next few years, Jim trained Paul to a high level in marketing, admin and fundraising, skills that were to prove invaluable in the coming years.

In early 2009, Paul was chosen as candidate in a local by-election in Swanley, on the outskirts of London. The campaign was relentless and sophisticated and after a hard slog lasting six weeks, which included canvassing in the snow and sleet, Paul was elected in a landslide with 41% of the vote. The election of the first BNP councillor in the South East of England caused a media frenzy and set the BNP up for its greatest triumph a few months later in the European Elections when it won two seats, despite a media smear campaign of apocalyptic proportions.

During this period, the BNP was completely outclassing UKIP in every way, so the BNP, despite its draw-backs, seemed like the only option for patriotic Britons who were fed up of mass immigration, the rise of Islam and political correctness.

Major disruption to the BNP's ascendancy came a few months after the European Election victory, when Nick Griffin was invited onto Question Time. Griffin's lacklustre performance destroyed his credibility and the party's in the process.Around one in three of all adults in the UK at that time were watching – an unprecedented audience that was squandered. After Question Time, it was all downhill, despite the general feeling that Griffin was 'ambushed' by a hostile panel and handpicked audience.

In May 2010, the BNP achieved reasonable results in the General Election, but its failure to actually win a seat in Parliament led to a collapse in party morale. This precipitated a split in the party, between those who wanted Nick Griffin to step aside for a 'fresh face' and who wanted further dilution of the party's policies and principles, and those still loyal to Griffin. This unnecessary civil war within the BNP effectively finished the party as a viable political force and precipitated an inexorable downward slide.

By now, Paul had been appointed 'Director of Communications' and had been given control of virtually the entire marketing wing of the party, including the media, publications and cyberspace. However, Paul was only too aware of the rapid collapse of the party from serious contender to infighting basket case and this, coupled with Nick Griffin's indulgence on the European Parliament gravy train, led to his resignation. Paul was also unable to stomach a group of talentless idiots Griffin had surrounded himself with, morons who would later depose Griffin and turn the BNP into an invisible, inactive farce. Paul spent less than a year in the political wilderness along with dozens of other senior party officials, including Jim Dowson. Many of these patriots had spent years grafting to engineer success for the BNP and were unwilling to watch as all the hard work was squandered and thrown away.

New organisations were emerging such as the English Defence League and UKIP was achieving national prominence. The political landscape was rapidly changing. The rise of Islam reoriented the focus of the 'patriotic right' towards the wave of Islamist extremism and terrorism that was barraging the Western world. The rise of social media would make it possible for the first time to bypass the leftwing corporate mass media. Rather than the sun setting on the 'right' of politics, a new storm was about to break and one that would propel the New Guard into the mainstream of political discourse. Paul Golding took the reins and lead this resurgence. This is his story…

1. Inception

It is sometimes said that the right wing of politics is its own worst enemy. A seemingly inexhaustible capacity for self-destruction has neutered every attempt to build a resistance since the early days of the 20th century. Widespread support at the ballot box has never been achieved. A genuine, nationwide, grassroots support base has never been established. The right wing in Britain - compared to the dizzy success achieved in other European countries - has been a laughing stock for decades.

Apart from the odd breakthrough or occasional media frenzy, what has patriotism in Britain achieved when compared to the Front National in France? Or the Freedom Party in Austria? The most successful patriotic party here in the UK, the British National Party, achieved moderate success with breakthroughs onto devolved assembly and European parliamentary levels, but then quickly fell apart.

Taking the BNP as an example, there seemed to be an almost religious commitment to repeating the same obvious mistakes over and over again without learning from them. Decisive action to root out idiots who bought the party into disrepute was never taken. Individuals with decades of Nazi or racist baggage were tolerated, even promoted. No attempt was made to protect and safeguard the party's public image. When a few morons burned a gollywog teddy at a BNP event, they were not expelled. There is a saying that 'a few bad apples spoil the bunch' and this sums up the BNP very well. Tolerance of a minority of malcontents and extremists destroyed any chances of becoming a mass movement.

On the flip side, out on the streets among the protests and big marches, the problem was alcohol and a tolerance of hooligan and moronic behaviour. Scenes of drunken hooligans carrying Stella cans in their hands slurring their football chants gave the impression that the only people who make a stand against militant Islam are inebriate morons.

Let us not delude ourselves: The BNP, a party that won seats in the European Parliament, imploded because the fringe elements and their antics allowed the media to paint the whole movement as racists and fascists. Likewise, the EDL was always doomed because of its love affair with public alcohol consumption and rowdy, messy, rabble-like behaviour and conduct.

If anything, the BNP and the EDL serve as lessons to future generations of patriots in how to sabotage your own chances of success. They literally snatched defeat from the jaws of victory. They serve as monolithic examples of how *not* to go about saving your country.

With every patriotic political party or street protest movement in the UK crumbling for the aforementioned reasons, the contingent of patriots that resigned from the BNP were determined, above all, not to repeat the same mistakes again. Enough was enough. If anything had been learned at all from recent experiences, it was this: If there was any hope of saving our country and building a future for our children, any new movement had to rigorously enforce discipline and eradicate any remaining traces of extremism or bad behaviour. If it didn't, it would end up with a toxic public image and toddle along in a self-made political ghetto with no hope of success.

After less than a year in the political wilderness pondering our options, Jim Dowson, myself, and other former senior officials were contemplating the rapid decline of the BNP and the dead-end that the EDL had put itself in. The establishment was so terrified of the BNP's success at the ballot box that it had started the process of promoting Nigel Farage and UKIP as a safety valve for patriotic votes. This process would hasten the demise of the BNP, but backfired on them spectacularly when Brexit became a reality. However, UKIP became the default repository for patriotic voters for many years to come and this effectively put a brick wall in front of the electoral path for any new movement.

By early 2011, Dowson, myself and Andrew McBride, the former South East Regional Organiser for the BNP, had made a firm decision that a new movement must be launched. Something must be done. The BNP was toxic and collapsing. The EDL was running out of steam and its leader was tangled up with various criminal charges, such as fraud. UKIP would eventually run out of steam once its objectives had been met with Brexit. All of this was correctly foreseen during that period.

In early April 2011, the three founding members mentioned above held a planning meeting in Dundonald, on the outskirts of East Belfast. The decision to launch a new movement had already been made, but the details had to be thrashed out. The name, the branding, the organisational structure and so on, were all agreed during an intense three days of discussion and plotting. This was not going to be just a regular political party, this new movement was going to be a complete departure from the mistakes of the past and would embody the ethos that made the British nation so great.

This new movement was to be political, as well as a street activist movement. There was a famous Republican term in Northern Ireland that summed up the Sinn Fein/IRA strategy - they would win via 'Armalite and ballot box' (the Armalite was an automatic assault rifle). Our strategy was to the 'boot and the ballot box', elections and street activities, conventional politics and militancy.

The new movement would rigorously enforce strict internal discipline. There would be zero tolerance for racists, extremists and drunken idiots. There would be a never-ending effort to resurrect the traditional gentlemanly ways of the Victorian and Georgian eras that modern liberals hate so much. If it was going to get done, it was going to be done *right* this time.

There was a general realisation amongst the original three founding members that it would take 3-5 years of hard graft in the wilderness before this new movement gained recognition and became a sustainable organisation. Nothing in life comes quick and easy - everything of value takes time and effort. While some pretenders launch a new group and expect success to fall into their laps, we knew that years of tedious databasing and consolidation of new supporters would be needed, with little initial reward.

The branding of the new movement was key and this took up a lot of the time of the initial planning meeting. For inspiration, we looked to Ulster loyalism. We dissected the parades, the organisations, the orders and the symbolism of Ulster loyalism, steeped as it is in our traditional native British culture and heritage. We unanimously agreed to adopt the traditional British lion as the symbol of our new militant movement. The lion was the key icon of the British Empire, evoking the former glory and power of Britannia. It is also the symbol of England, and the power, guts and glory of the English people. Nothing out there was more suitable.

Using a flip chart, we used traditional marketing methods to continually narrow down the use of certain words. The new movement was to be committed to the maintenance of the Union of the British peoples. It would be a staunch Unionist movement and would seek to mobilise the strength of the entire United Kingdom in the fightback campaign to which we were now committed.

After many hours of intensively thinking about the meaning of each and every possible name, and every word, we made a fateful decision. Cleverly we decided on a name that could not be abbreviated into a toxic acronym by a hostile media, much like 'British National Party' was condensed into 'BNP' etc. We also wanted our name to be a slogan, so every mention of our name would trigger instant recognition of the essence of what we stood for and wanted. The three founding members, satisfied that we had hit the proverbial jackpot, decided on the name of our new movement: Britain First.

This name has proved to be a superb decision. So easy off the tongue, so easy to remember and so easily entered into the sub-conscious mind, it has become a household name. Sooner or later, the sheer patriotic simplicity of the name would be copied by American President Donald Trump, who used 'America First' as his main slogan.

The idea that Donald Trump, a marketing genius, did not encounter, somewhere, the name of 'Britain First' – possibly via our vast social media success - at some stage, and that in turn inspired his use of the 'America First' slogan, is not likely.

Nevertheless, at this early stage of the game, the inception, Britain First was tiny, unheard of with no supporters or members.

The three founding members knew full well that we faced an almost impossible task: To start with nothing and build a mass movement. It was a daunting prospect, with a very real and terrifying possibility of failure that would leave us all destitute and demoralised. It was a colossal risk, but unperturbed by the sheer enormity of our decision, we grit our teeth and threw our fate into the hands of the Almighty.

Most supporters of Britain First are familiar with the big marches, the confrontations with Islamists and days of action in town centres, but for many years before there were any real activities to boast of, the three founding members struggled against the odds to keep the movement going. It was a fruitless, unrewarding slog that drained all of them to the point of nervous breakdown. But, without the first three years of draining, demoralising, sometimes terrible, hard graft, Britain First would not exist. It took three years of suffering and heartache before the movement reached critical mass and took off like a rocket. These years in the wilderness of failure, impotence and near bankruptcy, were instrumental in putting in place the foundations of the movement. Their importance cannot be understated.

Britain First was launched in early May 2011 by posting a magazine, welcome letter and signup form to several thousand patriots around the country. The result was abysmal, with only a tiny handful of folk joining up. Our membership, three months in, would have fit snugly into a phone box! That first mail-out was a complete flop. Britain First launched a futuristic website with petitions and complaint forms in order to capture new supporters and consolidate them into members and activists. But for that first year, everyone had their guard held high where the 'new kid on the block' was concerned. After the first year, Britain First was still microscopic, unknown and ended the year £20,000 in the red.

During the first year or two, the three founding members lived in abject poverty. Everything was poured into the new movement, time, money, everything. At some points, both Jim Dowson and I, living in Northern Ireland, didn't have two pound coins to rub together. A meagre existence was endured. The heating stayed off for weeks on end. Basic, plain, cheap food was consumed. Anything approaching a social life was non-existent. Most nights, for months on end, I slept in an icy, near derelict room, fully clothed to keep warm. It was a miserable existence that lasted several years. A life of poverty was eked out, with the very real prospect hanging over all of us that Britain First might fail and fail spectacularly. But nevertheless, the founding members kept going and going.

Britain First activities during the first three years consisted of publicity stunts (that were ignored), meetings (which hardly anyone attended) and online e-campaigns (in which no one participated). National speaking tours were organised, consisting of around 6-7 meetings, starting in Scotland and ending in Kent. By the end of the tour, at least four of the meetings ended with no one in attendance. The maximum attendance at a meeting during the first three years was approximately twenty individuals. Once again, the second year for Britain First ended with the movement horribly in the red financially.

During the first two years, Britain First was like a bath with the tap fully on, but with the plug out. Members would join, then disappear when they realised just how small and pathetic our organisation was. Activists came and went for the same reason. It was a grinding, fruitless struggle to put the movement on the map. The third year for Britain First followed the same pattern: Paltry growth, political irrelevance, small turnouts for activities and endless frustration. All the founding members had was an unshakeable, obstinate refusal to give up.

Then, on 22nd May 2013, everything changed. A terror attack in South East London, in Woolwich, only a few miles from where I grew up, rocked the nation to the core and transformed the situation. This terrible, shocking crime caused unparalleled revulsion, both at home and abroad. Few could have foreseen the consequences that would follow this barbaric attack. The gloves were off, the battle had begun, and the nation had woken up.

2. Lee Rigby

Lee James Rigby (25 years old) was a drummer and machine-gunner in the 2nd Battalion of the Royal Regiment of Fusiliers. Lee hailed from Middleton, Manchester and was born in July 1987. He served in Cyprus, Germany, and Afghanistan after which he assisted with duties at the Tower of London.

On 22nd May 2013, at around 2.20pm in the afternoon, at the rear entrance to the Royal Artillery Barracks on Wellington Street, in Woolwich, South East London, Lee was walking to report for duty after returning from the Tower. He was wearing a 'Help 4 Heroes' hoodie.

Lee crossed the road to visit a shop before he entered the barracks and as he did he was mowed down by two Islamic jihadists driving at approximately 40mph in a Vauxhall Tigra.

The jihadists, identified as Michael Adebolajo and Michael Adebowale, immediately jumped out of the vehicle and attacked Rigby with knives and a meat cleaver, hacking him to death in the process. They then attempted to behead him. Several passers-by then stood around Lee's lifeless body and tried to shield him from further harm, but it was too late.

Michael Adebolajo, covered in blood and still brandishing a meat cleaver, said the following to a bystander holding a mobile phone: 'By Allah, we swear by the almighty Allah we will never stop fighting you until you leave us alone. So what if we want to live by the Sharia in Muslim lands?'

Twenty minutes after the attack, armed police arrived. The jihadists charged at the police but were shot eight times, wounded but not killed. The jihadists were sent to hospital, the area was secured and Lee Rigby was identified.

This daytime attack on a serving soldier by Islamists triggered a furore unseen in modern Britain. The anger and disgust of the British people was palpable. A wave of anti-Muslim attacks and hostility swept the country. Mosques and worshippers were attacked. Muslims walking the streets were set upon by the hundred. Muslim businesses were targeted with graffiti. There were arson attacks on Islamic centres. Hostility to Muslims exploded on social media.

There was a tangible and widespread feeling of frustration among a vengeful British people. The British Armed Forces are sacrosanct and held in an unassailable high regard by the British people. This shocking, public execution of a soldier in such grisly circumstances by two bloodthirsty Islamist butchers struck at the very heart of the mutual devotion and love between the British nation and their armed personnel. However, there was only one organisation that was prepared to take off the gloves and make a stand. Everyone else who proclaimed to be 'patriotic' and 'counter-jihad' simply engaged in an avalanche of verbal protests and ineffectual posturing and grandstanding.

The slaughter of Lee Rigby triggered a serious and concerted fightback effort against Islamic extremism. There were plenty of other high profile Islamist outrages, such as the abuse directed at the homecoming parade of the Anglian Regiment in Luton, but this was the rod that broke the camel's back. The very next day after the carnage in Woolwich, I visited the scene on my own, having grown up only a few miles down the road and been a regular visitor to Woolwich all my life. Up to this point, Britain First was an ineffectual nonentity devoid of a serious following or activist base. But there and then, when I paced the kerbs of Wellington Street surveying the police cordons, a decision was made that would transform Britain First from a moribund laughing stock into a highly effective direct action movement with millions of followers and hundreds of activists.

Up to that point, opposition to Islamic extremism consisted of hordes of drunken football hooligans making fools of themselves in public while clutching cans of Heineken. What was needed was a highly organised, clandestine body of street activists that would wage an unceasing campaign of harassment and confrontation to known Islamists and their activities.

Little consideration was to be given for the consequences of our actions. The only thing that mattered was a determined effort to suffocate the activities of Islamists and their minions. To do so, our brave activists needed to get up close and personal with some very unsavoury and dangerous Muslims. They also risked the wrath of the politically correct police authorities who would not relish any group of British activists harassing the volatile networks of jihad in Britain. The risks were extreme, but if any further Lee Rigby style attacks were to be prevented, the Islamists needed to be shut down with endless confrontation. If anything, the videos of these high-octane confrontations would raise the general awareness of the problem to a point where police inactivity would become untenable. This strategy worked beautifully.

The problem was, and has always been, that the PC police allow, even facilitate, the most extreme displays of Islamism in Britain. Completely legal patriotic activities carried out by British citizens are subject to the most stringent restrictions and bully-boy interference, but when known terror suspects with long beards scream 'UK go to hell' outside an embassy, the police simply protect and shield them from public indignation. This biased approach was always going to backfire and Lee Rigby and others paid the price.

Both Michael Adebolajo and Michael Adebowale were known to the security services as prominent Islamists. Had they been subjected to the same scrutiny and pressure that the police always apply to patriotic Britons, then poor Lee Rigby would still be alive. Instead, Islamism is allowed to spread and blossom. It's almost as if the police are on their side. In a country determined to protect its citizens, such as Israel or Russia, an incident such as the public beheading of a soldier would attract a decisive and fearsome reaction. Everyone even remotely connected to the perpetrators would be instantly interned. The networks the perpetrators operated out of would be immediately dismantled.

In soft, politically correct liberal Britain, however, things are radically different. The infamous hate preachers that radicalised the killers of Lee Rigby were left untouched. No decisive action was taken to root out the poison of Islamic extremism. The government response to the ensuing crisis was limp-wristed and pathetic. The only consideration was to ensure that Islam itself was not subject to any opprobrium. The media and the body politic were propelled into overdrive, acting as public relations spokesmen for Islam. Islam wasn't to be allowed to take any blame whatsoever for the excesses carried out in its name.

The only consideration on display was for a perceived backlash against Muslims and how terrible it was that Islam was taking a degree of criticism. For many months, the subject of endless talk shows and news bulletins was a supposed spike in 'Islamophobia'. The public was led to believe, by the skilful manipulation of public opinion, that the real problem in Britain was not the growing prowess of Islamism, but the mythical 'Far Right'. Everything was back to front and upside down. This carefully planned reaction by the media and political establishment to turn reality on its head and hide the real problems in Britain was to be rolled out in the wake of every upcoming Islamic terror attack to hit the West, dozens of them. The politicians and journalists of Britain really are a contemptible bunch of traitors and liars. Scum, the lot of them.

By the time I left the crime scene in Woolwich that day, I was firmly resolved to do something decisive about this colossal problem. I realised that Lee Rigby wasn't the first and wasn't going to the last innocent victim of Islamic jihad. The Islamist networks that facilitated Michael Adebolajo and Michael Adebowale were still thriving and operating with impunity across Britain, but specially in London. The police seemed completely indifferent to their activities and presence in London. They couldn't care less. They were busy spending their time on diversity courses and targeting those despicable enough to park on double yellow lines.

That a growing and brazen network of Islamic extremists was threatening the life and safety of the citizens of the capital bothered them little. Hear no evil, see no evil, speak no evil. But one movement cared enough to put itself in the firing line. One movement was bold enough to go head-to-head with some of the most dangerous terror suspects in the country. One movement vowed to drive these Islamists off the streets. That movement was Britain First.

3. Preparation

In the Summer of 2013, Britain was awash with Islamic extremists. On 12 July, Lee Rigby was laid to rest at Bury Parish Church. Prime Miniaster David Cameron was in attendance. The media and political establishment simply waited for anger to dissipate, rather than do anything effective to stamp out or expose the problem.

All focus was applied to ensure that 'Islamophobia' did not gain any momentum in the wake of Rigby's death. The genie was firmly out of the bottle, so to speak, but the establishment cared little. The only consideration was to deflect righteous anger away from militant Islam. 'Multiculturalism' and political correctness were not permitted to take any of the blame for Rigby's death.

It did not take long for compromising photos to appear showing clearly that at least one of the jihadists, Michael Adebolajo, stood shoulder-to-shoulder on protests with the notorious 'hate preacher' Anjem Choudary. Choudary stood at the apex of a network of Islamists and jihadists that held regular provocative activities across Britain. Choudary was given a platform regularly by a complicit media. His face was well known thanks to his incessant TV and radio interviews. Choudary's influence rested not in directly training or ordering jihadists to carry out attacks, but in his ideological and propaganda efforts. He was the main recruitment sergeant for the blossoming Islamic extremist movement in Britain.

Choudary is directly connected to at least one hundred jihadists, either convicted or at large. He has been linked to multiple foiled terror attacks both in the UK or in Europe. After the rise of the Islamic State in Syria and Iraq, Choudary helped recruit hundreds of British born Muslims to go and fight for the caliphate. Choudary was a key figure in 'Al-Muhajiroun' before it was proscribed under terror legislation. Al-Muhajiroun then relaunched itself as al-Ghurabaa, which was then banned. He then led 'Muslims Against Crusades', which was proscribed, followed by 'Islam4UK' and 'Need4Khilafah'. All of these groups were continually banned by the government for their links to jihad.

Commander Dean Haydon, the head of Scotland Yard's counter-terrorism command, said of Choudary and his lieutenant Mohammed Rahman: 'These men have stayed just within the law for many years, but there is no one within the counter-terrorism world that has any doubts of the influence that they have had, the hate they have spread and the people that they have encouraged to join terrorist organisations. Over and over again we have seen people on trial for the most serious offences who have attended lectures or speeches given by these men.' If Choudary had been a white Englishman, he would have been serving life in Belmarsh, probably in solitary confinement. But because he was Muslim, he was allowed to operate with impunity.

On the Continent, the influence of Choudary was so pernicious that the Dutch intelligence agency, AIVD, described him as a key player in Islamic extremism and jihad in the Netherlands.

According to one leftwing think tank in the UK, 'Over the last 15 years he [Choudary] has influenced and inspired over 100

Britons who have carried out or attempted to carry out terrorist attacks at home and abroad.'

On a different occasion, the same think tank said of Choudary: 'In the six months following the creation of the Islamic State, Choudary was its biggest cheerleader in the English-speaking world and the network he helped create became the largest recruiter for IS in Europe.'

Hannah Stuart, of the Henry Jackson Society think tank, said: 'A quarter of all individuals convicted of Islamism-inspired terrorism and terrorism-related offences in the UK since 1999 had direct links with al-Muhajiroun (or its aliases), through public membership, al-Muhajiroun-linked activism or regular attendance at lectures and protests. One in 10 offenders had a proven personal relationship with Choudary in particular.'

It was clear to me that if a serious fightback against Islamic extremism was going to be mounted, it would have to focus on Anjem Choudary and his acolytes. This was a highly dangerous strategy that was fraught with danger, not just from Choudary's minions, but from the politically correct police commissars determined to keep Islamism protected and free to spout their bilge in public. Previous experience with the 'English Defence League' had shown that anyone who dared to confront the 'protected species' of Islamic extremism in Britain would face stiff and determined opposition from the corrupt authorities.

The initial problem was a complete and embarrassing lack of activists to carry out this campaign of confrontation. It was literally just me, on my own. If any fightback activities were to be carried out, they would have to be solo to start with. This ridiculous predicament compounded the dangers mentioned above. But, completely undeterred, I set about researching and plotting.

There is an old saying that 'a fish rots from the head down'. So, to launch this fightback effort, it would be important to adopt a policy of 'shock and awe' and start right at the top of the pyramid. This would gain maximum publicity and exposure, leading to growth and recruitment. It would be no use going after these Islamists in public, to start with, with such paltry numbers. We needed to hit them where it hurt, to unsettle them, to make them look over their shoulders, to 'freak them out', so to speak.

The first step was intelligence gathering. Where did they live? Where did they work? Where could they be confronted? The first obvious line of enquiry was media reports. When reporting on court appearances, the media typically names an individual complete with their home address road name. Upon scouring certain stories online, I noticed that one of Choudary's chief lackies, a notorious Islamist by the name of Abu Izzadeen, lived on Brierley Road, in Leytonstone, East London. It was a good place to start. Furthermore, other online stories described Izzadeen as working at a sweet shop in East London that was owned by the notorious family of Anjem Choudary.

A home address and a workplace, for one of Britain's most notorious Islamists. This was the beginning of what I called 'Operation Fightback'. No one previously had shown the courage to visit the home addresses of known Islamists until Britain First took the lead. Before this moment in time, all 'opposition' to Islamic extremism had consisted of big 'protests' where hundreds of football hooligans, most of whom were completely inebriated, walked the streets giving a hostile media endless ammunition to paint all patriots in a bad light. The clear majority of these so-called 'patriots' had never even clapped eyes on Islamists, let alone confronted them.

Abu Izadeen's real name is Trevor Brooks. He was born into a Christian family from Jamaica, part of the Windrush generation. The day before his eighteenth birthday, Trevor converted to Islam and adopted the name Abu Izzadeen. He then learned to speak Arabic, fluently. Izzadeen frequented the notorious Finsbury

Park Mosque and was radicalised by hate preacher Omar Bakri Mohammed, the chief ideologue of the UK Islamist movement. Shortly before 9/11, Izzadeen visited Pakistan and terrorist training camps in Afghanistan. A few years later, Izzadeen described the 7/7 bus and tube bombers as 'completely praiseworthy'. During this period, Izzadeen openly stated his wish to die as a suicide bomber. Izzadeen was most famous for disrupting a meeting of the then Home Secretary, John Reid. Izzadeen has stated in media interviews that his aim is to bring Sharia Law to the UK and was convicted for encouraging and supporting terrorism, serving many years in prison.

Izzadeen was second only to Anjem Choudary in prominence and influence among the burgeoning radical Islamic movement, so he provided an excellent starting point for a counter-jihad fight back.

His home address was given as Brierley Road, East London, but the newspapers never publish door numbers. There are dozens of houses in Brierley Road, so a level of surveillance and covert intel work was needed to establish which exact property Izzadeen lived in. Upon arriving in this quiet suburban road with only one other activist, and armed with a printed photo of Izzadeen, we politely questioned several residents we caught coming out of their homes and walking down the street. We were very careful to keep a low profile to avoid rattling Izzadeen. Very quickly it was established that Izzadeen lived in the very first house on the road, on the left side.

This was our first 'operation', the first of dozens aimed at harassing and confronting known Islamists across the country. It was a major breakthrough. A moment of great satisfaction. Here we were, two patriots in the heart of heavily-Muslim bandit country, and we had successfully tracked down a major Islamist leader. Izzadeen was completely unaware that a unit of patriotic activists were bearing down on him.

We did not rush into things, we took our time and collected as much solid data and intel as we could to dissipate risks. The next step was to confirm Izzadeen's workplace. Newspaper reports claimed he worked at a sweet shop in the heart of Muslim East London, an establishment owned by a member of Anjem Choudary's family. I thought this was strange as most Islamist activists are proud benefit scroungers. They openly laud the fact that they sponge off the British taxpayer. Rarely do you find a member of Anjem Choudary's retinue in full time employment. Choudary himself encourages reliance on the British benefits system. He was famously caught on a secret recording describing Job Seeker's Allowance as 'Jihad Seeker's Allowance'.

I remember scratching my head whilst investigating this situation. Here was a convicted jihadist and national spokesman for radical Islam, sitting all day working in a quiet sweet shop! Nevertheless, our unit sat on covert duty in the proximity of the 'Yummy Yummy' shop in East London and watched as Abu Izzadeen, a man who declared he wanted to die as a suicide bomber, walked into the sweet shop to start 'work'.

It was time to confront this public menace at his home and workplace, an action we calculated would make the Islamist network of which he is part sit up and take notice. It's one thing wondering around London on protests protected by hordes of police officers, and quite another having opposition activists descend on your home address and workplace! Our aim was to shock these cretins in the places they felt most safe, to unsettle them in the comfort of their own homes.

Once we started and intensified our campaign, as we fully intended to, we knew that we would draw the ire of these dangerous and fanatical Islamists. Our approach was deliberately 'in ya face' and was designed to trigger a massive, robust reaction. We would make their lives a misery. We would make them pay dearly for spouting radical, militant Islam in public. We knew that we were making ourselves prime targets for some of Europe's most dangerous Muslim extremists, but to say we didn't give a damn would be an understatement. On the contrary, we relished the opportunity to get 'stuck in' to these barbarians. No more Lee Rigby atrocities. No more 7/7 massacres. Enough was enough. The gloves were firmly off and we couldn't wait to get face-to-face with Choudary and his fellow tribesman.

4. Battle

Abu Izzadeen, a convicted terrorist and cheerleader for radical Islam, was sitting in his camp little sweet shop on a sunny day in the heart of the heavily-Muslim Whitechapel district of East London, when he must have spotted a group of English activists standing outside giving out leaflets.

He immediately sprang to his feet and marched out of the shop with hostile intentions. Standing there giving out leaflets to passers-by, were two Britain First activists, myself included. Completely unperturbed by the ethnic mix of Whitechapel, a former stalking ground of Jack the Ripper and the Krays but now a hotbed of Islamist activity, we knew full well that within the blink of an eye large numbers of growling Muslims could be mobilised from the warren of historic streets and alleys.

Nevertheless, as Izzadeen approached, walking with an overt display of confidence, the only thought going through my head was that violence was imminent. Instead, we stood our ground, gave Izzadeen a leaflet and told him to his face that he is a 'hate preacher' and that we knew where he lived and we'd see him shortly on his doorstep. Surrounded by a community of hostile Muslims, we warned him that we were nothing like the EDL, charging around the streets drunk, but instead we would take the struggle to his doorstep. Izzadeen put on a brave face, full of contempt, telling me he would 'eat me like a bonbon'. Obviously spending his days surrounded by tubs of sweets was affecting his mind! This was the first time in British political history that a group of English activists had tracked down and confronted a radical hate preacher – and you could see that Izzadeen was slightly confused by the incident.

Izzadeen retreated into the safety of the sweet shop and stayed put. After exhausting our supply of leaflets, we told him through the door we would see him very soon and left the area. A video of the whole operation was put together and uploaded to social media. The response was magnificent. For the first time, I could see the awesome power of social media and the potential it gave to the 'Patriotic Right' to bypass the controlled mass media and go straight to the populace, without the usual politically correct filtering and distortion. The video received tens of thousands of hits and patriots across the political spectrum were commenting in droves, typing messages of support and admiration of our bravery for going into the heart of Whitechapel and confronting one of Britain's most infamous Islamists.

Next stop was Izzadeen's home address and we printed special leaflets to distribute to every resident of the road warning them of the dangerous monster they had in their midst. Imagine if you found out that your next-door neighbour was a convicted terrorist who wanted to die as a suicide bomber!

We saw it as our duty to warn the other residents, most of whom it turned out knew who he was and supported our campaign to the hilt. We leafletted every single house on the road, including Izzadeen's. Once the leaflets were distributed and a short video message detailing our campaign had been filmed across the road,

I threw caution to the wind and decided to go across the road and challenge Izzadeen to come out and face me. I banged on the door for ten minutes solid, shouting at the top of my voice for him to come out and face me.

He was definitely at home as the curtains were continually twitching, but this warrior of the mujahideen refused to come out and face a single individual banging on his door. One thing I have realised over the years about Muslim extremists is that, unless they enjoy decisive numerical superiority, they are the most spineless cowards you will come across. I am pretty sure that if Izzadeen was sitting in his front room with a large company of bearded sidekicks he would have relished at the opportunity to come out and face me. Because we utilised the element of surprise, he was obviously on his own, perhaps with his wife, and thus refused to show his face.

Izzadeen must have been scratching his head wondering what the hell was going on. Organised direct action on this scale against any of Britain's bearded barbarians had never been seen before. Here he found himself confronted by hostile activists causing aggravation outside his workplace and on his doorstep. Surely, he must have thought about what would happen when he walked out his door and down the road the next morning for work: Would he be jumped and taught a physical lesson? What if next time they came back to his doorstep with a much larger team of activists? These questions and many more must have been racing through his cerebral cortex. Sitting in his front room watching TV or praying to Allah in his passageway would be very different now knowing that at any moment the flying squad of Britain First could turn up at his doorstep!

I make no apology for the discomfort we caused to the dozens of Islamists that we targeted. On the contrary, we set out fully intending to cause them as much exasperation as possible. These were the cretins who shouted 'UK go to hell!' on every street corner.

These were the savages that beheaded Lee Rigby. To hell with their feelings. Our only consideration was to wreak as much havoc in their lives as possible, obviously within the law.

We knew that Izzadeen would have relayed the details of our activities to the rest of his cohorts. Good, that means they would be wondering if they were next. I wanted them to be looking over their shoulders, anxious as to whether Britain First would be banging on their front doors. Regardless of who you are, no one enjoys being targeted in such a fashion. But these miscreants had it coming to them and we were only getting warmed up.

The biggest prize was of course Anjem Choudary. Targeting him at his home and harassing him in the street would rock the UK Islamist movement to its core. Like students learning our craft, we used resources like '192.com', electoral registers and press reports to narrow down the scope of our searches. Once we had identified a general target area, manned surveillance then took over. Choudary, unfortunately, was a difficult man to track down. He regularly moves address to avoid detection. We tried every trick in the book to try and generate leads to track him down. I deployed a surveillance unit outside the 'Yummy Yummy' sweet shop where Izzadeen worked but which was owned by the Choudary family. A surveillance unit was placed outside Izzadeen's residence in Leytonstone. A team of Britain First activists stood outside East London Mosque after Friday prayers, trying to spot Choudary to follow him home. All our efforts came to nothing, so we decided on a new tactic. We started stalking everyone connected to Choudary on Twitter and we came across information that Choudary and his groupies were to hold a mini-march from East London Mosque to the top of Brick Lane in protest at Muslims selling alcohol in the area. Perhaps we could follow Choudary home after the procession ended? It was worth a shot.

The day arrived and unfortunately it was only me and another activist in the middle of Taliban country. Two of us facing the hordes. Friday prayers ended and crowds of Muslims poured out of the East London Mosque into Whitechapel Road. Choudary and his gang were spotted making their way towards the start of Brick Lane to a grass area where a Christian church used to stand in Victorian times. Choudary used the open area to rally his troops and after giving a few media interviews, his procession crossed the road towards Osborne Street which led to Brick Lane. In amongst the legions of Muslims lurking about listening to Choudary, I paced in and out of small groups taking in the situation, at great personal risk to myself.

As Choudary and his group reached the corner of Osborne Street, I plunged forward and blocked his path, along with a few other patriots who had come along independently from me to oppose him. In the full glare of the media a small group of around 3-4 of us blocked Choudary's path and refused to let him turn the corner and up into Brick Lane. A Mexican stand-off commenced, with the police pleading with our small group to let the Islamists pass, but we flat out refused.

We hurled abuse at Choudary and his team and exhibited the maximum level of hostility we could muster. Here was the man who radicalised the killers of Lee Rigby and I was no further than ten feet from him. If it wasn't for the police line, I would have rushed him and his team. The stand-off continued, we wouldn't budge under any circumstances, despite the best efforts of the police to persuade us to let them pass. Over my dead body was I allowing Choudary to continue his dastardly procession. The scene was reminiscent of the 300 Spartans blocking the path of the Persians at Thermopylae. A tiny handful of English patriots blocking a much larger regiment of Islamic extremists in the heart of their stronghold of East London.

After a considerable amount of time stubbornly refusing to allow Choudary's march to continue, I found myself overwhelmed by his presence and I determined to get in his face at all costs. I decided to walk out into the road and round the side of Choudary's group. Here was a 'soft underbelly' with hardly any police and I managed to get to within a few feet of him. I pointed directly in Choudary's face and threatened him in front of news cameras and journalists: 'You should be ashamed of yourself Choudary. I'll found out where you live, you'll be seeing some more of me.' It was this moment that changed Britain First forever. The police quickly jumped on me and led me away. But the aftermath of that singular moment would soon propel Britain First into the big league.

The footage of me screaming in Anjem Choudary's face quickly went viral all over social media. The media covered the whole incident and included photos and footage of the confrontation. Following on from this incident, Britain First become a household name among the networks, groups and individuals who made up the 'Patriotic Right' of politics. Everyone was amazed at our bravery and our zeal. Everyone lapped it up. No one had ever confronted Islamic extremists in this way and it filled everyone with renewed hope. For the first time in Britain First history, a deluge of patriots wanted to sign-up as activists. By this point on the timeline, the BNP was evaporating and the EDL was in chaos, enduring a slow disintegration. Tommy Robinson had abandoned the EDL to go and work for a Muslim-led counter extremist group and what was left of that organisation quickly degenerated into a mess. Soon, Tommy was sent to prison for mortgage fraud. This left Britain First as the 'last man standing' and all eyes were now on us. Our hard work, perseverance and creative tactics had paid off. The years of hardship, poverty and obscurity had now paid dividends and the era of Britain First had arrived.

The top priority for me now was to consolidate the avalanche of new support, recruits and members into a functioning organisation. We had to move quickly to take advantage of our new-found notoriety and 'up the ante' so that we didn't slide back into obscurity. We were about to launch a Holy Crusade against radical Islam and as far as we were concerned, we were the modern-day Knights Templar, taking the war to the jihadi extremists with the aim of keeping our people safe. If we could suffocate the activities of Choudary's network, we could possibly prevent another Lee Rigby incident from taking place. That was our hope.

5. Jackpot

In early January, 2014, an activist meeting was held in Dartford, a small market town on the outskirts of South East London. For the first time, large numbers of patriots volunteered to get involved and help take the fight to the Islamists. These new recruits were impressed with our militant, intelligent approach and wanted to participate in these unique activities.

As we sat in a pub in Dartford, talking about the iron discipline and organisation of Britain First, most of these new activists were veterans of the EDL and the general feeling was that big protest marches were a waste of time and achieved little. They relished the chance to get confrontational with Britain's infamous hate preachers. This group of 20-30 new activists formed the nucleus of Britain First for a long time. I did not want huge numbers. I wanted a small, tight, highly organised but brave group of volunteers.

I could see the positives of using small, trusted and disciplined units, rather than relying on unruly swarms of drunken hoodlums, EDL style. We also operated in a particular way: The activities we engaged in we called 'operations' and they were organised along lines that would be familiar to the British Army, the IRA or the UVF. To minimise the risk of informers or touts telling the police authorities what we were up to, information was tightly guarded. I would typically call an operation by posting in a secret Facebook group. I would not give any advance information about what we were up to – all I would detail was the number of activists needed and the level of general danger.

All available activists would then assemble at our HQ pub at Dartford and hand their phones over to a commanding officer. Then, literally two minutes before we were to swing into action, I would outline the details of the operation and then we would immediately embark and set off. Dartford is immediately next to the A2 and A13 roads that lead directly to East London. Within 20 minutes we could be in the heart of enemy territory. Operating in this fashion protected the element of surprise and negated the ability of grasses to inform the authorities in advance of our intentions, not that we were engaging in anything illegal. No one had a clue where we were heading until their phones had been handed in. Then we were in action. It was a tight operation that worked for a long time.

Our first 'operation' in fact was a public protest against the Muslim Brotherhood headquarters in Cricklewood, North London. Although this was generally another pointless street protest, I am glad we went ahead with it purely because what I was told by an old lady that happened to walk past as we were assembling. This was the first Britain First street protest and I remember it well. About 30 activists attended and we intended to try and storm the HQ of the extremist Muslim Brotherhood. Our social media event graphic read: 'We want to show them they are NOT welcome here in the UK! Come and stand with us and show the jihadists that they can leave our fair country and go back to their own country and spread death and hatred! All sensible patriots welcome, please bring British flags. See you there!'

However, a large police and counter-demonstrator presence, coupled with barriers, ensured we could not get near their front door. A total waste of time, purely because we advertised in advance. I would not repeat that mistake again, not when we intended to directly confront Islamists.

When we were assembling at Cricklewood station for the protest, an old lady walked past and stopped to talk to us. I greeted her warmly and introduced myself as the leader of Britain First. We discussed our new militant approach and, completely out of the blue, she declared she knew exactly where Anjem Choudary lived! I could not believe our luck! What a spooky piece of fortune. If I would have called a demo anywhere else, we would not have crossed paths with this elderly woman. I pulled her to one side to guard the information she had and she told me the address in confidence and went on her way. I never saw the old lady again, but we were indebted to her in a huge way. If you ever find yourself reading this book ma'am, thank you.

Immediately after the Cricklewood protest, I swung into action. The address the old lady had given me was in Walthamstow, East London. The very next day I travelled there with a few activists to have a good look around. I drove up and down Bromley Road and surveyed the house in question, a quite large white terraced family house, number 1. The element of surprise was absolutely crucial in this instance, as Choudary could mobilise a huge number of nasty Islamists with the click of his fingers. All of his windows were blocked with heavy curtains which never moved. We dared not knock the doors of the neighbours to ask them for confirmation as they could be Muslims who would warn Choudary. Choudary has very young innocent children too, so we decided to approach this operation with maximum caution.

I left the area but immediately organised several surveillance units to gather the intel we needed to proceed. I even took part in the surveillance myself. I remember sitting across the road from Choudary's house in a car, waiting for him to emerge, doing my best to appear innocuous, when I was told that I was being called a crook and a thief by the EDL who were getting jealous of our growing popularity. Unfortunately, those who dare to call themselves 'patriots' have a nasty and incurable habit of attacking each other, even when the target of the enmity is engaged in honourable counter-jihad activities. I remember doing a video on my mobile while sitting there waiting for Choudary, calling out the EDL for their unnecessary hostility. Britain First makes its yearly accounts public every year. We have detailed accounts submitted either to the Electoral Commission or in the very beginning, Companies House. We have a section on our website which contains all of our annual accounts. The EDL, by contrast, has never produced a single sheet of paper with any financial details on it. All the hundreds of thousands of pounds from merchandise sales and donations that the EDL generated went into a black hole. No one has ever produced anything to show where the money went. But here was the EDL calling *me* a crook! You couldn't make it up - but unfortunately the hypocrisy was completely lost on the drunken hooligans of the EDL.

This is a recurring characteristic of 'patriots' when they attack each other: Someone always accuses the other side of being 'in it for the money'. Let's get one thing straight: There is no money on our side of the political fence. Being a patriot or a nationalist is perhaps the worst strategy for making money you can conjure! If I wanted money, then I would have joined the Conservative or Labour parties and stuck my nose in the taxpayer trough. Why, if I only desired 'money', would I decide to become a prominent 'far right extremist'? It doesn't make sense at all. Becoming an infamous far right activist virtually guarantees that you will never be able to make money in your career! So, I find it particularly nauseating when I hear numerous buffoons claiming that people like me are 'in it for the money'. There is no bloody money to be made when you take on the establishment and radical Islam – precisely the opposite in fact. Choosing the life of a chief of the 'far right' brings only poverty, misery, persecution, hardship and suffering. Even when patriots do manage to earn a few quid - perhaps from the sales of books or some suchlike - they have to endure endless adversity, calamity and torment. After a few days of solid surveillance, I got a call from one of our volunteers: He reported that Anjem Choudary had pulled up in a car and walked his family into the property. It was *definitely* him. I pressured the activist over and over again, 'Are you sure it was him?' He swore over and over again it was definitely him, 100%. I remember thinking, 'Jackpot'.

Muslim extremists do not drink alcohol and our activists have to work during the day, so with these two considerations in mind I decided the best approach would be to carry out our operation on a Friday night. I posted a call to action in our secret Facebook group and told them this was a very important operation and that they would not want to miss it. Around twenty activists arrived at our pub HQ in Dartford and we followed our usual procedures. Just before were set off, I briefed all the members of our unit on the operation at hand, with one detail left out: I said we were going to confront a famous and notorious Islamic extremist, but omitted to mention it was Anjem Choudary. I was terrified the information might leak, so I told them I would inform them who it was as soon as we arrived in the vicinity of his house. We jumped into a minibus and several cars and headed for Walthamstow.

Thankfully, in an adjacent road there was a small public car park which was conveniently positioned. We stopped in the car park and disembarked, immediately filming a quick intro to the inevitable video that was to be produced for the operation. With that out of the way, a mob of us marched the small distance to Choudary's house, a scene which could have come straight out of the film 'The Football Factory'. These operations are always 'hit and miss' and many of them in the future ended in failure. When we turned the corner into Bromley Road and arrived outside his house, to my horror the whole house looked dead and empty, no lights and no sign of life. I was extremely annoyed, as by this point we could have lost the element of surprise by one of the neighbours looking out their windows and wondering what the hell a large mob of men was doing outside number 1! They could have rung the police or told Choudary the next day. The whole operation looked like a flop and I was very depressed as I prepared to lead the troops away from the scene empty handed.

I was very disappointed, but then fate intervened. Suddenly our activists started shouting and hollering and running with haste towards the entrance of the road. A general rush began with loud shouts and frantic behaviour! Personally, despite being the commanding officer on the scene in charge of the operation, I did not have a clue what was happening. My activists, however, knew exactly what was happening and were acting without direction: Anjem Choudary himself had entered the road in a small Japanese car but had stopped when he saw our small army standing outside his house!

He was spotted when he tried to reverse out of the road in a blind panic and our activists simply rushed his car, like barbarians charging at the gates of Rome! Our brave activists surrounded his car – one even jumped on the car bonnet to try and prevent Choudary's escape! According to our activists, Anjem was terrified and desperately trying to swing his car round to make an emergency escape. God help him if our activists would have stopped his car. He thrust his foot on his accelerator and literally drove through our activists nearly running them over. He then completed his escape and drove off as fast as he could on the wrong side of the road to avoid traffic lights that happened to be red.

This was the start of the fightback against Britain's Islamic extremists! Here was the most infamous and notorious hate preacher in the UK, having to wheel spin away from his own home because a team of British patriots had ambushed him and given him the shock of his life. Given Choudary's prominence and the militant nature of what unfolded in Bromley Road, this operation really cemented Britain First into a feared organisation amongst the Islamist movement. The liberal-left were fascinated and horrified by the ascendency of this never-seen-before phenomenon. The media were desperate to cover our activities. The establishment were scratching their heads wondering where on earth this bizarre new group had appeared from!

The video of the operation ended with the famous Army portrait of Lee Rigby with the words: 'The day Lee Rigby was murdered, thousands of patriots were born. Rest in peace Lee Rigby. Rest in the arms of angels. The fightback has begun. We are the British resistance.'

The BBC was soon describing Britain First as the 'most dangerous far-right party' in British history. Our activists left the Walthamstow area with immense pride in what they had achieved and they deserved to be praised as true heroes. What they had done took guts and courage. We arrived back at HQ on a euphoric high, but utterly determined to accelerate and expand our campaign of direct action. It was us versus the Islamic extremists and we intended to hound them to the ends of the earth for as long as it took to drive them off the streets and into their proverbial caves. We wanted them quivering with fear and terrified to go out in public. Anjem Choudary, the man who radicalised the killers of Lee Rigby, was now driving around the streets of Walthamstow completely shell-shocked and unable to return home. A good night's work.

6. Backlash

That same night after our ambush of Choudary, the Islamist groups reacted with satanic fury. A group known as 'Islamic Emergency Defence' threatened violent reprisals unless their beloved leaders were left alone. Twitter was saturated with angry threats from every Islamist on the scene, including death threats and threats to retaliate in kind, by visiting our home addresses.

Over the next 24 hours the media publicity of the raid at Choudary's home address whipped up all of London's extremist Muslims into a frenzy of bitter recriminations. This kind of vitriolic reaction was new to us and was absent when we opposed Abu Izzadeen. This was something entirely different. Harassing their beloved leader and spokesman sent the Islamist networks into an orgy of anger and hate. 'Islamic Emergency Defence', in reality simply a cover name for every naughty terrorist wannabe surrounding Choudary, was pumping out warnings and threats of every kind. There were threats to me. My family. To my home address. Warnings of an imminent jihadi apocalypse unless I backed down and apologised. 'Islamic Emergency Defence' warned us not to return to Choudary's home as they had now deployed legions of inbred Taliban tribesmen to his address.

Our reaction to this tsunami of venom and vituperation was immediate: We got another team together and went straight back to Choudary's home address! Based on the endless conveyor belt of hate and threats over the last 24 hours, we expected Choudary's home to be a veritable fortress patrolled by his minions. However, when we arrived at number 1 Bromley Road in Walthamstow, to our surprise, we found the property and the general area surrounding it completely deserted! Choudary had fled. Despite the posturing and grandstanding, 'Islamic Emergency Defence' was nowhere to be seen. All that hot air and none of these brave warriors of Islam could be bothered to come out from behind their laptops! Bunch of whining morons the lot of them. No backbone whatsoever.

Just to prove a point, our team got back in the minibus and headed across East London to the home address of chief hate preacher number two, Abu Izzadeen. I jumped from our vehicle and banged on his door challenging him to come and face me. Again, the house looked completely deserted and devoid of life. Had our operations caused these ayatollahs of hate to flee London? This was supposed to be the 'cream of the crop' of radical Islam and here they were, getting a dose of their own medicine and instead of standing their ground and displaying their mettle, they had apparently fled to the moon!

To end the evening's rather disappointing activities, the team headed to finish the video of the operation immediately outside East London Mosque. Our video ended with the words: 'Britain First will respond to any threats or intimidation by striking back immediately. We will never be cowed into submission, ever.' By the end of the evening, it was clear that 'Islamic Emergency Defence' was a non-existent social media account, nothing more. Instead of waging a ferocious jihad against our movement, Choudary's underlings had evaporated into thin air. The Prophet Mohammed would be so proud!

Just for good measure, a few days later, our team returned to Choudary's home address and then to Izzadeen's. No sign of life whatsoever! We stood outside Izzadeen's house chanting, 'Terrorist scum off our streets.' For the first time ever, the media were in attendance with us, eager to cover as a story our unorthodox activities. We hurled our chants at the top of our voices, prompting the neighbours to look through their curtains with curiosity. I remember doing a full-blown TV interview in the road outside his house. Just as I finished the interview, a car full of Muslim men stopped at the top of the road, wound down their windows and stared in silence at our group. They then sped off. Was this the first sign of life of a Muslim patrol? Had the dreaded mujahideen finally decided to show themselves? Whoever they were, they did not return. Brave warriors indeed. These are the lowlife cretins who set off bombs on tube trains killing innocent individuals. There was one thing that was clear, extremist Muslims were cowards, pure and simple. This was a theme that was to repeat itself over and over again during the next few years.

At this stage, we decided to venture to a new area that was inundated with hordes of Islamic extremists: Bury Park in Luton. We tracked down the infamous Luton based hate preacher Saiful Islam to Kenilworth Road, home of Luton FC. Out of the blue we attended his home address, but despite twitching of the curtains, he refused to come out and face us. Saiful Islam was the most prominent of Luton's Islamists and a follower of Anjem Choudary and exiled Islamist Omar Bakri Mohammed. He is a vocal supporter of Osama Bin laden. He is also a founding member of Al-Muhajiroun, a group banned for the glorification of terrorism. According to media reports, 'It is Saiful's mission to overthrow the government and impose Sharia law in the UK, which he says will solve many of the country's problems.'

Since the infamous hate preachers of London and their followers had evaporated like a Nile mist, what were we to do now? By now Britain First was becoming a serious force on social media. Our efforts were concentrated on Facebook and by this point we had around 200,000 followers all over the world. Our brand of confrontational politics was proving immensely popular with the ordinary folk of the West. We started to attract a gigantic following in America, which soon would eclipse even our UK support base.

The total number of 'likes' on Facebook hides the really impressive stats from behind the scenes. Britain First loved to screenshot these analytics and post them for the world to see, leaving the media with gaping jaws. Britain First, with just 200,000 followers, was reaching anywhere between 20 and 60 million users per week with our videos and static posts. I remember one month where we reached a whopping 110 million unique users worldwide. These stats left the establishment flapping with terror, knowing that thanks to Facebook we were reaching more people every week than the BBC! That's true, organic power. We used social media to bypass the controlled mass media and took our message straight to the people, with dazzling results.

A few days after the final visit to Choudary and Izzadeen's home address, a large contingent of police officers arrived at my father's house looking to arrest me. Unbeknown to me at the time, this was the beginning of a campaign of persecution of epic proportions. Not anyone previously, Nick Griffin, Tommy Robinson and so on, would be targeted and harassed like I was. I knew on a basic level that there would be a backlash from the authorities to our activities, but when viewed from beginning to end, the efforts of the state to silence me and my movement would be apocalyptic and on a scale like Britain had never seen before.

My father let me know immediately what had happened at his

home. He sent the officers away packing, telling them that I did not live there. The next day I decided to hand myself in to see what all the fuss was about. I walked up the desk of the police station in the Dartford area and I was immediately arrested. I was taken by police car to Ebbsfleet Police Station in Gravesend. There to greet me were officers from a police division I had never heard of, but who would feature heavily in my life for many years to come. I was kept in a cell for a long time and then interviewed by officers from 'SO15 Counter Terrorism Command'. I remember chuckling to myself, had I unknowingly committed an act of terrorism? What were these jobsworths up to?

After an agonising silent interview, where I refused to answer any of their questions, I was released on police bail. They had arrested me for the ambush on Anjem Choudary. It is a standard rule within our movement that if arrested in the line of duty, you are to remain silent no matter what pressure or aggravation the police give you. The police are there to secure convictions, not to be your friend. These professional manipulators know every trick in the book. They have years of experience. They will lead you down a path that will incriminate you, if you let them. Their job is to convict you of crimes – they are not there to be nice and to help you. They are looking to shaft you, pure and simple.

If any of our activists speak during a police interview, they are immediately expelled from our movement. The mafia know how damaging it is speaking to the police during an interview. That's why they have their code of silence, the *Omerta*. To speak during a police interview will end with a death sentence in the mafia. Several of our activists have incriminated themselves over the years, simply by speaking in police interviews. Conversely, lots of us have escaped prosecution simply by keeping our mouths shut. Every activist in Britain First is told, keep your mouth shut, *always*. This is not because we are a criminal enterprise, but because we face corrupt and politically-motivated police attempts to abuse our civil liberties. Why help them secure a prosecution by talking to them?

No inference is draw in court by silence during a police interview. You have a right to silence. This is explained to you by police officers during every arrest, the standard caution given to everyone who is taken into custody: '*You do not have to say anything.* But, it may harm your defence if you do not mention when questioned something which you later rely on in court. Anything you do say may be given in evidence.' During my first interview by S015, I did not say a word.

I was released on bail and was immediately back to the grindstone. There was widespread outrage and shock that I had been arrested simply for harassing Britain's most notorious hate preacher. The authorities aren't very bright. They never calculate that with every arrest and act of harassment by the police, our support grows and consolidates. The reason for this is simple: Police psychological analysts always conclude that every human being has their own breaking point where they can take no more. Most of the time this threshold is very low.

So, the police work on the basis that all they have to do is drag a person through the barbed wire and make them endure enough hardship and their willpower to carry on will collapse. Arrests, prison, court, restrictions, injunctions, conditions, bail and sooner or later the subject that is causing them a nuisance will crack and give up. It has happened many, many times.

However, once in a generation an individual or small group of individuals come along that buck this general trend. Not only are they impervious to the most horrendous suffering and persecution the state can throw at them, but they seem to feed and thrive on being persecuted. These individuals seem to define themselves by the amount of punishment they can soak up and carry on with the fight. They are unbreakable and unshakeable and the establishment hates these types the most. A special place in hell is designated to them by the establishment. To be a leader, a real leader of men, you must be cut from this cloth or you will not last a season.

This war against the establishment and radical Islam is no joke. You will end up dead, in prison or ruined. The police hope that by subjecting every patriot to a dose of harassment, they will buckle and quit. All I can say is this: Britain First will never buckle, quit, surrender or back down. By the end of this book, you will be shocked at the level of dirty tricks, harassment, sabotage, disruption and subversion that the authorities have thrown at myself and my movement to try and stop us in our tracks. By the end of this work, you will be forced to admit that we no longer live in a 'democracy', but in a post-democratic, leftist-dominated political oligarchy where freedom of speech and political impartiality are dead and buried.

Speaking for myself, I do not recognise the word 'surrender' – it is not a word in my vocabulary. People do not understand what it entails being a 'leader' until you are in the driving seat yourself. It is not an experience that can be replicated or simulated. It is a unique type of brain-destroying stress that permeates your entire life. Your name and reputation are dragged through the gutter every day. You are subjected to the most vile, dishonest and disgusting smears imaginable. You are arrested, imprisoned and your freedom is curtailed. You face serious threats to safety and credible threats to your life. You cannot operate and live like a normal person. You face danger in public every time you venture out. You have to change vehicle regularly to negate being tracked down. You have to change residence every six months for the same reason. Those you counted as friends walk away and disown you. You lose access to children because of your notoriety. You find it impossible to find a partner because you are socially toxic. You end up living in relative poverty with no prospect of improvement. You are endlessly dragged through the courts on Mickey Mouse charges. Anxiety, worry, stress and hardship become your only true friends. You end up skint, hated and facing danger, estranged from your family and friends and mercilessly persecuted by the state.

If you manage to negotiate your way through this living nightmare without falling apart, then you can enjoy years of horrific struggle against monstrous odds with little prospect of success. All you really possess - and all that keeps you going - is the knowledge that you are 'doing the right thing'.

Ask yourself, right now, do you want to assume this level of responsibility? Do you fancy for yourself this horrendous lifestyle? There is not a day that goes by when people in my position don't dream of a 'normal' life. I positively despise and hate politics and politicians. I am an anti-politician. I would love nothing more than to down the tools and use my talent and drive to enjoy my own life. I think I would do quite well in the 'normal world'. But, that is not the 'code' that I live by.

I am nothing special. I grew up on a rough London council estate in a broken family with a single mother who raised us mainly on benefits. I left school with no education and had the chips stacked against me. I do not, however, consider this an excuse not to use my life in the service of my nation and God. We all perish and are eventually forgotten. The only thing that matters is that we sacrifice ourselves for our children and grandchildren.

That's what Britain First is all about: Sacrificing ourselves for future generations. We do not want money, or career, or advancement. To hell with all of that! All we want is to fight for our country against the evil vermin that are undermining it. If we have to suffer along the way, so be it. If we have to give our lives, then bring it on. Better to die on your feet than live on your knees. Better to fight and die than live and be a coward. Better to go down in a blaze of righteous glory than live a comfortable life of shame.

Unless you understand this aspect of our movement, you

haven't got a clue what we are all about. By realising that we have already decided to perish in the service of our people and nation, you will understand that no amount of persecution and sabotage by the authorities will dampen our spirits or hamper our fightback. There is nothing that will stop us in our tracks, except death. Even if death should catch up with us, there will be an endless supply of patriots ready to carry on the fight as our nation is overrun and dismantled.

Britain First is more than just a new set of policies, or a new manifesto for an election, or simply a new choice on the ballot paper. We are a new way of life, a new way of thinking and viewing the world. We are a spiritual, holy movement determined to carry out God's will on earth. We are a new philosophy, a new doctrine, a new creed. It is this that sets us apart from all other attempts to build a 'resistance' political party or organisation. So many have come and gone since Britain First was founded, but our movement has stood the test of time and pressure. We stand strong and proud and unbowed despite the best efforts of our powerful enemies. Understanding the factors that have been outlined in this chapter is critical to understanding not only our movement, but the rest of the story outlined in this book.

7. Patrols

After the initial operations against the famous hate preachers, most of the prominent Islamists went to ground. So, we decided to broaden our scope of activities. East London during 2014 was awash with Islamic fanatics and extremists. I did not want to confine myself to taking action against extremists only, but wanted to shake the communities that tolerated and facilitated them.

From 2012 onwards, East London was plagued by gangs of hardline Muslim vigilantes that roamed the streets harassing folk. These miscreants became known as the 'Muslim Patrols' or 'Sharia Patrols'. Many of the Islamists taking part in the patrols were acolytes of Anjem Choudary and Abu Izzadeen and some were from a group called the 'Sharia Project'.

These patrols walked the streets wearing hoodies and face coverings and confronted pedestrians with demands that they behave in an Islamic fashion. One report stated: 'They targeted prostitutes, people drinking alcohol, couples who were holding hands, women whom they considered to be dressed immodestly, and harassed others whom they perceived as being gay.'

Videos were uploaded to YouTube and social media by these Muslim patrols, causing universal outrage. Something had to be done about these unwelcome pests. The problem has always been that these Muslim patrols actually enjoyed a large degree of local Muslim community support. Forget the liberal garbage pumped out by the controlled mass media and the false, misleading protestations from Taqiyya-spouting Muslim 'community leaders'. Going into areas like Whitechapel to confront militant street gangs was a risky business, but we were more than willing to get the job done.

While finding these 'patrols' walking the streets carrying out their nefarious deeds would be difficult, we could always cause a stir within the community, raising awareness and drawing attention to the presence of 'Muslim patrols', prompting action from the police and local politicians. The presence of Britain First has always been the same, like pouring petrol onto a bonfire. If the authorities or local establishment refuse to take action to rid the area of Muslim patrols, we would highlight the situation to such a degree that firm decisive action would be *unavoidable*. Locking horns with aggressive Muslim patrols was right up our street and we couldn't wait to get stuck in.

Thankfully, one of the new activists that signed up beforehand owned a decommissioned British Army Snatch Land Rover. This vehicle had seen action in the deserts of Afghanistan. It was completely impenetrable to crowds of hostile, unarmed civilians. This new vehicle was a great way of keeping our activists safe if the situation spiralled out of control and had the added bonus of overawing the media and the local populace, who could not believe their eyes when a large crowd of flag waving Englishmen arrived complete with military vehicles. It made our counter-patrol activities far more newsworthy.

These armoured Land Rovers provided superb protection for our activists. Armour plated and sporting bullet proof windows with steel cages covering all outlets, if trouble kicked off within the heart of a hostile Muslim community, when locked inside our activists would be perfectly safe, even if a crowd of 1,000 screaming Muslims were trying to destroy the vehicle.

We had thousands of leaflets printed up, ready to be distributed. The Land Rover was fuelled up and prepped and our activists were briefed at our HQ pub in Dartford. We decided we would enter the beating heart of the East London area, Brick Lane, and carry out our own 'Christian Patrol'. The idea was simple: We would arrive in the epicentre of the area that had seen these Muslim patrols and our very public, loud and ostentatious activities would draw the local militants out of the shadows.

We developed some novel tactics too: We would leave a small group of white English activists outside East London Mosque drinking cans of (empty) beer, hoping to draw the ire of the Sharia gangs. These small gangs were left outside the Mosque, on Brick Lane and on Bethnal Green Road. Unfortunately, this tactic never worked, but it's always better to give good ideas a go as you never know what will work and what will not until you try.

By contrast, the patrols down Brick Lane created a furore. We started at the beginning of Brick Lane, which is actually Osborne Street, and two separate teams of activists walked on each side of the road giving out leaflets to the local - predominantly Muslim - population, with the Land Rover driving slowly along the road in the middle. It was a well organised, smooth running operation and discipline was never compromised.

The local Muslims stood in total shock as this solid formation made its way slowly up Brick Lane, their jaws gaping with the sheer brazenness of our display. I moved from one side of the road to the other for the length of the road, holding a radio to communicate with all our activists, watching for signs of trouble brewing. All I could hear from our activists was 'Christian Patrol, take a leaflet' on all sides.

Local Muslims stopped our activists and tried to claim that there were no such thing as Muslim patrols and that we were mistaken. The local Muslims were in complete denial, despite the Muslim patrol stories being reported universally across the media apparatus, even internationally. Sometimes our activists would lay down the law to these incredulous local Muslims: 'This is our country, you want to live here you have to abide by our laws.' The video of this operation ended with the words, 'The Christian British are in town, and we are not happy!'

The reaction by the media to our brazen activities in East London was explosive and widespread. Literally every single media outlet above regional level in the country covered the story and likewise across the Western World, in North America, Australia and Europe. Major entities such as the BBC, RT and so on were desperate to join us on our next 'Christian Patrol'.

The video uploaded to Facebook received hundreds of thousands of hits. The usual gaggle of local community 'leaders', politicians, MPs and faith leaders condemned our activity in the strongest possible terms. Our first march down Brick Lane caused a massive frenzy of support and condemnation. Patriots were pleasantly shocked that we had the gall and temerity to enter such a dangerous area of East London. On the political liberal-left, there was unbridled shock and outrage. Nevertheless, we intend to highlight the issue of Islamic extremism and patrols in East London and we succeeded.

Two to three weeks later, we decided to repeat the operation, again marching down Brick Lane through the heart of the local Muslim community. Again, the awesome spectacle of an armoured, camouflaged British Army vehicle was on display. This time, however, the local constabulary were ready and waiting for us. As we passed through the Blackwall Tunnel, a large contingent of police officers swooped on our convey. My best guess is that a marker was put on the registration number of the Land Rover and as soon as that pinged on the cameras in the tunnel, the police were alerted and swung into action.

The strange thing was that the police pounced on us almost immediately as we came out of the tunnel on the northern side of the River Thames. They must have been sitting there waiting to pounce, literally. The officers demanded they inspect our Christian Patrol leaflets and kept us stood there in a car park for a considerable amount of time. Where they giving their colleagues time to mobilise in Whitechapel? The officers knew our names and where we were going, which made me suspicious: Had someone snitched on us? One of our own activists?

This night we had an RT media team with us who filmed everything. After an inordinate amount of time talking waffle with the police officers, they let us go and we headed off into Whitechapel, flanked and followed by police cars. To be honest, I did not mind their presence. It simply meant that if there was any trouble that evening, the police would be immediately at hand.

Once again, a 'Christian Patrol' complete with military vehicle was making its way slowly up a packed Brick Lane. This time the police and media were with us, guaranteeing a greater impact than last time. There is a strange thing that happens every time Britain First is active in a Muslim area and the police are present: The Muslims in the vicinity become brave. On the first Christian Patrol the Muslims present in Brick Lane did not act aggressively or verbally abuse our activists. This time, because the police were present, things were different. The sight of police officers and the safety they provide, transforms most Muslim extremists into courageous warriors! No police, no trouble. Funny that.

Hundreds of leaflets were distributed again and our presence gripped the attention of the entire area. Diners and staff came out of restaurants and curry houses to watch our procession pass. The police stalked us relentlessly looking very nervous indeed. But there was nothing they could do – our activity was perfectly legal. The RT media team with their bright lights and huge shoulder mounted cameras flittered from one side of the road to the other, interviewing locals and our activists in quick succession. This operation led to another frenzy of media coverage and interest while the video of the activity led to hundreds of thousands of hits and thousands of new followers. Britain First was taking off like a rocket – all eyes were now on us while everyone else on the counter-jihad landscape melted away.

The reaction to our latest provocation was predictably ferocious. A spokesman for Scotland Yard said: 'Police at Tower Hamlets are aware of an internet video showing recent activity in the Borough. We will work with our partners in policing the diverse communities in Tower Hamlets to provide a safe environment for those who live, work and visit the borough. The Metropolitan Police Service takes these incidents very seriously and any activities that may raise community tension will be monitored.'

A spokesman for the East London Mosque said: 'Britain First's patrol does not represent Christians, just as Al-Muhajiroun's patrols did not represent Muslims.' As expected, some of the media reports were peppered with outright lies and falsehoods. For example, the Daily Express accused us of walking down a 'Muslim street' giving out 'booze' – a complete lie which *never* happened. Our video ended with a call to action, urging British patriots to stop playing 'toy soldiers' and to join our resistance movement that was growing into a serious and disciplined organisation.

The end result of our 'Christian Patrols' was a massively increased awareness of the problems of Islamic extremism in East London. The local media, MPs, clergy and community councillors were all stunned and could only offer as a response stiffly worded condemnations. It's funny, because in all my searching and research, I could not find evidence of such vociferous condemnations from any of these politically correct characters to the Muslim patrols.

There was a key difference of course: The Muslim patrols intended and succeeded in harassing the local community. Our patrols were simply designed to counteract the pernicious presence of the Muslim patrols. We did not harass or intimidate the local population. We did not verbally abuse local revellers, homosexuals or women. We simply warned the local population of the presence of Sharia Patrols and urged them to get in touch with us if they had any advance knowledge of their activities.

Our processions down Brick Lane sparked global media interest. Our HQ was swamped with media enquiries and requests for media teams to join us on any of our future activities. Britain First was, of course, widely mocked on the political left during this period. But, within the space of a few months, we had struck effectively at the hate preachers and convicted terrorists of Al-Muhajiroun and had caused a mighty stir across East London. We had attracted international publicity and a gargantuan new following on social media. We had propelled ourselves into pole position among the disparate groups and organisations on the 'Patriotic Right' of politics.

Then, to my astonishment, I received a phone call from a senior officer of SO15 Counter Terrorism Command. The case against me for ambushing Anjem Choudary had been dropped – no further action. The officer informed me that Choudary had actually decided *against* pressing charges.

I had by that point managed to get my hands on Anjem Choudary's mobile number and immediately phoned him to ask him what he was doing. He answered and simply said that he did not want the police involved. I immediately challenged him to a face-to-face debate. Such a debate would be a blockbuster for both the media, the patriotic movement and of course even for the Islamist networks. He agreed, to my surprise. I got in touch with a journalist who had reported on Britain First in a fair manner and offered him the role of chairing the debate. He accepted with glee.

The night before the debate was to take place, I received a phone call from this journalist who said that Choudary was now demanding a guarantee that - if the debate went ahead - I would promise not to insult the Prophet Mohammed. I replied that I would be asking probing questions about the Prophet Mohammed otherwise, what kind of a debate would it be? Surely Choudary did not want a sanitised discussion?

I said that I agreed to this debate on the basis it would be 'no holds barred' and would not agree to any restrictions on dialogue. I did not want any 'taboo' topics. Early the next morning, Choudary pulled out of the debate. I was furious. What a coward. No backbone whatsoever. It's easy standing on a street corner surrounded by police officers chanting 'UK go to hell!' and quite another sitting across a table from an obstinate and tough British citizen who will bat the argument back. I'm quite flattered to be honest that the great and knowledgeable Anjem Choudary, spokesman for radical Islam in Europe, chickened out from a face-to-face debate with me.

The confrontational approach of Britain First was obviously shaking the tree when it came to radical Islam and they must have been rocked by our visits to their homes and workplaces. We had also succeeded in unsettling the situation in their typical stomping grounds of East London. The next task on our to-do-list was to drive them off the streets completely, or at least to physically confront them every single time they came out in public.

It was around this time that Choudary and his network decided to roll out a series of protests on the streets of London. Our job now was to keep up the pressure on these reprobates at all costs. Whether that was at home, at work, on protests, out shopping – it didn't matter. Where they went, we would follow them and confront them. They would not be permitted any respite or peace. These degenerates had enjoyed a free run for far too long and Lee Rigby had paid the price.

8. Headfirst

On 26 February 2014, Michael Adebolajo and Michael Adebowale, the jihadi killers of Lee Rigby, were sentenced to life imprisonment. On that day, multiple groups held simultaneous protests outside the Old Bailey. Britain First was the biggest group with about 35 activists, but what defined that day was the disgraceful behaviour of the other so-called 'patriot groups'.

At the top of the Old Bailey road stood a pub and most of the assortment of 'patriots' from the EDL, South East Alliance and others spent most of their time downing pints of Stella before they emerged for their protests. General hooligan behaviour was on offer, with most of these idiots acting in a disgraceful manner. One of them was filmed by a TV crew baring his arse for the cameras. Only Britain First behaved with dignity. I remember condemning the general behaviour of the motley crew of 'patriots' that day outside the Old Bailey. Lee Rigby and his family would be ashamed of these degenerates.

Anjem Choudary and his followers put on a good face after our onslaughts at their homes, but judging by the reports I was fed by our surveillance teams, they were taking precautions due to our continued presence. They were seen looking around before getting out of vehicles outside their homes and they appeared fidgety and anxious. I must admit to a general feeling of satisfaction during this period. Making Islamic extremists apprehensive and jittery gave me a perverse sense of pleasure.

Despite our efforts to target these savages where they felt most vulnerable, the whole motley crew surrounding Choudary still felt bold enough to organise regular street protests. The first of these we were able to confront was a protest outside the Natural History Museum on Cromwell Road in the West End of London. Choudary held this demonstration to protest the supposed treatment of Muslims at the hands of Christian militants in the Central African Republic. The protest was held opposite the embassy of this African nation.

This was a beautiful opportunity: Choudary and all of his top lieutenants would be out in public on a busy London road. Easy targets for our robust teams of patriot activists. The weather that day was atrocious: Non-stop torrential rain poured from the heavens but did little to dampen our enthusiasm to tear lumps out London's most feared Islamists. After a short wait the number of bearded fanatics on the opposite side of the road started to proliferate.

These medieval creeps were holding big placards with the words 'Islam will dominate the world!' and 'Muslims rise up and establish the Islamic State' emblazoned on them. High profile Islamists like Choudary and Abdul Mahid were on full display. Despite ostensibly holding a counter protest on the opposite side of the road, we persistently tried to cross the road, prompting harsh verbal responses by the police officers present. One way or another, we gave the police the run around trying to get to the other side. We gave them no peace. We were damned if we were expected to watch graciously as these lowlife jihadis shouted 'UK go to hell!'

without a vehement response. In response to our determined and troublesome behaviour, the police parked two large vans across the road blocking not only our view of the protest but also our ability to get across the road to confront them.

At some point, a foreign tourist came over to our small counter-protest and informed us that he had been assaulted by the Muslims on the other side, purely because he told them they were in the wrong. The police witnessed the assault but did nothing. Typical politically correct double standards at play again. Imagine if a group of white 'far right' activists had assaulted a Muslim? The riot police would have been summoned. In response to the police inaction over this assault, I decided to throw off all restraint and quietly whispered into the ears of everyone present that upon my signal, they were to charge the Muslim extremist demo with full force.

I quietly and covertly made the preparations and then when I felt the police were at their most relaxed, I shouted at the top of my voice 'For England!' At this moment, the 20 or so activists in our company ran across the road and filtered through the gaps in the police vans, their Union Jack flags flickering in the confusion and bustle. General mayhem broke out and the police were quickly overwhelmed by our 'Charge of the Light Brigade' tactics. For a few chaotic minutes, the police struggled to maintain order and hold our activists back. Some of our activists managed to get to within a metre or so of Choudary and Mahid before they were rugby tackled to the ground by overzealous police officers.

Gradually, the police regained control of the situation but the Muslim extremists were utterly startled by our sudden onrush! Mahid could be heard shouting on his loudhailer for the Islamists to remain calm while the police subdued our activists. Two of our footsoldiers were arrested for breach of the peace and led off to the nearest police station. The police took no chances after that and formed an iron curtain of police officers directly in front of us to prevent another charge. Shortly after both protests dissipated and everyone headed off home. But that first dash across the road to physically confront the UK's top extremists was legendary and we felt that we had successfully ruined their demonstration with our incessant harassment. A bloody good day's work indeed.

Immediately after the chaos on Cromwell Road, I decided on the adoption of a kind of Britain First 'uniform' for our activists. We decided on military green activist jackets and old fashioned British flat caps. The military green jackets were chosen to convey our unique brand of nationalist militancy. The flat caps were chosen because they oozed an old fashioned, rustic, working class quality and that was precisely what we stood for.

During our monitoring of Twitter accounts connected to Choudary and his followers, we learned of a new initiative called 'Islamic Roadshow'. This was a kind of travelling circus of Islamist 7th Century barbarism. The first such 'roadshow' event was to take place in Forest Gate, East London. However, Choudary and his chums must have been getting fed up by our constant intrusions because they only announced this activity on Twitter a few hours before it was to take place in the hope we could not mobilise quickly enough to oppose it. Luck would have it that on that particular day, we were having an activist social at our HQ pub in Dartford and we were able to swing into action very quickly indeed.

We parked a few streets away from this 'Roadshow' and sent scouts round to see who was present. Anjem Choudary, Abu Izzadeen and a whole range of mad mullahs were giving speeches on a PA system, blissfully unaware of the storm that was about to break. After briefing the activists, we crept undetected to within thirty feet of the event. A bearded crazy was waffling about Sharia Law when suddenly a large group of English activists screamed 'Terrorist scum off our streets!' and hurled themselves round the corner and paced frantically across the road directly towards a startled Choudary and his team. Forest Gate is a heavily Muslim area, so our team of about 10 activists were heavily outnumbered. The Muslims countered our chants by screaming 'Takbir' which means 'Allah is great'. The police were startled and did not know what the hell was going on.

Our activists were heavily outnumbered, even by Choudary's team, let alone the wider local Muslim community. Nevertheless, we broke out a rendition of 'God Save the Queen' on our loudhailer until the police surrounded us and forced us back across the road. The police frog-marched us across the road and threatened to arrest us if we dared to cross it again. Here they were again, the Muslim Protection Squad! Doing all they could to keep the local Taliban safe from indignant native Britons. For the first time ever, our activists chanted our newly adopted main slogan, 'Britain First, Fighting Back!' The whole street was dominated by the sound of Abu Izzadeen on the microphone shouting 'La ilaha illallah!'

That day we had travelled to Forest Gate in the armoured Land Rover and unbeknown to us, during our counter-protest a famous Islamist and ex-boxing champion by the name of Anthony Smalls had slipped off from the 'Roadshow' and slashed its tyres. Shortly after this he was arrested for criminal damage and eventually convicted. Just for good measure, after the counter protest had ended we decided to go back to Anjem Choudary's home address and leafleted all of his neighbours for the first time letting them know exactly who they had living amongst them. Unknown to us, the local council had whisked Choudary off to a brand-new taxpayer-funded house in a different area of East London, all as a result of our activities. If only local law-abiding English residents were looked after like this!

The next Islamist protest was to take place outside the Lebanese Embassy on the Bayswater Road in the West End. This demonstration was to protest the treatment of Sunni Muslims in the predominantly Shia Lebanon. The assembly point was Notting

Hill Gate tube station and unknown to us, this was where many of Choudary's gang were meeting. Fifteen of us stood there passing time while extremist after extremist unwittingly walked into our presence. A young new Islamist was collared just outside the tube station and I spent a good ten minutes tearing into him verbally. He was completely meek, almost fragile. He supported radical Islam. so he was fair game as far I was concerned.

Then, to our great delight, prominent extremist, Muslim patroller and Choudary right-hand man, Abdul Mahid, emerged from the tube station. He was accompanied by another infamous extremist, Mohammed Rahman. Immediately we surrounded him and harassed him for a considerable distance up the Bayswater Road, screaming in his face 'Terrorist scum off our streets!' We literally chased these cretins up the road hurling abuse at close quarters. The police already had a fenced paddock waiting for us across the road from Choudary and his rabble, which we duly occupied.

After half an hour of chanting and taunting the Muslim extremists, we had another stroke of luck. My old foe Abu Izzadeen and another eminent Islamist, Mikaeel Ibrahim, were making their way to the Islamist protest, but on our side of the road. What followed was one of the most iconic scenes of anti-Islamist harassment in the history of Britain First. Izzadeen and Ibrahim, both big, stocky black men, seemed un-fazed by our presence and walked straight through our activists to get to Choudary and co. Big mistake. They were immediately surrounded and our activists exhibited the usual display of rabid hostility. Izzadeen and Ibrahim struggled to make their way through our activists – as soon as the police removed one activist from their way another took their place. It was a miracle Izzadeen and Ibrahim were not pulverised by our activists. With considerable difficulty and massive police assistance, these Islamists managed to negotiate their way to the other side of the road, but were obviously quite shaken by our onslaught.

What followed next was classic Britain First militancy. Choudary and the rest of his morons started chanting 'UK police go to hell!' and of course the police officers present did nothing. Then they started chanting 'UK go to hell!' and we had had enough. I quietly whispered to our activists that on my signal we were to break the fences down and charge at the Islamists as hard as we could! Seconds later, with the police completely unaware of our impending blitz, I shouted at the top of my voice 'For England!' and charged across the road aiming directly for Anjem Choudary. Our activists charged with full force, but the police reacted quickly and only three of us were able to reach the opposing fences behind which stood Choudary and his minions. The police swooped on us and dragged everyone back to our fenced area. No one was arrested. It was almost as if the police were expecting our headlong charge.

After this particular counter-demo, I tried to imagine myself in Choudary's position. He must have been apprehensive every time he ventured outside his house. He must have been concerned when he left home and travelled to the local tube station to get to one of his demos. Even when he held a protest, we were there making aggressive charges across the road to get to him. He must have felt as though he was being stalked all the time and that was precisely the effect we hoped to achieve. No respite for these villains - that was our strategy. And to be honest, we were having great fun in the process!

Harassing hate preachers was great amusement for us. But generally, this was a serious business. Our aim was to strangle and suffocate their activities so that we could prevent any more Lee Rigby type atrocities. Someone had to do it. Every other 'patriot' group in the UK thought they could combat radical Islam with alcohol consumption. Rampant political correctness permeated our police guardians to the point where they would rather let wannabe jihadists operate unrestrained throughout our capital city rather than do their job. It was left to Britain First to clamp down on radical Islam. We were the 'frontline' of this important battle and the stakes were daunting.

9. Arrests

Choudary's next public demonstration was outside the Indian Embassy on the Aldwych in central London, protesting the treatment of the Muslim minority in India. The problem we always had was that all our volunteer activists held down honest employment while Islamic extremists are generally benefit scroungers. Choudary and co always held their protests on weekdays somewhere in London as they faced no employment related problems restricting their movements. Our activists on the other hand found it difficult to attend because they had full-time jobs.

Before the confrontation outside the Indian Embassy, a man from Swanley joined our team called Matt King. I met Matt while staying in a guest house in Swanley which he ran as manager. Matt was an Ulster loyalist with a background in the feared and notorious 'C Company', run by Johnny 'Mad Dog' Adair. Matt had long ago left Belfast and set up home in the Kent area. We got chatting at the guest house and within a whisker of time he was a full member of our inner circle. I appointed Matt my chief bodyguard and the confrontation outside the Indian Embassy was his first taste of the

Britain First fightback that was under way.

That sunny day in London was to be an eventful one. We always made it our business to arrive well in advance of the Islamists so we could harass them individually one-by-one as they trickled into the area. This tactic was first used on the counter-demo on the Bayswater Road. Our activists fanned out on the Aldwych and Strand stretch of road and to our surprise we found a lone young black Muslim convert standing on his own waiting for Choudary. His name was Brusthom Ziamani. We did not know it at the time, but this newly recruited Islamist was to become very, very famous within a year. We lost no time however racing up to him to confront him.

Waving a microphone in his face, I questioned him in front of the cameras of the media about his support for jihadi Islam. He said he only wanted to demonstrate peacefully and had no words to offer when I pointed out he would be rubbing shoulders today with hate preachers and convicted terrorists. The video footage of me fulminating in Ziamani's face would be broadcast universally throughout the media shortly after, but more on that later. After a few minutes of me sticking it to Ziamani, the police intervened and led him away from our raucous activists.

Once again, the police had constructed two separate fenced paddocks for our respective protests and we made our way to ours. Then one of our team noticed two men walking towards us from the opposite direction wearing Muslim garb. We immediately launched into action by rushing towards them with hostile intentions shouting, 'Terrorist scum off our streets!' One Islamist was immediately identified as Abdullah Deen.

Abdullah Deen was a notorious ginger-haired white convert to Islam. A former Millwall fan and drug dealer from Bermondsey in South London, he has convictions for violence and called Lee Rigby's killer Michael Adebolajo a 'friend'. A self-employed perfume salesman, he was recruited into Choudary's following around the same time as Adebolajo. He also frequented a Lewisham mosque with Adebolajo and joined Adebowale at self-defence lessons.

Deen gave an interview with the 'Sun on Sunday' where he described Adebolajo as 'kind and considerate' and believes the killing of Lee Rigby was justified as supposedly Britain and Muslims are at war. This scumbag even said, 'Some people may have been terrified by it, horrified by it [the slaughter of Lee Rigby]. But I believe it was an act of war. I hope Lee Rigby's family might be guided and accept Islam.' Deen accused Jesus Christ of being a paedophile and said the UK was 'full of paedophiles and whores'.

Deen and the killers of Lee Rigby were part of an Islamist cell known as the 'Greenwich Dawah' and he was arrested during the 2012 Olympics after he abused soldiers that were on duty protecting the games. The 'Greenwich Dawah' was disbanded after the slaughter of Lee Rigby but Deen sustained his public Islamist activities along with Anjem Choudary and others. When we saw him walking up the road with another unknown Muslim extremist, we simply charged him at full pelt.

The two Islamists were driven back some twenty to thirty feet and the police were unable to hold our activists back. This warrior of Islam looked like a frightened rabbit and his usual jihadi persona was non-existent. We forced Deen and his friend into the busy road and they were forced to cross over to the other side and walk the long way around us to get to Choudary and the protest. Deen managed to summon up the courage to threaten to cut my head off but only once he was safe behind the police.

Once Deen was safely ensconced within the main Islamist demo, he transformed into a wild beast, screaming profusely from behind the barriers that he was going to 'bust my face' and cut my head off! We really had shaken him and he didn't like it one bit. During Deen's colossal bitch fit, we simply kept laughing and telling him we would soon be descending on his home address. The difference between the frightened and startled Abdullah Deen who was surrounded by our activists and the foaming-at-the-mouth wild man who was safely behind the police barriers could not have been more stark! It was a source of great amusement to us during the remainder of that day.

For the first time, Matt King seized the microphone and started to verbally assault the Islamists who held placards sporting the words 'Democracy go to hell!' and 'Islam will dominate the world!' I challenged Deen as to whether he condoned the killers of Lee Rigby – he simply slithered around the questioned without answering it directly. He also refused to answer whether he supported Osama Bin Laden. Once again, it was too much to take, watching the dopey PC police facilitate yet another hateful Islamist activity on the streets of London. I walked around covertly briefing all those present that on my signal they were to charge the paddock opposite and rush headfirst into Choudary's demo. Everyone was ready and the police suspected nothing.

When I gave the signal, one of our activists pushed open the metal barriers of our pen and out poured a mass of patriots who charged towards Choudary and his minions. Some of us managed to reach the barriers and we leapt into the air to grab some of the Islamist placards. But the police were surprisingly quick to swing into action and within five seconds we were all pinned against a large police van. I was dragged around the other side out of sight along with several others. Once again, the Muslim Protection Squad had excelled themselves!

Three of us were arrested for 'breach of the peace' and forced into the police van. The situation, viewed retrospectively, was an outrage. Here were convicted terrorists and extremists shouting, 'UK go to hell!', and they are left alone, protected and guarded. When citizens try and confront these hostile enemies of Britain they are arrested and bundled into a police vehicle.

To say that the police are on the side of Islamic extremists is simply to state an obvious and incontrovertible fact. The Islamists and their poisonous followers were allowed to continue their despicable protest while our activists were forced to disperse. They were told by the police they had to leave the area immediately or face arrest, a 'Section 35' notice. They all left the Aldwych and headed to Holborn Police Station, less than a mile away. Me and two other activists were taken there after our arrest and within a few hours, we were released without charge.

After our dash towards Choudary and Co, the police simply wanted to neutralise us from causing any more trouble. This was my second arrest for confronting Islamic extremists. I was left with 'no further action' on both accounts, a splendid example of the use of police powers to protect Islamists if ever there was one!

Without the battalions of politically correct police officers protecting them, our brave activists would have run all Islamic extremists out of London within a few months – that's not hyperbole, that's simply stating an undeniable fact. It was the determination of the police to shield Islamic extremists from public indignation that allowed them to operate, recruit and prosper.

It is my belief that, because of the police policy of protecting Islamists, and allowing them to recruit new extremists, that many innocent victims died due to terrorism that otherwise would not have died. When it boiled down to an argument between the civil rights of innocent victims and the civil rights of foaming wannabe jihadists, the authorities always put the jihadis first.

At any given time and in any given set of circumstances, the authorities could have initiated a decisive clampdown on the activities of Islamic extremists in Britain, saving dozens of innocent lives. How many times do we hear that a terror attack that claimed the lives of innocent victims was perpetrated by a man 'known to the authorities'.

There are only two plausible possibilities here: That our government is guilty of incompetence on a galactic scale - or that there exists an unwritten, unspoken government policy of politically correct tolerance towards Islamic extremism, regardless of the consequences. I am convinced that the latter is the truth. The government doesn't care how many die at the hands of Islamism, only that Islam itself doesn't face any criticism whatsoever. Nothing must be allowed to interfere with the inexorable march of multiculturalism or the Islamification of Britain.

If anyone should dare to point out that Islam is not integrating or that there exists industrial scale grooming of thousands of young underage non-Muslim girls by Islamist rape gangs, for example, then these vocal champions of truth must themselves be neutralised using the full power and might of the state. Even if that means allowing a situation to exist where Islamists are given free rein and rape gangs allowed to operate on a grand scale but that British citizens simply voicing 'opinions' are arrested, harassed and jailed.

The establishment doesn't care about the outrageous double-standards of this official approach, only that Islam must be safeguarded from criticism. Islam is the 'protected species' of the British state and will never be allowed to attract even a justified critique without the Muslim Protection Squad rolling into purposeful action against the transgressor! No other ethnic or religious minority in the UK enjoys such sacrosanct status as Islam.

Choudary's next demonstration was outside the embassy of Saudi Arabia, in the Mayfair district of central London. They were protesting the domination of Saudi Arabia by the House of Saud, which I found ironic considering that the Saudi royal family pumps billions into mosques, madrassas and cultural centres throughout the Western world, spreading their unique but medieval version of Wahhabi Islam in the process. In fact, the blame for the rise of extremist Islam throughout the entire world can convincingly be laid at the feet of Saudi Arabia, a Sunni Muslim country that subjects its citizens to a brutal and 'pure' version of Sharia Law.

We mobilised a strong band of activists and headed for Mayfair, meeting at a tube station in the vicinity. We arrived at 3pm expecting to see Choudary and his retinue but the ground surrounding the embassy was deserted. I rang the official mobile number for the 'Need4Khilafah' (Need 4 Islamic State) group which Choudary led and challenged the Islamists to come and face us, calling them cowards in the process. It was at this point that around five activists from the EDL arrived wearing embarrassing gimp masks – they looked *ridiculous*. I challenged them to remove the face coverings, arguing that real patriots are courageous enough to show their faces while defending their country. They refused - no surprise there. However, I did not hold a grudge because after the day's festivities had ended several of these EDL activists jumped ship and joined Britain First, impressed by our bravery and discipline.

Quite sneakily, the police had moved Choudary and his gang of freaks to the rear of the embassy, hoping we wouldn't spot them and simply give up and go home. Here was another example of the police going out of their way to facilitate the activities of London's hate preachers.

Immediately upon discovering this devious manoeuvre, we marched around the side of the embassy and round to the rear end, all the while escorted and hemmed in by a huge police presence. Here they were, the famous Muslim Protection Squad in all their glory! Once again, the police had ready two separate fenced paddocks, one for Choudary and the Taliban and one for us. This time, a 'Charge of the Light Brigade' would be impossible, as a solid and impenetrable wall of police officers stood facing us with their backs to the Islamists who were shouting 'UK go to hell!' and waving jihadi flags in the air. Even a local Muslim, shocked by the situation, came and stood with us and shouted expletives at the Islamists surrounding Choudary!

Standing with Choudary was a roll call of Britain's most prominent Islamists: Abu Izzadeen, Abdullah Deen, Mikaeel Ibrahim, Abdul Mahid, Mohammed Rahman, Brusthom Ziamani and so on. Unable physically to confront this posse of scumbags because of the heavy police attendance, I got on the powerful PA system and challenged Mikaeel Ibrahim to a charity boxing match. Ibrahim is, physically speaking, the biggest and most muscular of Choudary's gang. Nevertheless, I would have relished the opportunity to jump into a boxing ring and pound seven bells of shit out of him.

I kept on and on at him, taunting him and challenging him. I shouted across the street that I would not allow Ibrahim or his ilk to carry out another Lee Rigby style killing on our streets. At that precise moment, he looked at me and made a hand gesture of the slitting of a throat directly at me before he was pulled away by another extremist. He had clearly threatened to chop my head off, ISIS style, and we had filmed the whole thing on camera. I showed it to the police on the spot but they refused to arrest Ibrahim. Imagine if I or any other Britain First activist had made a death threat to a Muslim – we would have been immediately seized and sent to Belmarsh forever! Different rules exist for British citizens and Islamic extremists.

After chanting 'Terrorist scum off our streets!' for a good hour and a half, my vocal cords were straining under the pressure. I was desperate for someone else to take over the relentless chanting. Unluckily for me, no one volunteered to grab the microphone. It was then that our new recruit, Jayda Fransen, stood forward and offered to give the Islamists a verbal lashing. This was the first time Jayda would be in action. Jayda's amplified voice echoed from wall to wall, deriding and mocking the Islamist rabble. 'You're worshipping a false prophet, you're all going to hell!' and 'The only way to heaven is through Christ and there will be no virgins greeting you!'

Towards the end of the day, I decided to interview Matt King on camera. Here was a man who had fought the IRA and here he was on the streets of London taking action against the Taliban. I loved the way he spoke in a thick Belfast accent: 'We beat the IRA and we're gonna beat these uns'. Britain First was based on Ulster Loyalism and so it was very welcome having these battle hardened ex-paramilitaries onboard. Not that we were breaking the law, but here were strong men who had defended Britain once before and would be more than happy to do so again, although this time politically and with street activism.

I remember during this period I was on police bail for harassing an Al-Qaeda terrorist and was banned from entering the Greater London area. Choudary announced a demo outside of the Egyptian Embassy in support of the toppled Islamic Brotherhood government and for once, I could not turn up to oppose him! Jayda volunteered to lead our activist team and a counter protest was quickly organised.

The team arrived in Mayfair, just off Park Lane, and immediately stormed up to Choudary and co who were praying on the pavement. Jayda got to within two feet of Choudary and almost snatched a Koran he was holding. It was then that the Muslim Protection Squad swung into action, leaping on Jayda and dragging her away with brute force. They arrested her for 'breach of the peace' and took her away to a police station. I was updated on this development by the rest of our activists and immediately broadcast the news across social media. She was later released without charge.

Anjem Choudary then held a meeting where he ridiculed Britain First for our efforts to harass him. He poked fun at the new police restrictions placed on us, particularly mocking the fact that I could not even visit my own mother who lived within the Greater London area. Even now when watching Choudary's video you will get incensed by his gloating of the way the police were cracking down on us and leaving him and his merry band of savages alone.

Unbeknown to us, this would be one of the last times we would be going head-to-head with the Choudary network vis-à-vis protest and counter protest. We could feel very proud that we had been there to confront them every single time, putting ourselves in great danger and facing the wrath of the Muslim Protection Squad, otherwise known as the Metropolitan Police.

Believe me, if we could have, we would have charged at them at every opportunity. We wold have physically driven them off the streets. Had it not been for the Muslim Protection Squad, London would have been an Islamist free zone. The only reason Anjem Choudary and the rest were able to carry out their venomous activities was because of the Iron Dome of protection provided by the police. The British public would have been more than happy if the brave activists of Britain First would have run the lot of them out of town. The only thing stopping us was the police. I have repeatedly called them the Muslim Protection Squad and that is what they are.

10. Confrontation

During the period where our activists were locking horns with London's radical Islamists, I ordered several socials to be held so we could bind our troops together not only in the trenches, but also on a personal level. So far it was all work, no play. So, we organised several 'Britannia Balls' in our HQ town of Dartford. These events were not only a disco and knees up, but an opportunity for the leadership to reward our frontline footsoldiers with specially created Britain First activist medals.

Our activists were extremely proud and honoured to receive these medals, and it was the least our movement could do to honour their bravery and courage. Some of these activists had been arrested or cheek-to-cheek with the likes of Izzadeen or Ibrahim. They had marched proudly up the Islamist-stronghold of Brick Lane and Whitechapel Road. Besides the general revelry and awards ceremonies, we invited a traditional Ulster loyalist marching band to perform. This was a first taste of fiercely British loyalist culture for most of our activists, but they lapped it up and loved it.

Shortly after the last Britannia Ball, our deputy leader Andrew

McBride was forced to step down due to ill health. I had been at Andy's side for years and he was a founder member of Britain First. But now his health was in steep decline. With much regret he decided to step down. I was gutted to see Andy go, he was and always will be a real hero of the British people. He was a capable and talented organiser and leader of men and proved his worth in several organisations. Britain First owes him a debt of gratitude for helping found our movement and making sure it grew during the hardship of the early years.

The media interest in Britain First by this point on the timeline was enormous. Documentaries and news reports oozed from every TV channel and private production company. TV crews followed us around London into Muslim ghettos or to the home addresses of famous Islamists. Vice TV did a full one-hour documentary on our activities, called 'London's Holy Turf War'.

The documentary painted a picture of a battle for the streets of London between radical Islamists, led by hate preacher Anjem Choudary and Britain First, led by me. Many of the opposing players were interviewed and followed around London, including me, Anjem Choudary, Abdul Mahid and several others. The documentary pitted Islamic fundamentalists against Christian patrols - and that at least was accurate. An otherwise entertaining production was ruined at the end by an attempt to apportion some of the previously mentioned bad behaviour outside the Old Bailey to Britain First, when it was in fact the EDL and its splinter groups. Leftwing journalists simply have to tell lies and distort the truth – it's in their DNA.

Vice TV was blacklisted due to this act of deceit and we have never dealt with them since. They have attempted to obtain our cooperation under various false guises since but we always tell them to sod off once we unmask them. When media outlets resort to dishonest reporting with Britain First we simply blacklist them.

Why should we supply them with exciting news material when they cannot even tell the truth? We don't mind being subjected to tough scrutiny, but why tell lies? Why twist and distort actual events so that they become a falsehood? Why claim something when you consciously know it is not true? Thankfully, in the modern era, the mass media's credibility is all but destroyed and the level of general trust in the veracity of the 'news' is dissipating as time marches on.

The final street confrontation between Britain First and Anjem Choudary's gaggle of terrorists, wannabe jihadists and extremists came when he announced on Twitter he would be holding a small meeting outside the Regent's Park Mosque (also known as the London Central Mosque). His strange change of tactics was obvious: Holding a protest was becoming a headache because of the guaranteed presence of Britain First. So how about holding a demo outside a gigantic mosque after Friday Prayers when thousands of Muslim worshippers would be on hand to pulverise the small group of Britain First activists? Nevertheless, we decided to go and confront him anyway! To hell with the obvious potential for carnage. To hell with the guaranteed prospect that we would be hideously outnumbered.

Regent's Park Mosque is a 5,400 capacity mosque and is packed to the rafters every Friday, the Muslim holy day. I tried to get as many activists to attend as possible, but this was Good Friday and a long bank holiday weekend. Many of our folk had plans to go away for a relaxing break.

In the end, we could only muster 25 activists, but this would have to do. Despite being outnumbered and with the certainty of violent opposition, I simply could not allow Choudary and his minions to hold a public event under *any* circumstances. I remember thinking that if we could rattle his cage under these suicidal odds, then he would be quite dispirited. We arranged to meet at the Regent's Park tube station – a short walk away – and it was a gloriously sunny day.

Perfect for some Taliban hunting.

When we assembled and walked to the vicinity of the mosque, we noticed that the EDL had turned up too. Some of them had the infamous gimp masks on to hide their faces. The police positioned two fenced paddocks next to each other opposite the mosque and the EDL managed to occupy the one closest to the entrance to the mosque. I remember the EDL activists being virulently hostile to us, something they would later retract when the going got tough. Luckily, Britain First had a powerful PA system which pounded out a whole string of patriotic anthems and hymns, including 'Jerusalem', 'I Vow To Thee My Country' and 'God Save the Queen'. The Muslims in the giant domed mosque must have been able to hear our music blearing outside as they were praying.

Once Friday Prayers finished, I knew that a tidal wave of angry Muslims would be pouring out of every entrance and occupying the street between us and the mosque. At around 2pm, Choudary and the rest were spotted at the gates of the mosque using a loudhailer to speak to worshippers who were like a human avalanche coming out of the mosque. It is hard to describe in writing, but standing in a group of 25 activists, however brave, watching literally thousands of opponents rushing out of a building and surrounding you, is a surreal experience! What followed was a true Rorke's Drift situation. Some 25 Britain First and next to us around the same number of EDL, surrounded by an endless sea of Muslim heads, all agitated and foaming at our presence. Imagine a swarm of at least 1,000 Muslims and in the corner of your eye, a tiny handful of patriots holding a few Union Jack flags!

We were outnumbered in a horrific way. It was literally 25 of us versus 1,000 of them, minimum. There could have been anywhere between 1,000 and 5,000 Muslims surrounding us, but there was no way of knowing what the real numbers were. The police commander quickly came to see me as the man in charge of the Britain

First contingent and told me candidly that he was summoning reinforcements but that if the Muslims decided to rush our small group, there is no way the tiny number of police present could hold them back. He advised me in the sternest manner possible to avoid provoking the Muslim horde besieging us.

Our response was simple and instant: I grabbed the microphone and started to shout through the PA system that we were not scared one jot and that the prophet Mohammed was a paedophile who took a six-year-old bride! We started to sing 'God Save the Queen' and I remember the police commander looking at me with a look of disbelief in his eyes. Suddenly missiles started to rain down on us from the block of flats behind us.

Far from avoiding acts of provocation with the crowd in front of us, our activists did all they could to anger and inflame them. We were not scared, not in the slightest. During the general chaos one of the EDL members who had been so overtly hostile to us at the start of the melee slipped into our paddock and asked me that in the event of a serious lapse into violence, both Britain First and the EDL would 'join forces'. I replied to him with a smirk on my face that in such an event, Britain First would of course protect the EDL activists!

What followed was horrendous: The police struggled against all odds to keep the baying Islamist hordes away from us. Choudary, Izzadeen, Ibrahim and Deen infiltrated the Muslim ranks and forced their way to the front, the first such instance where they found it comfortable enough to get mouthy to us up close! We held our ground without flinching for a long time, giving as good as we got. Despite the missiles raining down on us and being horribly outnumbered, we still managed a confrontation of sorts with Choudary and the bearded inbreds that follow him. Choudary is an intelligent man and he must have thought to himself that we were stark raving bonkers being so belligerent in such a hopeless situation!

Eventually, the police slapped their usual 'Section 35' dispersal notices on us, forcing us to leave the area under threat of arrest. But it wasn't that simple! Blocking our departure were thousands of enraged Muslims who were determined to rip our heads off. So, the police used their reinforcements to create a small fenced pathway for us to move along and out away from the army of Muslims. They blocked the Muslims from following us, but at least a hundred of them managed to get through this barricade. As our activists made their way down Park Road, we came under attack by these small groups of Muslims. The police quickly arrested several of them for launching a violent attack on our retinue.

The day had been high-octane and fraught with danger, but we had made our point. We would confront Choudary and any radical Islamists even if they had thousands of cohorts at their disposal. No army of Islam, no matter how gargantuan, would be enough to keep us away. Thus, Choudary's plan had failed. Not only had we refused to give him a clear run, but we had turned up anyway and insulted their poisonous ideology outside their London HQ despite being ridiculously outnumbered. Britain First was a movement of fearless British Lions who could not be intimidated or cowed into submission. Our activists took 'No surrender!' to another level.

11. Trial

In March 2014, it was reported by the media that an Al Qaeda terror suspect had set up a primary school in East London. The man in question was called Sajeel Shahid, born in Britain but who moved to Pakistan to run an Al Qaeda terrorist training camp where he taught combat and bomb making skills. He was later detained and sent back to the UK.

Shahid called for attacks on the British Armed Forces and tutored terrorists on how to make bombs and fire rocket-propelled grenades. One of the terrorists he trained was Mohammed Siddique Khan, ringleader of the tube and bus bombers who killed 52 innocent people on 7/7 2005. Shahid also trained four convicted terrorists who tried to attack Bluewater Shopping Centre in Kent and London's Ministry of Sound nightclub. Shahid was also connected to Choudary's Al-Muhajiroun network.

Despite being a known Islamic extremist, terrorist and member of Al Qaeda, Shahid was allowed back into the UK and, incredibly, given permission to set up an independent Islamic primary school! He reportedly employed his brother who also had a long history of extremism. Britain has literally lost the plot and instances like this exist to prove the point. After reading all the relevant information in the media, I resolved to do something about it.

Our intel team immediately got to work, digging for information on home addresses, movements, Twitter accounts, known associates, surveillance, the lot. We discovered that Shahid was registered to an address in Chafford Hundred, a small town near Lakeside Shopping Centre in Essex. Our surveillance units watched as Shahid frequented this address – something that was later confirmed in court by a neighbour. Whether he lived in Hepburn Close or not, he was registered there and frequented the address regularly. The Islamic primary school mentioned by the media was actually registered to the address in Hepburn Close. The prosecution later tried to claim in court that Shahid had no connection whatsoever to the address, but that was easily disproved by simple online searches.

One sunny evening, I led a team of Britain First activists to Shahid's registered address in Chafford Hundred and we started our operation by leafleting all of the residents of Hepburn Close alerting them to the dangerous terrorist they had in their midst. The local residents we spoke to were shocked to learn this news. With the leafleting out of the way we decided to knock on his door to try and confront him. Unfortunately, he wasn't present at number 13 but one of his female family members was. I told the woman in polite terms that I would be back to see him and that we do not want Islamic terrorists living among our people. At no point did I raise my voice or speak in harsh colourful tones.

The next day the Muslim Protection Squad a.k.a Essex Police turned up at my father's address again looking to arrest me. I was notified immediately. I decided to go over to Grays Police Station and hand myself in. I was accompanied by a media team and Matt King. I entered the police station and announced myself to the front counter, upon which I was told to sit down and wait. I managed to give a considerably long interview with the TV crew inside the police station before two uniformed officers came out to see me. They immediately gave me the good news: 'Paul, you're under arrest for racially aggravated harassment, you do not have to say anything....'

I was quite shocked by this arrest, my third in a matter of a few months. All I had done was give out some leaflets and speak politely to a woman through a door. No threats or menacing behaviour had been dished out. Nevertheless, the Muslim Protection Squad saw fit to arrest me and charge me with harassment of an Al Qaeda terrorist.

Just for good measure, they also charged me with wearing a 'political uniform' contrary to the 1936 Public Order Act! This archaic law was brought in during the volatile 1930s to combat the growth of the uniformed Blackshirts under Oswald Mosely. This piece of legislation bans the wearing of political uniforms. On that particular day, our activists were wearing our usual military green activist jackets and flat caps. But some weren't wearing these items of clothing. Britain First activists usually wear all manner of varying official merchandise, but they do not wear a 'uniform' by any understand of the word. There are only a tiny handful of individuals who have prosecuted for wearing political uniforms: Oswald Mosley, an IRA terrorist, Paul Golding and Jayda Fransen! That's it, the entire roster of this exclusive club!

The Old-Gang political parties are always campaigning in the streets wearing official party merchandise and the police *never* arrest them. However, the police were developing new tactics for dealing with the rise of Britain First. The Muslim Protection Squad would arrest us for anything, no matter how ridiculous, and then apply 'bail conditions'. These bail conditions would usually be nothing to do with the offence which led to the arrest but were designed to hinder and curtail our legitimate political activities. For example, I was arrested for harassing Sajeel Shahid in *Essex* but my bail conditions stipulated I was not to enter the Greater London area. What one had to do with the other is a mystery, except when you accept the police were abusing their powers to stop me entering London to combat Anjem Choudary and his followers.

The next tactic was to shift the emphasis away from the terrorist, hate preacher or rapist we were genuinely targeting to a wife, girlfriend or family member so they could proceed with harassment charges. They have pulled this trick on me several times, but it started with Sajeel Shahid in Essex. After I gave a silent interview to Essex Police I was released on bail with a whole range of conditions that if I broke them, I would be re-arrested and slung into prison.

After a short while, the much more serious 'racially aggravated harassment' charges were dropped and changed to a Section 42 offence of the Criminal Justice and Police Act 2001, 'Harassment of a person in their home'. I was charged with causing harassment to Munazza Munawar, the woman who I spoke to through the door and the sister-in-law of Sajeel Shahid. This particular offence, Section 42 of the Criminal Justice and Police Act 2001, was created to deal with the animal rights movement who were targeting the home addresses of those employed in the animal testing facilities such as Huntingdon Life Sciences. Now they were using this legislation against Britain First to protect Islamic extremists.

This prosecution could only proceed because of a single technicality revolving around certain words we used on our leaflets.

Section 42 of the Criminal Justice and Police Act 2001 stipulates an offence occurs when the person present at a home address demands the following from the resident:

(i) that he should not do something that he is entitled or required to do; or

(ii) that he should do something that he is not under any

obligation to do;

Because our leaflet had *demanded* that Al-Qaeda operator Sajeel Shahid move *out* of the area – something he is not under any legal obligation to do – we broke this particular law. It was a ridiculous technicality that allowed the police to prosecute me in the Magistrate's Court. Unlike my previous arrests, the police were not going to give me a 'no further action' but were determined to see me convicted. There were several reasons that explain why the authorities decided to start prosecuting me for every Mickey Mouse offence they could.

Legal cases cost money, sometimes lots of money. Dragging us into court at every opportunity would drain our resources. Likewise, the more times we were we arrested and prosecuted, the more likely we were to give up and throw in the towel. Lastly, with every new conviction the weight of bad character in law increases and can be introduced as evidence of bad character in future prosecutions. But the police had something specific they were aiming for on this particular occasion.

At a pre-trial hearing, I entered a plea of 'not guilty' to all the charges and a trial date was set for Monday 5th January 2015. When the day of the trial came at Chelmsford Magistrate's Court, I attended with approximately 25 activists and the key witness, Munazza Munawar, sister-in-law of the Al Qaeda boss Sajeel Shahid, gave evidence through a video link. The day was a total farce. People have a strong delusion that British courts of law can be relied upon to be impartial and fair – the truth is they are politically correct and dodgy. When someone like me arrives before a leftist judge, all pretence of the law disappears and decisions based on political bias are made. I have been stitched up multiple times by bent judges, some of who were under pressure from the justice department and Home Office to convict me no matter what the evidence says.

As was totally expected, I was found guilty of both charges:

harassment of a person in their home and wearing political uniforms contrary to the Public Order Act 1936. I received a £1,000 fine but now had a criminal record which was to get a lot bigger over the ensuing years! One of the witnesses for the prosecution, a neighbour in Hepburn Close, gave evidence in the stand and confirmed that she has seen Sajeel Shahid coming in and out of the house in question many times. Never mind, still find Paul Golding guilty of harassing his sister-in-law! The law is stupid and crooked at times and always favours the criminal or terrorist over the victim or patriot.

Then the police and prosecution dropped a bombshell which exposed their blatant political motives. They applied for an ASBO with a whole series of restrictive and repressive conditions, to last for several years. To our unbridled shock, the judge told the police and prosecution to sod off! The judge actually said the terms and conditions of the proposed ASBO were 'extreme' – a direct quote.

Some of the conditions were ridiculous, such as barring me, a political party leader, from speaking to a political gathering. The police and prosecution threw their toys out of the pram in protest but the judge was adamant: There would be no ASBO on his watch! The police were visibly gutted. They had missed their one chance to shut me down for a number of years. But this was the now the pattern of persecution we were subjected to for many years: Arrest followed by restrictive bail conditions, followed by prosecution and a new criminal record. Each time the punishments get worse and worse and your 'bad character' in law grows ever more alarming.

Most of the prosecutions we have been subjected to have been dragged out for as long as possible so that the bail conditions hinder our activities for as long as possible. Even being arrested for a non-imprisonable minor offence brought in their wake bail conditions fit for an international war criminal or terrorist. The authorities in Britain abuse police powers to try and shut down legitimate political activity, a policy fit for any of the tyrannical dictatorships that our

Prime Minsters like to condemn on the world stage when they are grandstanding for popularity.

While all of this is happening, a mass of dangerous individuals the size of a British Army division walk the streets of the UK spreading jihad and terror and are left alone. They can recruit and spread hate under the protective shield of the Muslim Protection Squad otherwise known as the UK police and are left alone to foment mayhem and death. Should you, however, as a British citizen, blow the whistle to expose this scandal, the powers of the state will come down on you like a tonne of bricks to silence you.

Make no mistake: The 'Powers That Be' have already decided that Islam will be allowed to grow and consolidate in our country and nothing or no one will be allowed to criticise or oppose it. Islam is the 'protected species' of the state and the political Left and this also includes - judging by experience - the fundamentalist and jihadist variations. Oppose Islam and the social and extremist problems it brings in its wake and you will be subjected to a campaign of sustained harassment designed to silence you.

My first prosecution for 'harassing' an Al Qaeda terror camp operator was simply an act of politically motivated repression. In a sane, healthy society, the likes of Sajeel Shahid would have been rotting in a stinking prison or deported to his land of family origin. But in Britain he was welcomed back from terrorist activities in Pakistan and allowed to open a primary school for young children! Am I the only person who thinks our country has gone mad?

If Britain was a medical patient, that patient would have been locked up long ago for reasons of mental illness. Britain would be put into a straitjacket and placed in a padded cell for being stark raving bonkers. I am sure this is how many of the normal nations in this world view us, as a country that is run by lunatics who have lost the plot.

12. Invasions

After the showdown outside Regent's Park Mosque, Anjem Choudary and the rest of the extremists went quiet. The police were starting to pile real pressure on them and one by one they started to be arrested and thrown in prison. Through social media Britain First generated somewhere in the region of 50 million views of videos that exposed these wannabe jihadists.

Britain First was putting every Islamist activity into the public realm in a big way. We were raising awareness and shining the spotlight on their repulsive and sordid activities and best of all, demonstrating beyond all doubt the craven acquiescence of the police in the face of their hateful enterprises.

Britain First by this point had grown to vast proportions on Facebook, sporting some 600,000 followers. This was a source of extreme panic for the media and the politicians. How could Britain First possibly grow so big on social media and attract so many followers? While serious leftist groups recognised that they had a monster on their hands, the childish elements did their best to convince anyone who would listen that Britain First was buying 'likes' in contravention of strict Facebook rules. It was complete codswallop of course. If Britain First had been purchasing fake 'likes' then Facebook would have relished the opportunity to remove them or worse still, remove the page completely.

The reality was at odds with the hysterical leftwing lies. Our 'likes' grew gradually and steadily, in an upward trajectory, for years on end. Any monkey watching our page on a daily basis could see this. To this day, I am not even sure if it is possible to purchase fake 'likes' on Facebook. What use would fake Facebook 'likes' be to us anyway? Would they join Britain First? No. Would they donate? No. Would they become activists? No. So, sorry to disappoint any leftwing mongrels reading this – our support on Facebook was entirely organic and naturally accumulated over time.

Anjem Choudary and his Al-Muhajiroun network were no longer active on the streets organising Dawah activities, so we decided to embark on a novel but brief new strategy. Our incursions into the East End of London had caused real outrage among the Muslim community. But they had sat on their hands as the local extremists formed Muslim Patrols and beat up or harassed local tourists or revellers. The local Islamic elders and spokesmen were conspicuously silent, despite the real presence of extremists causing problems.

Having literally driven Choudary and his followers off the streets, causing them to live in a state of alarm with our direct action operations and physically confronting them at every street activity they organised, we opted to do something new and outrageous. We also decided to expand our operations to the north of England. Up to his point, our activities had centred almost exclusively on London, the national hub of radical Islam.

What we needed was a strategy that would force the Muslim community to sit up and listen to our concerns. A radical approach that was so controversial it would generate such an hysterical response that we would be given a national platform to shine the spotlight on radical Islam. For several months, our units engaged in what we called 'Mosque Invasions'. If a local mosque was connected in any way whatsoever with extremism, we would turn up and invade the precincts of the mosque, filming ourselves along the way. Some of these mosques were empty, some were packed with worshippers. Nevertheless, our campaign caused a massive furore within the Muslim community and their collaborators in politics and the media.

On a single day, I took a team to every single big mosque in the towns of Bolton, Rochdale, Blackburn and Burnley and filmed our escapades. The reaction to our intrusions was so vehement that I knew we were on to something. The problem was that virtually all local Muslim 'communities' simply ignore or gloss over the activities of extremists. Not once has any Muslim community taken decisive and highly vocal action to combat extremism, grooming or radicalisation. Our strategy was designed to cause such a reaction that we could highlight this laid-back approach to their own problems. We would achieve this by entering their most sacred buildings and posting videos of us doing so online.

That first round of mosque invasions across the North West attracted the ire of virtually all local politicians. Cretins such as Gordon Birtwistle, the Lib-Dem MP for Burnley, who said: 'This group [Britain First] is not welcome in East Lancashire. People should not be deceived by this group's Christian façade.' The Lancashire Telegraph published a condemnation with the headline, 'Far Right group Britain First told to stay out of Blackburn'. Like that was going to happen.

The next stop on our national tour was Bradford, a well known stronghold of Islamism in the north of England. Two car loads of activists accompanied me as we criss-crossed the entire town, visiting and 'invading' every single mosque within the town. Bradford at that time was suffering with a bad Muslim grooming gang problem, so we intended to 'trigger' the local political and Islamic establishment with our actions to highlight the problem that was being covered up. Halfway through the day, word was spreading that Britain First was in town and that we were invading all the local mosques. We spotted a Labour Party office and so we invaded that too, warning the local Muslim councillors to get a grip on the problem of grooming gangs.

Britain First was mocked by some of its opponents during this campaign that we only visited mosques while they were empty. This is simply not true. Not only did we not know until we entered a mosque whether it would be empty or filled to the brim, but a lot of the mosques were packed with worshippers. Watch the video we published of the Bradford mosque invasions and you can see that some of them are literally bursting at the seams.

To end the day of action in Bradford we turned up at the mayor's home address looking to speak with him about the Islamic-related issues in the town. He refused to come out and speak with us, preferring instead to send his wife out to slam the door in our faces. The mosque invasions across Bradford that day caused a colossal stink. Not only had we entered mosques and, in the eyes of Muslims, disrespected their sacred buildings, but we had distributed hundreds of British Army Bibles that we had with us.

Towards the end of the day, the local police were in a blind panic! They rang our mobile phones and begged us to relent and leave the area immediately, claiming that local Muslim criminal gangs and gangsters were scouring the town intent on inflicting serious harm on us. We told them to sod off and tell these Muslim gangs that they could go to hell. We were not in the mood to be driven out of a British town by a gaggle of Islamist barbarians.

The campaign led to a wave of media publicity and condemnation by local MPs, councillors and newspapers. To hell with the lot of them! These were the lowlife animals who covered up for Islamist grooming gangs and consigned thousands of underage

English girls to predatory paedophiles.

The most vociferous denunciations came from arch-traitor George Galloway. Galloway made a career out of pandering to the Muslim block vote and is a lover of all things anti-British, including Islamist terror groups, communist dictators and the IRA. In a sane country, someone like Galloway would be executed as a traitor. Galloway took to Twitter to denounce Britain First for 'desecrating' all the mosques in Bradford.

Galloway went on TV and gave endless interviews pleading with the government to proscribe Britain First for our campaign. I reacted immediately by ordering a search for his home address and any offices he operated. However, before our intel team turned up any solid leads, George Galloway was attacked and beaten to a pulp by a 'Britain First supporter'.

Neil Masterson was a 39-year-old former BBC manager and had - according to the media - a 'pathological loathing' for Galloway. Masterson saw Galloway and instantly attacked him, causing Galloway injuries. Masterson was jailed for 16 months. Media records stated: 'The Scottish MP is now unable to hug anyone without pain and claims he now cannot go anywhere without bodyguards.' Masterson described Galloway as an anti-Semitic 'serpent' and 'enemy of Judaism'.

One other motivating factor for the attack was that earlier that year Galloway had described his parliamentary constituency as an 'Israel-free zone'. Masterson was a big fan of Israel. When he was arrested, Masterson was wearing a pink hoodie and a tshirt sporting an Israeli Defence Force motif. Masterson had only signed up as Britain First activist the day before the attack, *literally*. He acted on his own impulse and did not receive any orders or direction from our organisation.

Typically, I consider MPs as sacrosanct representatives of the people. But I must admit I did not shed a tear when I heard of the attack on Galloway. This man is a criminal traitor and collaborator of radical Islam. He has made endless inflammatory statements against Jews, Israel, Britain and patriots. He is a professional race baiter and servant of Islam. Imagine if any MP - of any party - would have declared an entire parliamentary constituency a 'Muslim free zone'. There would be international tumult. The UN would be involved. A cataclysm of moral outrage would be unleashed by our political elite. The media would broadcast endless bulletins condemning 'Islamophobia', for months on end. But, since Galloway said 'Israeli free zone', that's fine. Sorry to say, you reap what you sow, and Galloway had it coming. He deserved a good kicking. If I was Prime Minister, he would have been sent to the gallows long ago!

The activist team I led around Bradford then headed north and we drove to Scotland for the first time. We decided to head for the famous Gorbals area of Glasgow and entered Glasgow Central Mosque, which resembles a spaceship from outside, such is the strange shape of its dome. I stood and spoke with the elders for a while discussing our leaflets and our issues of concern. These elders were actually very polite and listened to our concerns.

Contrary to hysterical media and leftist distortion, unless we were provoked we acted towards the Muslims in these mosques with restraint and good manners. We then headed to Cumbernauld where we visited a huge new local mosque that was proving unpopular with the locals. We spoke for a while to the Muslim worshippers and their imam before leaving on good terms.

By now, the big media and TV channels wanted to cover our mosque invasion campaign. So, we met up with some of these TV crews and took them to the East End, where we walked, bold as brass, into the infamous East London Mosque and distributed about a hundred leaflets to worshippers inside the building until the staff rang the police and forced us to leave.

There were at least a hundred Muslims inside the mosque but

none of them did anything to eject us. We did not give a damn about the chronic danger that we placed ourselves in. We only cared about the honour of our nation and we wanted to show these newcomers that the East End was still 'our area'. After all, the Whitechapel area was bombed to bits by the Luftwaffe and Churchill had walked around this area surveying bomb damage. The East End, despite the demographic catastrophe that has overtaken it, is still British soil. Then we returned to the Islamist stronghold of Bury Park, Luton, to cause a furore there. We appeared outside Bury Park Mosque and despite a heavy Muslim presence, we boldly walked past a multitude and into the prayer precinct. The Muslims did nothing to stop us entering their mosque and stood dumbstruck as we left.

Once again, our actions caused a major local backlash, with a whole spectrum of politically correct councillors and appeasers lining up to condemn our actions. Most nauseating of all were the white 'Christian' community 'peace activists' who loved to make public statements cosying up to Islam in the town. These miserable idiots are about as 'Christian' as Anjem Choudary. Specimens such as Peter Adams, a gormless publicity seeker who spends much of his time trying to impress the Muslim inhabitants of Bury Park, are deeply contemptible. All the 'Christian' clergy of Luton would shortly line up against Britain First in their efforts to kiss Islamist backside. Shame on the lot of them. Jesus would be appalled.

There ended our mosque invasion operations, a short and brief campaign to trigger a hysterical response from our liberal politicians and the Taqiyya-spouting 'Muslim community'. This campaign led to an avalanche of publicity and attracted cataclysmic enmity from PC politicians and traitors, such as George Galloway. It managed to sustain the momentum in the media that arose from our clashes with the Islamists in London. It wasn't everyone's cup of tea, but it worked. It raised awareness of extremism in mosques and gave us the opportunity, through social networks and the media, to highlight problems of radicalisation and grooming.

Shortly after, Britain First held a day of action in the town of Derby, in the Midlands. We marched into town with our flags held high and a banner at the front of the procession. The local English population was very supportive but as our march made its way down the high street, a bearded Muslim appeared from nowhere and approached me in a menacing fashion. He got extremely close to me and as I was forced to push him away and as I did, he threw a punch at me. Chaos ensued as the police tried to contain the situation and my security rushed to defend me. I was pushed into a doorway by the police until they made checks and liaised with the town centre CCTV operators.

After five minutes being held by the police, both myself and the Islamist who threw a punch at me were arrested and carted off to the local police station. I was released without charge shortly afterwards while the police carried out an investigation. It turned out the Muslim who attacked me was a notorious local Islamist and part of a gang called 'Allegiance' which posted 'Gangster Rap' pro-Islam music videos to YouTube. This gang also sold Islamic clothing. I found some of the YouTube videos of this Islamist gang rapping and training in martial arts, and after I stopped laughing, I was certain that they were all homosexual. I posted a video mocking this group to our social media, which had the disclaimer, 'We apologise for the street slang and illegible rubbish being spouted by this camp gang of Islamists. We also apologise for the embarrassing display of amateurish martial arts and jumping in the air ninja style'.

It turned out that this particular Islamist, Uthman Ali, had carried out 'Muslim Patrols' on the streets of Derby with his camp friends and loved to pose for photos with the black flag of jihad. He actually released a video claiming that I headbutted him! After a short while, all concerned were given a 'no further action' by Derbyshire Police. To my surprise, all the CCTV from the town centre that day did not capture the incident. A very mysterious event considering Derby town centre is saturated with CCTV.

Despite the fake news emanating from the deceitful mass media, Britain First was stronger than ever. We now had around 750,000 followers on Facebook and we were unchallenged on the 'Patriotic Right' of politics. However, one sad event blackened an otherwise rosy general picture. My bodyguard and close associate, Matt King, was suddenly taken ill with chest pains and rushed to hospital. Deputy leader Jayda Fransen and another one of my bodyguards rushed to the hospital to be with him, along with Matt's daughter. Matt was sitting in his bed talking to Jayda and after a while, our activists took time out to go to the local shop to get Matt some supplies. Then disaster struck. Upon their return to the hospital, Jayda and Matt's daughter were taken to a side room and told that Matt had suddenly died of a major aneurysm of the heart. It was a crushing, sudden blow to all of us. Jayda was devastated. She was good friends with Matt and had been with him shortly before his heart gave out.

The whole of Britain First went into mourning and Jayda, me and several others could not believe what had happened. Matt had been so unexpectedly taken from us. It was a demoralising blow to our inner circle. What made matters more heart-breaking, is that Matt died only a few days after we returned from the trip to Bradford and Scotland, invading mosques. This was his last weekend and he spent it in the service of Britain First. He told Jayda and others that he had thoroughly enjoyed himself. He said he felt like he was back in Belfast battling the IRA with his loyalist comrades during the good old days. At least we were able to spend that final glorious and action-packed weekend together before he departed this earth. Britain First was much poorer because Matt had left us. But it was his time. We still miss him dearly. A true patriot.

13. Elections

In May 2014, elections to the European Parliament took place. The clear majority of my political career up to that point had consisted of traditional politics and election campaigns. Britain First was effectively locked out of the political rat-race by the growing dominance of UKIP. As a result of UKIP's hegemony, we focussed on street activities. But, European parliamentary elections provide a great opportunity to pump out vast amounts of propaganda at minimal cost.

Britain First took part in the Euro Elections but did not entertain ideas of getting candidates elected or achieving good results. We participated purely to use the election to output broadcasts and leaflets. It was a recruitment drive. We devised a clever strategy too. We decided to stand in Wales and Scotland as for the cost of £5,000 for each region we were entitled to TV broadcasts. To achieve broadcasts in England it would have cost somewhere in the region of £55,000. An added bonus to standing in Wales and Scotland was that the TV signals overlapped into England by around 25%. So, for the small sum of £10,000, Britain First would be beamed across

Wales, Scotland and big areas of England.

Despite the indifference we felt to achieving good results in this election, we still attracted around 20,000 votes in Wales and Scotland. The monster that was UKIP trounced all opposition in the election and achieved the highest number of total votes, some four and a half million, beating both Labour and the Tories. Clearly if Britain First was to make any kind of headway into the political arena we would have to wait until UKIP was a spent force. This day would eventually arrive, but not for some years.

The second tactical foray into electoral politics was the Rochester parliamentary by-election, caused by the resignation of Mark Reckless who defected to UKIP. He resigned to seek re-election under his new party. I decided that Britain First would contest this election for one reason only: To use the resulting publicity as a platform to campaign against the Gillingham mega mosque planning proposal that was causing a furore in the area.

Britain First had already claimed ownership of this campaign, holding multiple days of action in the Medway towns distributing thousands of leaflets. Our activists also invaded Medway Council offices and demanded to speak with the planning officers. I still remember standing outside the council holding a huge 'No more mosques!' banner. Our activists also attended and entered several of the existing mosques across the Medway area and spoke to the imams.

Jayda Fransen was selected as our candidate and she took the lead in many of the activities. From the very beginning of this campaign, we had no intention of asking for locals to vote Britain First. Quite to the contrary, we told everyone who would listen to vote UKIP! We only wanted media attention to highlight the Gillingham Mega Mosque issue. We didn't give a damn about garnering votes or achieving a good percentage. On our days of action and leafleting sessions, we spread the same message: Vote UKIP! We were only interested in the mega mosque.

Britain First utilised our usual explosive mix of publicity stunts and confrontation to grab attention. Jayda invaded the Conservative campaign office on Rochester high street and gave these treacherous Tory careerists a good verbal bashing! The footage of Jayda terrorising the Conservative campaign staff and taking them to task over their support for the Gillingham mega mosque went viral.

After the showdown at the Tory campaign office, our team headed to the Jamia mosque on Canterbury Street to confront the hordes of Muslims who were pouring out of the building after Friday Prayers. Despite hundreds of Muslims flooding out of the front doors, Jayda walked in and out of the groups of men giving an impromptu speech. The Muslims watched in shock that a single English female was condemning the spread of mosques in Medway right in front of them, while vastly outnumbered.

Anyone who stands in a parliamentary election is entitled to free delivery of election leaflets by the Royal Mail to every home in the constituency. We promptly printed 45,000 leaflets so that they were ready for distribution by the local postmen. Our election leaflet was hard hitting and controversial, with a Muslim woman in a niqab on the front and a heavy focus on the proposed Gillingham mega mosque.

The sneaky Royal Mail waited until very late in the process and then told us flat out that they would not be delivering our election leaflets! We immediately sought legal advice and it turned out that the Royal Mail were breaking the law. However, to enforce our democratic rights would cost in the region of £15,000 to drag the Royal Mail into the High Court. With our limited financial resources and the very slender time frame we decided to simply crack on with our campaign, minus a free leaflet going to every home in Rochester. No other political party received this illegal treatment from the Royal Mail, only Britain First. So much for democracy. Even the

Electoral Commission refused to help us.

One sunny day during the campaign, a large team of Britain First activists bumped into some of the UKIP team while campaigning in Rochester High Street. By and large, every time the rank and file of UKIP and Britain First have come into contact, our counterparts in UKIP always say they support and respect the bravery of Britain First and our street activities. It was the same in Rochester high street and our two teams posed for a photo. When this harmless photo was posted to social media, UKIP head office went into meltdown. The UKIP volunteers were disciplined and told never to pose for a photo with us again. Pathetic, childish behaviour from a supposedly patriotic political organisation.

During the campaign Britain First held two protest marches, meeting at the local train station with the intention of making our way up the high street to an area where we could make speeches. Obviously, the announcement of the first march met with fury from the local leftwing groups, who vowed to come out and oppose us. Great, the more the merrier.

When the day of the first march came, a large multitude of leftwing idiots, weirdos and degenerates turned out to block the route. I will never forget the sight of an almost exclusively white middle class hippy gaggle of leftists shouting, 'Racist scum off our streets!', while we stood opposite. At one point, a black Britain First activist took the microphone and gave the leftists a dressing down.

However, arguing or debating with white liberals is perhaps the biggest waste of anyone's time. These zombies know only one thing, to shout 'Racist!' over and over again like a broken record, even if some of the so-called 'racists' they were targeting were black or Asian. Trying to reason with white liberals is like trying to have a constructive conversation with those intractable hordes of deceased zombies in the Living Dead movies. You might as well try and explain yourself to the nearest lamp post - you would have more success!

Upon leaving the train station, our procession was immediately blocked by the leftist hippies who managed to halt us in our tracks for a short while until I told the police commander that if he didn't move them out of the way, we would. The police lined up and forcibly pushed the leftists out of the way and our march continued. We made our way to the rally point, where we gave speeches. The police did not have the situation under control and the leftists and Labour activists opposing us were able to get to within ten feet of us. What ensued was not an ordered rally, but a colossal slanging match! Regardless of the heated situation, the wimps of Labour and the Left did not take this opportunity to physically attack us. We stood facing them laughing at the top of our voices as they dished out the threats but in the end, they were too cowardly to act on their impulses.

Two weeks later, we held a second protest march but this time the leftists called in reinforcements from all over. Once again, an explosive and incendiary confrontation was brewing. The leftist counter-protest was even more decadent than last time. White converts to Islam, transgender oddballs, hooded teenage 'Antifa' morons, and much more, was on display. These miscreants were no match for our rugged activists, but they did try their best. After we left the train station, we had to force our way once again through the leftist gangs and into the beginning of the high street. In my opinion, the local police commander was given a ticking off for allowing our previous march to proceed up the high street to the rally ground. This time, the police did everything they could to sabotage us.

About halfway down the high street, the leftists formed a road block of sorts and the police reinforced it. The march came to a halt. A Mexican stand-off commenced, with the police refusing to move the leftwing rascals out of the way. I told them again that if they were not moved out of the way, we would simply do it for them.

Unlike last time, the police were refusing to budge. I decided to give them a warning, so I walked through our ranks and whispered to every activist to prepare to push our way through the police and leftwing lines. With preparations complete, I gave the signal and our entire phalanx of activists pushed forward with great zeal.

The police reacted quickly and were sandwiched in between us and the leftwing idiots on the other side. Our activists pushed and pushed, and just as the police line was about to collapse and all of them fall on their arses, I gave the signal to cease pushing and fall back. Had we pushed for another five seconds, the police would have been swept out of the way and we would have charged into the opposing leftwing rabble.

I did not actually want things to go that far, but we had shown the police that we were a force to be reckoned with and that if they did not do the right thing, things would be different next time.

Immediately after our robust forward manoeuvre, the police reversed a long transit riot van between the lines, blocking the route of our march. Now we were knackered. There was no way we would topple a police van and force our way forward. Our route was blocked. The police started to draw their batons and aim them at our activists when we stood our ground. The police were adamant now that we were not going any further down the high street. But we were not ready to give up quite yet.

We were only about one hundred yards into the high street, so once again I decided on a radical approach. I briefed everyone again on the sly and prepared. Our plan was to turn around, face away from the police and leftists, and sprint away from them and around into the dual carriageway that ran parallel with the high street, outflanking them. On my signal, everyone turned and ran away from the police who were thunderstruck and startled. The police, utterly confused at what was happening, ran after us in small groups, desperately trying to grab and restrain any Britain First activists they could. What followed was absolute chaos!

Imagine a hundred Britain First activists being chased by dozens of police officers down a high street with flags and placards flickering in the air. Everywhere you looked, police officers were rugby tackling our activists to the ground. Batons were drawn and used on our activists. It was like a giant, wild game of tag in the middle of a town centre. I will never forget the sight of the police chasing a parliamentary election candidate down a dual carriageway!

Believe it or not, but the only activists who had made it past the police gangs were Jayda and me. We ran until we were panting for breath. When we made it to the war memorial – the part of the high street we were due to hold our rally - we stopped running and realised it was only the two of us that had made it! Everyone else had been grabbed, tackled and battered by the thuggish police bullies. Me and Jayda were on our lonesome surrounded by small gangs of leftist opposition. Shortly after, the police caught up with us and frog-marched us back to our activists. They then slapped a 'Section 35' dispersal notice on all of our activists, threatening us with arrest in the process.

The footage from the day clearly shows the police brutality. They would never act like that with leftwing protesters or Muslims, never. But the British gestapo never hesitate to use heavy-handed aggression when they are dealing with patriotic Britons. The police completely sabotaged our legal political activities that day. A situation made even worse by the fact that Britain First was participating in a parliamentary election.

The police strategy was simple: Allow Britain First the bare minimum of a procession that was humanly possible. Then, allow the leftwing opposition to block our path. The police would then cravenly surrender to this artificial and easily-removed leftwing road block. The headlines would then be something like, 'Local residents block Britain First march'. Britain First would be embarrassed and look silly. Unfortunately, this kind of political policing is rampant in Britain. More examples will be provided later.

It is doubtful however that the police expected us to react with such obstinate ferocity as we did on that day in Rochester. What could have been an embarrassing flop, with leftwing protesters blocking our path, turned into triumph when our activists literally pushed a police line on their arses and then had them chasing us down a main road. The police looked like tyrannical bullies. Britain First acted with bravery and determination. It was a day I will always remember.

14. Proliferation

Britain First was now expanding on a national scale. Our Facebook page was rapidly approaching 1 million 'likes' and branches, groups and teams were popping up all over the country. This allowed for a big proliferation in activities around the country, but I also tried to keep a strong grip on all levels of the movement. I maintained strict discipline with no exceptions made for anyone.

Any officer or activist who embarrassed the movement was unceremoniously expelled. At times, I remember expelling entire regions of activists, thirty at a time, for refusal to follow HQ directives. Britain First was never a free-for-all. We raised the bar high on standards of behaviour and enforced it. The result of this approach - which we lauded at every opportunity - was that our movement looked completely undesirable from the outside to the football hooligan lads looking for a piss-up.

This situation was naturally intolerable for the lager louts and hooligan types. I remember entire EDL divisions defecting to Britain First, like Hull division. When I and a team travelled to the city for a launch meeting, these ex-EDLers were drunk and snorting cocaine in the toilets. They were rowdy and unruly and badly behaved. Just like football hooligans. I was not impressed.

I gave the usual speech about our brutal ban on all alcohol consumption prior and during activities, outlined our strict, disciplined approach based on good behaviour and I could see by the look on their faces they were horrified. The EDL-types were only interested in a boozy, exciting day out – the typical activity type of the EDL. I would never tolerate anything like that in Britain First. We would not be racist or Nazi like the BNP and we would not engage in alcohol-fuelled hooliganism like the EDL. Britain First was a serious, committed and fanatical movement for grown-ups.

Britain First was expanding not just the geographical localities of our activities but also diversifying the type of activities. We still exhibited the same level of fierce behaviour to our opponents, but the age of harassing hate preachers and terrorists was coming to an end because we had driven them off the streets and the police were starting to imprison them, one by one.

Hizbut Tahrir are a radical Muslim movement who aim to create an Islamic government ruling the Middle East and the rest of the world. Terrorists all over the world have been linked to Hizbut Tahrir and they recruit rigorously on British university campuses. The UK government was exploring the possibility of proscribing them at one point.

Hizbut Tahrir announced that they would be holding an international conference in South West London with an abundance of hate preachers and extremists in attendance. This was too good to miss, so we organised a contingent of activists and headed for Southall. When we arrived, we attracted support from the local Indian population which is big in Southall. The police forced us to the opposite side of the road but we refused to stay put, our activists trying to walk across the road and off to both sides to outflank the police. We gave them the run around for a long time and it caused them serious annoyance.

It was time for another textbook Britain First street charge! I whispered to everyone on the sly to get ready and upon my signal, everyone suddenly charged across the street! The police were taken by surprise and total chaos ensued. Activists were being rugby tackled by the Muslim Protection Squad all around me.

Our activists were being dragged, pulled and thrown in all directions. I remember one activist, Northern Paul, as we called him, being dragged to the floor, when he placed his arms underneath himself and refused to be arrested. It took the police at least five minutes to get him to his feet and out of the middle of the road!

The police then formed an unbroken line of officers in front of us to prevent another charge. We ended up surrounded by a large group of local Indians who could not believe the police were allowing an Islamic extremist conference to take place in their community.

Shortly after, we learned that a cinema in a shopping centre in Birmingham had implemented a 'Muslims only' evening, so we decided to go to Brum and kick off. When we talk about the 'Islamification' of Britain, this is exactly the kind of thing we are talking about: The warping and bending of the British way of life to accommodate Islam.

Our activists arrived at Star City and found the manager of the cinema (a Muslim). We warned him that if he discriminated against non-Muslims again he would know about it. We walked around the Star City complex distributing leaflets before the mall security jumped on us and asked us to leave. We then visited Birmingham Central Mosque with a huge 'No more mosques!' banner for good measure.

Our attentions then turned away from Islamic issues and we visited a troubled area of Doncaster in Yorkshire. Hexthorpe, for some reason, was literally overrun with Roma gypsies from Eastern Europe and the locals were on the verge of revolt. They had actually warned the local police and media that they would riot if any more of these gypsies were placed in the small suburb.

We turned up to leaflet the estate and the press reports were correct: The place was swarming with Roma gypsies. Why had the council decided to place them all in Hexthorpe? It was a horrible sight and I felt great concern and solidarity with the English locals. The Roma were extremely hostile to us and harassed us as we went from road to road leafleting. Talk about being bloody swamped with immigrants!

Something more substantial was needed than six activists leafleting, so the following week I organised a protest march through the area. We thought it was best to let the police know we were coming so we duly notified them. Big mistake. The police told Doncaster council and the Labour councillors notified the local Roma hooligans and the usual leftwing opposition groups. Nevertheless, we arrived, formed up and marched with a banner through the estate, up and down residential roads shouting 'Roma gypsies off our streets!' and the local English folk were very supportive. The Roma hooligans and their leftwing fellow tribespeople tried to attack us but the police kept everyone back. We stopped in the heart of the community and gave speeches. Local English residents came to us when we finished and thanked us for coming to Hexthorpe.

Then, the migrant crisis arrived and TV news bulletins were dominated by the chaos in Calais and the Balkans. Endless lines of migrants crossing fields and invading trucks were broadcast for months on end. Europe was being invaded by a human tidal wave of phoney 'refugees', upwards of 85% of them being fighting age Muslim males from the Middle East. An armada of boats from the north African coast were making their way across the warm seas of the Mediterranean carrying millions of scrounging migrants. This nightmare scenario was foretold by the French author Jean Raspail in his famous book 'The Camp of the Saints', which depicts the destruction of Western civilization through Third World mass immigration to France and the West.

The town of Dover in Kent was the entry point for this invasion of foreigners, so we decided to hold multiple days of action in the town. Around thirty of our activists assembled and marched into town with flags, music and leaflets. The local residents of the town were very, very supportive, with only a tiny minority of leftwing (white) idiots in opposition to our presence.

All races and ethnic groups supported us, including black and Eastern European (mainly Polish) locals who were very vocal in their support for us. I remember a single, white, gormless liberal man turning up with a home-made placard sporting 'Not in my name!', before he was surrounded by an assortment of dear old ladies and young black men who told him he was an idiot! It is amazing how far from reality the traditional leftwing portrayal of the racial situation in Britain really is. Britain First has drawn support consistently from black, Asian and Oriental origin British citizens who support our patriotic, anti-establishment, anti-political correctness stance.

We held a rally with speeches in the middle of the high street with a crowd of locals watching intently. We then headed off to the ferry terminals to leaflet all the of the truck drivers waiting to board the boats, who, once again, were very supportive of our message. The following week we held a second day of action and this time a large group of aggressive leftists were in town to 'teach us a lesson'. This brave group of socialists walked past us and called a female activist of ours a 'slag', prompting me and our burly security volunteers to confront them. Let's just say that in the ensuing drama, this group of leftwing hard men were 'dispatched' with minimal effort and limped off with their tails between their legs!

Then, a major scandal unfolded that shocked the nation and prompted an indignant reaction from the public. In a small town in South Yorkshire called Rotherham, it emerged that over 1,400 children had been groomed, exploited, raped and tortured by Islamic Pakistani paedophile gangs over a sixteen-year period. The local social services, council and police authorities refused to take action against this tidal wave of paedophilia because they feared they would be called 'racist'. Instead, they did nothing to halt the terrible crimes happening in the town.

An official report laid the catastrophic situation bare. It was international news and the general public were completely unaware of the scale of the Islamist grooming crisis that was hidden by officialdom all around the country. Better to abandon tens of thousands of young non-Muslim girls to predatory Islamic rape gangs than do something about it. We don't, after all, want anyone to criticise Muslims, do we? Shielding Islam from criticism is more important to our masters than protecting tens of thousands of young girls.

All departments of the town's establishment were involved in a conspiracy to cover-up the scandal: Social services, councillors, police commanders, literally everyone knew that industrial scale grooming of non-Muslim girls was taking place by Muslim grooming gangs. The word 'racist' and the general fear of it paralysed any attempt to tackle this vast tide of criminality. When the scandal broke, it rocked the nation and the liberal-Left swung into action with a myriad of excuses and spin to deflect any criticism of Islam.

The fact remains, the grooming gangs only targeted *non*-Muslim girls. Muslim girls were left completely *alone*. So, there was a religious or cultural factor in these grooming scandals. It was Muslims targeting *non*-Muslims. That's why patriots and commonsense commentators refer to this problem as a *Muslim* grooming scandal. The media, however, always refer to them as *Asian* grooming gangs, tarring the Sikh, Hindu and Indian communities with the same brush all in an effort to protect Islam.

It is not, however, 'Asians' that are responsible, but *Muslims*. If

Muslim girls were targeted along with white, black and other Asian girls, then you could convincingly call this a general paedophile problem. But Muslim girls are *never* targeted by these gangs, who are made up of Muslim men. So, if the perpetrators are Muslim and the victims are non-Muslim, then you can claim with certainty this is not an Asian problem, but a *Muslim* problem. For heaven's sake, just look at the collages of perpetrators that the police consistently release during one of these scandals! All the gang members are Muslims, not 'Asians'.

Everyone knows who is responsible, but because it is Muslims that are the problem, officials and police forces refuse to take action due to the likelihood of being called 'racist'. Whenever Muslims are the problem, the political Left leaps in to lie, spin and distort the situation to protect Islam from criticism. The grooming scandal confirms that - where the establishment is concerned - Islam is more important than tens of thousands of underage girls being raped, drugged, tortured and abused. It was even the case in many towns that the police punished the *victims* of grooming while refusing to take action against the gangs themselves.

The problem is not confined to Rotherham. There have been major grooming scandals in Rochdale, Telford, Blackpool, Newcastle, Oxford, Bradford and many, many others. The towns affected by this phenomenon are too numerous to list here. The BBC produced a drama series about the Rochdale scandal while Telford was described as the child abuse capital of Britain! The Rotherham scandal has been described as the 'biggest child protection scandal in UK history'.

Britain First swung into action when this scandal hit the headlines. A team of our activists invaded the council offices in Rotherham and demanded to speak to the head of social services. We gave them a big dose of verbal hostility until they rang the police who appeared quickly from across the road. I remember shouting at the staff that the vermin responsible for the grooming scandal were working in the building and that we wanted to confront them. We held a small protest at the customer services desk with a banner that said, 'Justice for the victims of Muslim grooming!' The staff pleaded with us to leave but we refused to budge until the police threatened to arrest us.

After our ejection from the council building, we travelled up the road to Shipley, to the home address of the head of Rotherham children's services, Joyce Thacker. This was the woman primarily getting the blame for the scandal in the town. She had ignored countless young children reporting the grooming gangs to her department and left them to suffer. After the report was published by the official enquiry into grooming, she was called upon to resign, but she refused. So, we went to her home address to confront her and leaflet her neighbours. Her neighbours were disgusted with Thacker's actions and took our leaflets with enthusiasm. The police promptly turned up and forced us to leave the area. Nevertheless, the operation hit the headlines and Thacker must have been apprehensive because shortly after we arrived at her home she duly resigned.

The stage was set for our first big public protest march and for weeks our activists leafleted pubs and residential homes in Rotherham to attract participation. We blasted the details of our proposed march to the hundreds of thousands of supporters we had on Facebook and when the day came, hundreds of patriots have arrived from all over the country.

This was the *first* big march that we had organised and it was markedly different from those that came before. Unlike the wild, undisciplined marches of the EDL, we banned alcohol and had a big contingent of security volunteers to keep order. Unlike other groups, we distributed hundreds of flags which were prepared beforehand. The sight of hundreds of flags made a beautiful spectacle as our march made its way through the town's twisting roads. At the front stood our leadership and in front of us, three flag bearers hoisting heavy Knights Templar flags into the air. It was a great sight as we progressed to the rally point in Rotherham town centre.

Two weeks later, we held another protest march through the town and this time, our leftwing friends decided to oppose us. A pathetic group of Muslim extremists tried to block our path but were quickly and decisively moved out of the way. The pace of activity in Rotherham was driving the local establishment barmy. It wasn't just Britain First. Almost every patriotic or counter-jihad organisation in the country, big and small, were descending on Rotherham.

The general level of behaviour from these other groups was so dire in Rotherham that I decided to detach Britain First from the ongoing campaign in the town. It was a tactical decision that I felt must be taken, however annoyed I was at leaving the 'battlefield'. Organisations or movements can become 'toxic' overnight and rarely can they recover their reputation. Guarding your public perception from damage is paramount for a patriotic or nationalist movement that strives for great things. With a heavy heart, I decided to continue campaigning elsewhere, but we would return to Rotherham eventually.

15. Harassment

In the autumn of 2014, Britain First held its first annual conference and what an unforgettable event it would turn out to be, but not for the right reasons! Around one hundred patriots turned up from around the country and the venue was a conference suite in Swanley, Kent.

Britain First, like all organisations of the political Right, struggle to get venues for meetings of any kind because of the intimidation and harassment that landlords suffer from leftwing fascists when they host our meetings. We always book our venues under a range of cover names to avoid the inevitable cancellations that occur.

When we held our first conference in Swanley, we booked the venue under a cover name and the local Labour town councillors found out about our meeting, probably from the crooked police. Completely disregarding all pretence of democracy and freedom of association, they immediately swung into overdrive to sabotage our conference. Fancy that, a political party formed over a century ago that has held the reins of government many times doing all they can to deny freedom of speech to another political party. But that was the reality of it.

About halfway through the agenda, a contingent of Kent police officers pushed open the door and interrupted our policy debates, telling us we had to close the meeting immediately. I was forced to hand the mic over and walk outside to confront these gestapo idiots. When I walked outside our hall, there were about ten police officers waiting for me asking me to vacate the premises. I politely told them to sod off and that we would be finished in about an hour and a half.

I took myself back into the hall and we tried to carry on with proceedings. Then, to our total astonishment, all of the delegates watched in horror as the police started to push listening devices through a side door! They didn't even try and disguise what they were doing. Imagine if the police harassed the annual conference of the Labour Party like this? Imagine the deafening uproar that would produce. Imagine if the police pushed listening devices with long wires through a side door of the Conservative Party conference? It would be unthinkable. But this is what patriots put up with on a regular basis in a supposed 'democracy'.

I immediately walked outside again to confront these Stalinist jobsworths and this time they were filming me and gave us an ultimatum: Close the conference and clear off or face arrest. Then they cut the power to the room! I told them again to sod off or follow through with their pathetic threats. Sometimes you have to call their bluff and face the music. After all, when incidents like this happen you have a sacred duty to defy the authorities who are trying to sabotage freedom of speech. We powered through the next half an hour and finished our policy votes and then ended the conference. Funnily enough, despite the volume of video evidence we disseminated over social media, Kent police actually *denied* trying to shut our conference down at all when questioned by the media!

Millions of our ancestors have given their lives for freedom of speech and democracy. We have fought the ambitions of tyrants from Philip of Spain to Adolf Hitler throughout hundreds of years of bloodshed to maintain Britain as a beacon of rights, the rule of law and representative government. In the last few decades, however, a dark cloud of tyranny has crept up on our country. Nowadays, our 'rights' are being eroded and civil liberties are being abused. The judiciary is no longer impartial or neutral, but politically biased. The media is tightly controlled and hostile to certain viewpoints, engaging in slander, lies, distortions and character assassination of anyone opposed to establishment orthodoxy. The police make decisions based on political correctness, not the immutable word of the law. Britain is sliding ever so determinedly towards censorship and leftwing fascism.

A new term has been invented to *override* freedom of speech and suspend all political debate when it doesn't favour the liberal-Left: 'Hate speech'. 'Hate speech' is simply free speech that the Left doesn't like. Opposition to a whole range of leftwing fetishes and dogmas is now categorised as 'hate speech'. Opposition to mass uncontrolled immigration is 'hate speech'. Criticism, however justified, of radical Islam, is 'hate speech'. Free and fair comment on the new 'LGBT' social Marxist poison invading our schools and TV sets is condemned as 'hate speech'.

Opposition to most leftwing policies is 'hate speech'. It is a clever but totally dishonest method of closing down legitimate political discussion. A state of cognitive martial law is imposed when 'hate speech' is pointed out! Freedom of thought, of conscience and of speech is suspended when the Left declares an issue to be 'hate speech'.

The usual drivel from social networks, the courts or the police is that, freedom of speech is wonderful and should be protected, but 'hate speech' cannot be allowed. Who determines what is 'hate speech' and what is not? The political Left of course. It is yet another system of *control*, just like the word 'racist', 'fascist', 'homophobic', 'Islamophobic' and so on. These bogey words are designed to silence free debate on issues the Left doesn't want discussed.

Shortly after our conference, several of our activists attended a mosque in the South West town of Yeovil and asked the imam why he worshipped the prophet Mohammed when he took a six-year-old as a bride. The imam called the police and our activists were arrested for 'racially aggravated harassment', including the regional organiser. They were later given a 'no further action', but that didn't stop the Muslim Protection Squad from swinging into action once again on behalf of a mosque leader!

According to the history of Islam itself and their sacred scriptures, Mohammed *did* marry a six-year-old and had sex with her when she was nine. Asking a Muslim about this verifiable historical and religious fact is now a crime? That's how absurd the politically correct police protection of all things Islamic has now become. Although I have borne the brunt of the establishment suppression of our movement, many of our brave activists have been arrested over the years. They deserve recognition.

Next stop on our national crusade was Northern Ireland, a country that is still overwhelmingly populated by the British people but where Islam is starting to make its presence felt. The issue of Islam was never on the radar in Ulster, where the traditional conflict was sectarian in nature, between Catholic and Protestant Christians. The narrative in Northern Ireland has always been dominated by the carnage of the Troubles, by the issues of a united Ireland or maintenance of the Union with Britain, and so on.

Thanks to the continual conflict in Northern Ireland and the necessity of maintaining your culture, traditions and heritage in the face of a hostile opposing community, Ulster is a country that is still fiercely pro-British and perhaps the only part of the kingdom where our customs and way of life still hold sway. The British way of life has been so polluted by social Marxist policies on the mainland that it is hardly recognisable. But Ulster is different. The loyalist and unionist struggle against Irish republicanism has ensured the survival of our martial heritage. Patriotic parades on a scale unseen for decades on the mainland and overt displays of British flags, artwork and culture within every single community leaves Ulster as the only remaining part of our country that is still 'British'.

Because of this culture of rugged British patriotism, Britain First has always enjoyed popular support in Northern Ireland. Britain First is not – and never will be – sectarian or anti-Irish. Catholics in Northern Ireland constitute a big chunk of our support base. I will not tolerate any sectarian hostility within Britain First. We have greater, more frightening and more alien problems to deal with in the future than engaging in sectarian conflict among different denominations of Christians. If the peoples of the British Isles are to survive, we must move on from ancient conflicts and unite – or at least cooperate - to save our collective nations from the dangers of Islam, mass immigration and demographic suicide.

When I lived in Northern Ireland for about a year at the beginning of Britain First, in 2011, I attended a huge church in North Belfast called the Whitewell Metropolitan Tabernacle. The main minister of this church was a man called Pastor James McConnell, who later would become the focus of a scandal involving Islam in Northern Ireland. I had no idea at the time that the man I was listening to would be the first to lock horns with Islamic extremism in Ulster.

Long after I stopped attending his church and moved to the mainland, Pastor McConnell gave a sermon where he condemned Islam as a religion 'spawned in hell'. He described Islam as 'Satanic'. Once again, the Muslim Protection Squad swung into action and arrested this elderly Christian and charged him with, yes you guessed it, 'hate speech'. It caused a seismic furore in Northern Ireland. At his trial for, yes you guessed it, 'hate speech', he was found not guilty by the judge who told the police not to overstep the mark again with regards to freedom of speech. If Pastor McConnell thinks Islam is Satanic, then that's his right. Everyone is allowed their own opinions. Remember the immortal words of Evelyn Beatrice Hall, 'I disapprove of what you say, but I will defend to the death your right to say it'.

It then turned out that the man who made the complaint against Pastor McConnell was one of Northern Ireland's most prominent Muslim leaders, who attracted widespread condemnation when he said that an Iraqi city (Mosul) - seized by Islamic State - was 'the most peaceful city in the world'. Dr Raied Al-Wazzan of the Belfast Islamic Centre later said he was 'sorry' for any offence he caused following his comments about Mosul. Al-Wazzan said relatives living in Mosul had told him life was better since the city was taken over by Islamic State. Then he tried to claim that Islamic State was 'less evil' than the Iraqi government.

In response to these developments in Northern Ireland, we decided to get active there for the first time. We travelled to Belfast and invaded the Belfast Islamic Centre, looking to confront Dr Raied Al-Wazzan for his pro-ISIS comments. We burst into the Belfast Islamic Centre looking for him, but luckily for him he wasn't there. We spoke to one of the other mosque imams and offered to pay Al-Wazzan's plane fare if he wanted to go and live under ISIS rule in Mosul!

We then headed to meet about a dozen new Ulster activists in the loyalist town of Newtownards, east of Belfast. One of the activists told me at the meeting that there was a mosque around the corner in this staunchly unionist area. I said I didn't believe him, that I would have to see it with my own eyes. So, he offered to show me and off we went. After a very short drive a few streets away, there it was, the Newtownards Mosque! It was nothing more than a residential house converted into a mosque.

I decided to film a short video for Facebook outside the mosque, flanked by our new Ulster activists. I had only just finished talking into the camera outside the mosque when a 'people carrier' type vehicle pulled up no less than fifteen feet from us. Out poured a burly looking team of young Muslims with tank tops on. 'What are you doing outside our mosque?' one of them asked. I told them I was filming a video for social media. We stood our ground. It was obvious to me what was happening: Someone had seen us outside the mosque and reported this to a network of local Muslims who, within a very short time frame, had mobilised a 7-seater vehicle full of young men to come and confront us. The speed with which they mobilised was shocking.

This video caused a huge stir within the unionist and loyalist community. Most folk in Ulster had no idea whatsoever that there were any mosques in the whole of the country, let alone one in Newtownards, a quiet, medium sized town that was bombed by the IRA during the Troubles.

The sight of a Muslim gang confronting us outside this new mosque in Newtownards shocked many of the people in Ulster. It really was a wakeup call for many. Thousands of comments on our Facebook page displayed people's disbelief that this could happen in Northern Ireland of all places. I told everyone who I could that it was time to wake up and realise what was creeping up on them.

The authorities in Northern Ireland – dominated as they are by the sectarian bigots of Sinn Fein/IRA – would soon come down on Britain First like a tonne of bricks in a desperate attempt to halt the rise of our movement in Ulster. Northern Ireland was - and still is - a strange country where the rule of law is 'flexible' and where stitch-ups are a regular occurrence. There have been multiple instances where the rule of law is simply turned on its head, all for the sake of continuing and protecting the flawed 'peace process'.

Regardless, radical Islam has arrived in Northern Ireland and the Sinn Fein/IRA establishment – with the complicit silence of the 'Unionist' DUP – is determined that it will sink roots under the protection of the state. God help anyone who stands opposed to this official state policy. From Pastor Mcconnell to Britain First, nothing or no one was to be allowed to criticise the spread of Islam from the mainland to Northern Ireland.

16. Media

It might seem absurd to most people that an entire chapter of a book detailing a political struggle against radical Islam, the leftwing establishment and political correctness should be devoted to the mass media, but I feel it is absolutely critical.

In recent times the credibility of the mass media has taken a severe battering, with the emergence of the term 'fake news' becoming a popular epithet for journalists and dishonest media channels. Trust in the veracity and honesty of the media is now rock-bottom, and rightly so. We live in an unparalleled era where even the President of the United States attacks the mass media on a daily basis, helping to chip away at its credibility and shine a light on the rampant dishonesty and duplicity of this mega institution. I believe that the media is the number one factor in the destruction of Western civilisation and hence it is crucial to comprehensively understand this evil beast, inside and out.

It is fashionable for historians to theorise that a particular event or invention represents the start of a new era for mankind. History books are replete with such claims: The first fixed human settlements, the first stirrings of agriculture, the advent of monotheistic religion, the industrial revolution, the space age. All these and more are debated as the multifarious turning points of human history, the dividers between old eras and new ones. Life, we are told, was never again quite the same as it was after these colossal historical events.

It is the author's opinion, however, that the most significant and far reaching event in human history went entirely unnoticed, and continues to draw little attention. The emergence of this particular phenomenon truly changed the world. This phenomenon was the emergence of the mass media.

For thousands of years, throughout innumerable civilisations, religions and epochs, mankind generally held fast to the *natural* ways of the world. Regardless of religion, the principles that underpinned society, namely patriotism, race, tribe or nation, family and procreation, community and duty, all went unchallenged as the natural foundations of a healthy functioning world.

With the emergence of the mass media - at its beginning comprising newspapers, then with the additions of television and radio – there was suddenly an apparatus whereby ideas (of whatever variant) could be implanted into the national consciousness on a vast scale and continually repeated in a way that the world had never witnessed before. Before the onset of the mass media, news or ideas spread via word of mouth, public oratory, small circulation books, or public notices. This lack of mass dissemination ensured that the healthy, natural ways of the world were never successfully *supplanted* by false ideologies, to a large degree.

It is no coincidence that mankind starting to go adrift a split second after the emergence of the mass media. Here was a means whereby entire populations could be successfully brainwashed into believing almost anything, regardless of how absurd it would have seemed in previous, healthy times. With the advent of the media, a new dawn for mankind had indeed began, one to rival anything in significance to the events that the history books love to fuss about. Before delving into the workings of the mass media and its effect and influence on society, the most important thing to examine is how the human mind actually *works*. Once this is explained sufficiently, everything falls into place.

The human mind is comprised of two parts: The conscious and the sub-conscious. The conscious mind is the thinking, calculating, reasoning part. If someone lobbed a brick at your head it would be the conscious mind that analysed the situation and reacted to it. The sub-conscious mind is a filing cabinet. If you did something regularly enough your sub-conscious mind would store all the occurrences to produce automatic behaviour in the future, to take the workload off the conscious mind in everyday life. Breathing is an excellent example: Imagine having to concentrate on breathing all the time, and if you stopped concentrating, you stopped breathing! This is the purpose of the sub-conscious mind, to produce automatic behaviour for the things that occur *regularly*. Ever kept your phone in a certain pocket? Can you recall a time when you reached into that pocket to get your phone out without even realising it when you wanted to make a call? That's your sub-conscious mind at work.

Why is this relevant? Because media propaganda is aimed specifically at the sub-conscious mind. The sub-conscious does not reject information if it considers it wrong or false. It takes in information and accepts it dispassionately. The sub-conscious mind is accessed by *repetition*. The media repeats the same basic messages time and time again until they become entrenched, and once entrenched, they produce *automatic* behaviour. A good example of this would be the hordes of brainwashed lefty zombies who strut around calling people 'racist' on the flimsiest of pretences. Why is it that voters automatically elect the same degenerate political parties time and time again, even though if forced to reason they would find a million negative things to say about them! Understanding how the media exploits the workings of the human mind is the key to fighting back against its malignant influence.

This is what is meant by the term 'brainwashing'. The media acts as a *brainwashing* machine, aimed primarily at the sub-conscious mind, which it accesses by churning out the same politically correct mantras relentlessly and repeatedly. We are all familiar with these: Racism, extremism, human rights, the benefits of immigration and the EU, and so on. The result is a population mass that sub-consciously accepts the most ridiculous leftwing views as 'the norm', these views being beamed into people's heads at lightning speed by the media apparatus. Politicians shamelessly exploit the receptive nature of the sub-conscious mind when election time comes and they spew forth endless catalogues of 'vows', 'promises' and 'pledges', all designed to flood and poison the mind of the masses with their garbage.

There are essentially two types of person: The first group, which amounts on average to a puny 5% of any given population, has a strong enough intellect and powers of reasoning that they possess the ability to make their own judgements and decisions, particularly with regard to political matters. This group is less susceptible to brainwashing, fashion or prevailing trends, and generally retains an independent consciousness.

The second group is the remaining 95% - the 'sheep', to use a traditional harsh criticism. This group, while containing an enormous array of differences, all tend to be dominated in thinking by whoever has a monopoly on the information they receive, which is the mass media. The mass media aim the phalanx of their attack against this group, and utilize every trick in the book to brainwash the sub-conscious mind of the 95% to turn them into a pliable mass that will carry out any bidding – or vote for any party!

Obviously control of the mass media apparatus would be an attractive prospect for anyone wishing to control and manipulate entire populations, hence the democratic process as well. The black American activist Malcolm X had it spot on when he said: 'The media's the most powerful entity on earth. They have the power to make the innocent guilty and to make the guilty innocent, and that's power'.

With absolute control on all information reaching the public, the media bosses are *immensely* powerful individuals. Their media empires are highly regimented and tightly controlled. The idea that newspapers and TV stations allow their staff to report and to review *independently* is pure fantasy. 'Freedom of the press' is one of the most laughable statements ever muttered!

Here we come to the crunch of the issue: There exists an organisation, controlled by individuals who are unelected, that has almost absolute power to shape the climate of a nation's internal life and achieve almost any effect or trend possible, and which is being used directly to undermine Western civilisation.

Is this merely sheer paranoia on the author's part? Is the media really this influential and significant? At the dawn of the media age, one of the great figures of history and a man of enormous power and achievement, Napoleon Bonaparte, said the following: 'Four hostile newspapers are more to be feared than a thousand bayonets.' What prophetic words from a historical giant.

Two centuries ago this man recognised - albeit while the media machine was still in its infancy - the profound and enormous power it would one day yield over the world. The primacy of the media, wielding far more real power than that enjoyed by elected representative politicians, is a fact. 'For a politician to complain about the press is like a ship's captain complaining about the sea', said Enoch Powell, referring to the fact that in many respects, the media and the sham circus of 'debate' and news coverage it provides, *is* the political process, and the votes cast by the populace, merely the end result.

The patriotic movement needs to do more to destroy the credibility of the mass media. The attack must not cease, but on the contrary, should continue for years on end, until our basic message that the media is dishonest and crooked enters the national subconscious mind. Thankfully, in recent years, a tidal wave of anger and criticism of the media has been gaining momentum. Fuelled by populists such as US President Donald Trump and assisted by scandals like phone hacking, the media's reputation is being relentlessly ground down. The clear majority of your average population hold negative views about journalists and the media when asked.

Britain First has been mercilessly maligned by the media since its formation. Our leaders have faced dishonest and disgusting character assassination at the hands of corrupt journalists. Our movement has been called every negative name under the sun. We have been blamed for the deaths of babies and MPs, have been called racist, fascist, Nazi, homophobic, Islamophobic, anti-Semitic, militaristic, violent and so on.

We have been accused of fomenting and perpetrating terrorist attacks on Muslims and Members of Parliament. I have been falsely accused of being a sexual predator, of being accused of sexual assault (like Donald Trump) and conspiracy to cover-up attempted rapes. 'In late 2017, accusations were made against Golding by a female under the age of consent, who attended one of the group rallies protesting against the sexual abuse of young girls, that Golding had sexually abused her,' is one example of this noxious poison.

Wikipedia describes me as an 'advocate of British Fascism' and a 'convicted criminal'. The media have falsely claimed I am a former member of the National Front and that I was expelled from the British National Party for head-butting an ethnic minority councillor! All lies. Pure invention. You name it, I have had it thrown at me relentlessly. I am at the point now where I am completely numb to the lies, distortions and falsehoods of the mass media. If they haven't got something quasi-credible to lash you with, they simply make stuff up. They invent narratives and inject them with little white lies that – repeated over time – build up in the minds of the populace, poisoning them against me and my movement.

The worst thing about this situation is that almost everyone across the West is powerless against the lies and falsehoods of the media. Even the billions of dollars and global fame of Donald Trump didn't save him from taking a ferocious pounding when faced with the sustained efforts of the fake news media to destroy his reputation. Even when Trump overcame the avalanche of dishonesty from the media to become president, he is still under constant, daily barrage and faces indefatigable efforts to undermine his popularity.

The only refuge from the spin and bullshit of the mass media has been social networks, a phenomenon that has completely undermined the dominance of the traditional news outlets. Content travels freely and organically without censorship on social media. Britain First was the first movement of the political Right to recognise its tremendous power. Britain First was so dominant and prolific on Facebook that it caused alarm and despair at the highest levels of government. I remember being told of secret meetings at the Home Office where the then Home Secretary Theresa May had invited an assortment of leftwing groups to come along and discuss with her how to combat 'the rise of Britain First'. Hope Not Hate, a very professional leftwing campaign organisation, said that Britain First was the 'second most liked Facebook page in the politics and society category in the UK – after the royal family.'

Our social media efforts allowed our movement to *bypass* the traditional media and head straight to the masses. Our Facebook page topped out at 2.1 million supporters, more than double the size of our nearest political rival. We literally conquered Facebook in the UK. Sometimes we were reaching 30 million people within the UK every single week with our memes, videos and news links. That's one-third of the entire population, *weekly*.

We screenshot and publicised these stats and it left the establishment panic stricken. To their credit, for many years Facebook refused the requests of the UK government and the likes of Hope Not Hate to take down our fan page. Believe it or not, but the UK government applied *enormous* pressure to Facebook to take down the fan page of a registered political party, that's how crooked and disgusting this situation was. Outrageous fascist behaviour from a government posing as a 'democracy'.

The establishment was appalled that Britain First was side-stepping the traditional mass media and going straight to the people, without any distortion or spin from the usual gaggle of biased, lefty 'journalists'. Our message greeted the people without any meddling by the usual leftwing media censors.

This situation was simply unacceptable to an establishment that had enjoyed an unchallenged monopoly on public information for decades. Every so often, intel would filter its way to me from leftwing sources that efforts to shut down Britain First on social media had failed again and that the liberal-Left was aghast at our organic, genuine popularity.

For years, the political Left was forced to 'suck it up' until one fateful day when Britain First simply got 'too big' and a single incident triggered a chain of events that led to our movement being banned from every major social network in the world, including Facebook. Our own attempt to build our own mass media had been so successful it ended in frantic and violent censorship. We will discuss this in further detail in a later chapter, suffice to say that Britain First, through dynamic and relentless effort, had built the biggest and most powerful social media machine that Europe has ever seen.

17. Headlines

After a long absence from the Islamist dominated stronghold of East London, I received new intelligence that Abdul Mahid and his gaggle of miscreants were up to their old tricks again, organising 'Muslim patrols' but this time not aggressive and belligerent. This time, they merely roamed the streets in large groups distributing literature about Sharia Law and preaching Wahhabi Islam.

Once again, we deployed the armoured Land Rover and held a 'Christian Patrol' march down Brick Lane. By this point in the timeline, however, Britain First was a household name and especially in the Islamic strongholds such as Luton and East London. Unlike the first forays down Brick Lane, this time we encountered instant fierce opposition. As our activists walked down each side of the road small groups of Muslim men shouted 'this is a Muslim area'. We managed to reach the end of Brick Lane, but only by the skin of our teeth. As we turned right into Bethnal Green Road the police pounced on us and pulled us to the side of the road. Several Muslims saw this and decided to harass us as we were questioned by the police on the kerb.

We were surrounded by about fifteen police officers and I remember shouting at them, 'Is this the usual response when people leaflet in East London'. As usual, the reaction from the Muslim Protection Squad was over-the-top. Suddenly a Muslim passer-by called a female activist a name I do not care to repeat, and then launched at me with violent intent until he was restrained by the police. The Muslim idiot in question was actually allowed to return to within a few feet of me and flicked a live cigarette in my face, scorching part of the area under my eye. A clear case of assault if ever there was one. The Muslim Protection Squad, however, refused to arrest him and simply told him to leave the area. This wouldn't be the first time I was attacked by a Muslim thug and the attacker let off scot free.

Six months later we would return to Brick Lane for the last time. The local Muslims were fed up with our intrusions into 'their area' and this time their reaction was ferocious. On this occasion, we had a big contingent of activists and we made our presence felt using a large number of flags and Christian crosses. The police knew we were coming this time (somehow) and they turned up in droves to keep order. They struggled to keep aggressive local Muslims away from us and things turned nasty very quickly.

Muslims poured out of the curry houses and off licences all along the road. Within the blink of an eye we were hideously outnumbered by hordes of angry, quarrelsome Muslims. The police officers present panicked and begged us to hurry up and leave. We would not be budged and we kept walking down the road giving out newspapers and leaflets, all the while stalked by a rapidly proliferating small army of Muslims who wanted to do us harm. By the time we reached the railway bridge, about two-thirds of the way up Brick Lane, a line of police held back about two to three hundred apoplectic Muslims that were foaming at the mouth! If they had broken the police line – which they could have done with ease –

they would have charged us and torn us to pieces, so outnumbered were we. Our repeated incursions into East London led to a large number of international media reports, including on big networks such as RT.

In response to the escalating danger facing our frontline activists, I decided to hold activist training sessions, teaching them everything from boxing, MMA, Ju-Jitsu, Krav Maga and grappling. I have a background in martial arts myself and have been training boxing, Muay Thai and MMA since I was a young boy. I used to help train fighters at my previous gyms and I enjoyed imparting self-defence skills. It was the least I could do considering the danger we encountered when I led our troops into dangerous Muslim areas. Our activists were very enthusiastic about these training sessions and they thoroughly enjoyed adopting new combat skill sets. Unfortunately, a lack of gyms willing to accommodate our sessions was a crippling drawback. We held some of these sessions under cover names but this only led to establishments threatening us with legal proceedings if we didn't bugger off. For a long time I wanted to purchase or rent our own facilities so I could hold regular training sessions, but it never materialised. One day, I hope to open a dedicated Britain First activist training gym.

In March 2015, Britain First hit the headlines in a massive way when my old foe Brusthom Ziamani - a teenage Islamist follower of Anjem Choudary - was sentenced to twenty-two years for plotting to behead a British soldier. Footage of me confronting Ziamani and waving a microphone in his face featured on almost every single TV report and news bulletin. You may remember this was the extremist I confronted outside the Indian Embassy on the Aldwych in central London some time ago. On that day, I was arrested for breach of the peace, but the footage and photos of me getting stuck into Ziamani were iconic.

Believe it or not, but I remember members of the public

ringing up our head office phone line and complaining at our use of these photos because I was white and Ziamani was black. This just shows how deep politically correct brainwashing has penetrated the national consciousness. When we explained that the black fella in the photos was a Muslim extremist these angry supporters reversed their position, but it was a sad indictment of the sorry state of morals and values in modern Britain.

Ziamani has been busted by anti-terror police while making plans to behead a British soldier, Lee Rigby-style. Had I known at the time I had confronted him that the Islamist in front of me wanted to chop off a soldier's head, I probably would have rammed his head through the nearest wall.

Ziamani was born into a staunch Jehovah's Witness family and was only nineteen years old when he was sent to prison. Ziamani was arrested on a London street carrying a knife and hammer in his bag and said at his trial that he was on his way to behead a soldier. The judge at his trial said he had been 'adopted and totally absorbed by a twisted interpretation of the holy Quran'. Shortly before the arrest, Ziamani showed his weapons to an ex-girlfriend and said he planned to kill British soldiers, telling her he thought Michael Adebolajo, one of the men who murdered Lee Rigby, was 'a legend'.

Ziamani said at his trial that he first became interested in Islam aged fifteen via rap music. Believe it or not, he was arrested for the first-time months before he plotted his attack. On that occasion, the police found a ripped-up letter in his jeans pocket in which he wrote about mounting an attack on a British soldier and expressed the desire to die a martyr. He was arrested for this and bailed. Imagine that: This Islamist was apprehended with a letter describing his murderous intentions but he was released on bail! I am one-hundred percent sure, that if a white activist was arrested with a letter detailing his intent to launch a terror attack on a Muslim he would be banged up in Belmarsh quicker than you can say Allahu

Akbar!

After being asked to leave home by his parents, Ziamani linked up with militant members of Anjem Choudary's network, who gave him clothes and a place to stay. He attended their discussions and took part their demonstrations. Ziamani posted comments on Facebook saying that he was 'willing to die in the cause of Allah' and 'Sharia law on its way on our streets. We will implement it, it's part of our religion'.

Ziamani was born to Congolese parents and converted to Islam less than a year before his arrest. To be brutally honest, I actually feel sorry for this young man. He was only nineteen years old when he was sent to prison. He had his whole life ahead of him. He could have gone on to live a normal life, got married, raised a family and contributed to society. But at a very impressionable age he was radicalised by members of Al-Muhajiroun, led by Anjem Choudary.

Choudary and his hangers-on literally poisoned this young man's brain with their Wahhabi ideology and within a very short time frame, he had been brainwashed and then plotted acts of terrorism. The real blame in the case of Ziamani lies with Anjem Choudary and the network he led. A big share of the blame also lies with the politically correct authorities who allowed Choudary to operate with impunity for so long.

Ziamani was an innocent victim of Islamic extremism and political correctness. Yes, Ziamani planned to carry out unspeakable attacks on British military personnel, but he was only a teenager, a young boy. He was turned into a monster by the likes of Choudary. To this day, I am proud that I confronted Ziamani in such a forthright and belligerent fashion on the streets of London.

But the human side of me feels regret that this young black man had his life ruined by the likes of Anjem Choudary. If the police had taken care of Choudary at the beginning of his long career of extremism, then this young man would never have had his life sabotaged. It is a sad episode in the sordid history of radical Islam in Britain.

On the morning of 7th January 2015, two Islamist brothers - Saïd and Chérif Kouachi - burst into the Paris offices of the French satirical weekly newspaper Charlie Hebdo armed with assault rifles. During a barrage of gunfire, they slaughtered twelve innocent workers and severely injured another eleven. The terrorists claimed to belong to Al-Qaeda's branch in Yemen. Other the next few days, more terror attacks plagued France, leading to more deaths, including four Jews at the Hypercacher kosher supermarket siege.

The French Army was deployed to on the streets. A huge manhunt ensued to seek out the Charlie Hebdo terrorists who had gone into hiding. When they were found, a stand-off developed until the brothers emerged from the building they were hiding in firing their guns. They were quickly shot dead.

The Charlie Hebdo magazine operation fearlessly exposed the innate intolerance of radical Islam. Using French 'hate speech' laws a consortium of Islamic organisations unsuccessfully sued the magazine for repeatedly publishing cartoons of the Prophet Mohammed in 2006. Depictions of Mohammed are banned under Islam. Cartoons or caricatures of Mohammed typically send Islamic populations around the world into a frenzy when they emerged.

In response to the publishing of cartoons of Mohammed, the offices of Charlie Hebdo have been firebombed. Cartoonists working for Charlie Hebdo have been added to Al Qaeda death lists and have faced multiple assassination attempts by Islamists.

The Charlie Hebdo massacre shocked the world and caused an unparalleled outpouring of grief and condemnation from world leaders. Shortly after the massacre, my intelligence team informed me that – to my utter shock – thousands of Muslims were planning to demonstrate *against* Charlie Hebdo for publishing cartoons of their prophet! How insensitive, crass and heartless!

Not a single demonstration was organised in the UK by the Islamic population protesting the massacre by Al Qaeda in Paris. Instead, they virtually joined in the horror by protesting against Charlie Hebdo. I was speechless. Do these lowlifes not watch the news? Were they not aware of the shocking terrorist atrocity that had just taken place? Their first instinct was to ignore the massacre carried out in their name and protest against a magazine that had just suffered death and carnage at the hands of their co-religionists. These Muslims were not bothered by the rise of ISIS or by the massacres in Paris, no. They were propelled into action by a few cartoons! Words escape me sometimes when it comes to some Muslims.

I was determined to oppose this protest against Charlie Hebdo by thousands of UK Muslims. The only problem was that it was due to take place on a Sunday, which is a terrible day to mobilise activists. The Christian day of rest is so engrained into our native culture that Sunday has always been considered by me to be a day to avoid activities at all costs. Britain First is and always will be a Christian movement and so we take the fourth commandment very seriously, 'Remember the Sabbath day, to keep it holy. Six days you shall labour and do all your work, but the seventh day is the Sabbath of the LORD your God. In it you shall do no work: you, nor your son, nor your daughter, nor your male servant, nor your female servant, nor your cattle, nor your stranger who is within your gates. For in six days the LORD made the heavens and the earth, the sea, and all that is in them, and rested the seventh day. Therefore the LORD blessed the Sabbath day and hallowed it.'

When the day came, I had managed to mobilise a mere twenty-five activists, some coming all the way from Cornwall in the South West. We met at Charing Cross station and walked into the mouth of Whitehall and down towards Downing Street and the Cenotaph. There we caught glimpse of the enormous Islamic horde that had arrived outside the Ministry of Defence building. There must have been anywhere between 3,000-5,000 Muslims, and opposing them were less than thirty of us! Nevertheless, it is not in our DNA to back down when hideously outnumbered so we got as close to their ranks as possible and refused to budge. We were stupidly outnumbered! It was even worse than our 'Rorke's Drift' moment outside Regent's Park Mosque.

As soon as we approached the first big group of Muslims, we started to shout, 'Terrorist scum, off our streets!' The police immediately jumped on us and forced us back. I remember a group of young Muslim men shouted out 'racists' at us and so I charged across the road filled with rage at them until I was rugby tackled by the police! Several of our other activists who charged after me where set upon by the police and ended up face first on the tarmac. During these days, we were utterly *fearless*.

Our puny group screamed 'Taliban scum off our streets!' but we were outnumbered to the point of insanity. Nevertheless, we held our ground on the other side of the road and when groups of ten or so Muslims came over to us we gave as good as we got. We then noticed that some of the Muslims across the road were kicking the poppy wreaths that lay at the base of the new black memorial to the women of the Second World War. This sent me apoplectic. These bastards were showing no respect whatsoever to the memorial. They were kicking and treading all over the wreaths. I lost my patience and told a police officer if he didn't sort out this disgusting outrage then we would.

The police actually buckled and removed all the poppy wreaths from the base of the memorial. For once they did the right thing, even though we had given them an ultimatum. The Muslim crowds were screaming 'Allahu Akbar' and 'Takbir' and they were hanging off the General Bernard Montgomery statue showing no respect whatsoever. By this point we were surrounded by aggressive young Muslim men who were hurling abuse at us. The police gave us a Section 35 notice to disperse and threatened us with arrest if we didn't clear off. They walked us back towards Trafalgar Square but we were completely surrounded and under siege by hundreds of aggressive Muslims. The police struggled to keep the peace. We still engaged in a ferocious battle of hostile words with the Muslim hordes as we walked back to the station.

We never back down or go silent with fear when under siege – to the contrary, we always acted with complete bravery and bravado, even when stupendously outnumbered. That day in Whitehall was one such example where our small group acted with a cocky, intrepid and confident demeanour. Britain First grew to such monolithic proportions on social media because millions of users admired our courage and obstinate bravery.

In the face of such dedication and will to victory, the authorities can do little. How many times have you heard someone comment that Britain has lost its backbone? Probably thousands of times. Our job, as we saw it, was to lead by example and put that backbone back into our people. Leading from the front and going where no one else dared to tread was our forte. Relentless activities and dauntless bravery was in our DNA. These values ran through us like a stick of seaside rock.

18. SO15

SO15 Counter Terrorism Command is a specialist operations branch within the Metropolitan Police, based in London. According to Wikipedia, SO15 was 'established as a result of the merging of the Anti-Terrorist Branch (SO13), and the Special Branch (SO12) in October 2006, bringing together intelligence, operations and investigative functions to form a single command.'

SO15 has over 1,500 officers and staff as well as a number of investigators based overseas. According to the SO15 website, their supposed responsibility is to disrupt terrorist activity. SO15, although based in London and part of the Met, is, in practical terms, the leading anti-terrorism division in the UK. What all this essentially means is that SO15 is the last line of defence against the avalanche of Islamist terrorism hitting our country.

SO15 have foiled dozens of terror plots that would have wreaked untold carnage on the streets of Britain and led to certain civil war. SO15 is the agency responsible for monitoring the estimated 23,000 known Islamic extremists and the hundreds of returned ISIS fighters that roam free in our country. To be honest,

I admire the work that these amazing police officers do. They help to keep the British people safe and have prevented an avalanche of Islamist terror attacks. Without them, literally thousands of our people would have perished and the UK would be knee deep in civil strife.

However, sometimes SO15 is forced by its politically correct superiors to interfere in politics to harass and silence political dissidents. Despite the catastrophic scale of the Islamist threat, the Home Office thinks nothing of deploying these specialist anti-terror police to hound and badger patriots. I can testify, through personal experience, that much effort and time has been wasted by SO15 pursuing myself and Britain First for Mickey Mouse offences that are usually not even the domain of your local police CID! Despite the official UK government terrorism threat level hovering at 'severe – attack imminent', I know for a fact that huge resources have been wasted by SO15 as they lock horns with our legal political movement.

It is not only myself or Britain First that has been pursued for silly offences by these elite terror cops. Nor is it only our movement and leadership that have been subjected to their relentless pressure and dirty tricks. SO15 and the other elite branches of the Met Police have been variously referred to over time as 'Special Branch', a much more commonly known term.

There have been at least ten occasions where 'Special Branch' has approached my activists or senior officers and pleaded with them to snitch on me or provide ongoing intelligence about my activities. I am not concerned with any of my subordinates that come forward and tell me about these nefarious approaches, it is the ones who do *not* come forward that concern me. How many Britain First officers have SO15 got on their payroll? How many snitches infest our movement? I know from the ones that come forward and inform me straight away that there is a big operation underway to subvert the leadership of our movement.

I keep asking myself why, considering we are simply a legal political movement. The answer is simple: At any given moment, someone who has been awoken by our movement can take the law into their own hands and carry out a terrorist outrage against a mosque, for example. The only way the 'Powers That Be' can minimise this possibility is to infiltrate patriotic organisations that have grown to huge proportions, such as Britain First. These imperatives, passed down to SO15 by the politically-controlled Home Office, ensure that our movement is subject to regular efforts of infiltration, penetration and intrusion.

Usually the efforts to 'turn' our activists happen when they fall foul of the law. For example, I remember one senior activist that spends a huge amount of time at my side got into a bar fight on a night out and got arrested. Let's call him Dave, just for the sake of this example. Suddenly, Dave was faced with one of the arresting officers claiming that he had assaulted him. This was total nonsense of course, but faced with an assault charge against a police officer - which is pretty much a guarantee of a lengthy prison sentence - most poor souls would buckle immediately. That's the technique, to escalate the pressure quickly using false charges and evidence. Dave was facing a serious criminal charge and then, to his surprise, he was taken into a room and was greeted by officers from SO15. They did their best to 'turn' him, promising to cancel all charges against him. All he had to do was to provide 'inside' information on me and Britain First activities. To his credit, he told them to 'fuck off' and as soon as he was released, he rang me immediately to tell me everything that had happened.

Another example would be that which took place immediately after I was sent to prison in 2018, after our trial for 'harassing' migrant paedophile gang rapists in Ramsgate, Kent. As soon as our cell doors closed, SO15 contacted multiple activists and pleaded with them to snitch on us. I do not know how many were contacted, but I was told by at least three of our activists that they were contacted. I wonder how many folded and didn't tell me what had happened after my release? Who knows, unfortunately intelligence service infiltration is extremely hard to detect and root out by its very nature.

One of the elite divisions of 'Special Branch' is known as the 'Metropolitan Investigation Bureau', but I think in fact this is simply a made-up cover name and the people behind this supposed unit are SO15. Whoever the 'Metropolitan Investigation Bureau' really is, they are desperately interested in me. Tommy Robinson, the former leader of the EDL, wrote in his book 'Enemy of the State' that he was approached in prison by SO15/Metropolitan Investigation Bureau. According to him, they promised to make his problems go away if only he would spy on me. Robinson claimed that these spooks wanted him to return to be leader of the EDL so that they could control it. Seems highly likely to me – this is classic Special Branch tactics, to infiltrate and control what they perceive as a threat.

Robinson wrote, 'I also think they were worrying about this Paul Golding character, who had started another protest movement, Britain First. He's the man you might have seen in the news but mostly on social media networks storming into mosques and taking his followers into the fray quite a bit more forcefully than I ever did at the EDL.' These claims seem, to me, to be the truth. At that point, when Robinson was in prison for fraud, Britain First was indeed freaking out the government and we were growing to gargantuan dimensions on social media. It seems entirely reasonable that Special Branch would do whatever they could to worm their way into our ranks.

Robinson continued and expanded upon the approach made to him in prison later in his book: 'And then they told me they needed my help and started talking about what was happening not just in the EDL but the far right generally, especially Paul Golding and Britain First. They were talking about fragmented groups, no control or leadership and then they came right out and said they needed my help in rooting certain people out. They wanted help dealing with Golding. They thought I could command the respect of the entire far right – which I took issue with, as I have always done – and when they asked me what I was going to do when I got out of jail, I told them I was going to work, to get on with my life. Not the right answer, Tommy. They wanted me to help with what they called troublesome people, at which I said no, what you want is for me to become a police informant.'

Shortly after his licence conditions ended, Robinson asked for a meeting and when we arrived at the pub in the countryside outside Luton, he had a man with him who by his own admission, 'worked for the Home Office'. He looked very 'official', if that makes sense. I was immediately on edge and our guard was up. At this casual meeting in the beer garden of this particular pub in the Bedfordshire countryside, Robinson explained the whole sordid approach while he was in prison, saying that SO15 asked him to 'get close to me' after his release.

I am not claiming here that Robinson turned informer because to be brutally honest, there is no way of knowing anyway. If he had, we wouldn't know. If he had not, we wouldn't know for certain. Robinson vociferously denies it. Robinson has been persecuted by the authorities himself relentlessly and has been subjected to the same kind of Gestapo tactics as I have. He was thrown in prison in 2018 for supposedly breaching a reporting ban on a grooming trial and was later released on appeal. Since then, the Attorney General has confirmed he is to be arraigned again in court for the same offence. The only thing we know for certain is that he *was* approached in prison – by his own admission – by the security services and they asked him to help bring me down. That obviously worries me and I am eager to know the full story. But that will never happen until we are in power one day.

The fact is, nobody knows what the hell is happening in the murky world of the security services! I simply do not trust anyone. I am always on the lookout for strange patterns of behaviour.

I have an iron rule that I have lived with for the last seven years, since the inception of Britain First: If I detect any suspicious behaviour from anyone in my vicinity, then they are simply denied any important information. I prefer to keep people *close* who I am certain are working for the Old Bill. If you remove them completely, then SO15 will simply try to 'turn' *other* activists and for a length of time, you may not know that that particular person has been compromised. Better to leave these traitors in position and just control them and starve them of information. Better the devil you know than the devil you don't. Remember the famous quote from the Godfather film, 'Keep your friends close but your enemies closer'.

There have been many times when I have strongly suspected a wrong-un within Britain First and I have simply left them alone but at the same time, kept them at arm's length. To be honest, Britain First does not engage in illegal activity so there isn't anything to report to one's handlers except protest preparation and leafleting session preparation! But I am very skilled at looking for the *patterns* of dodgy behaviour that typically walks hand-in-hand with police informers and have several very experienced advisors from the 'Old School' who help me with tactics and strategy.

The security services will never give up trying to infiltrate and control Britain First – that much I know. My job is to spot the traitors and minimalize them. To render them *ineffective*. Sometimes in the past I have fed these informers false information that we were organising a major, incendiary activity only to find that, when a small incognito surveillance team arrived at the scene, the police were already there waiting. That's confirmation enough for me!

Sometimes these informers are fed false information that, surprise surprise, ends up on social media. Sometimes I have bugged suspects with recording devices and actually confirmed they were *not* informers. There's a hundred tricks out there for dealing with subversion and treachery, too numerous to name here. It is a strange world when dealing with subversion!

SO15 like to waste resources dealing with Britain First, that's for sure. I remember the time when we tracked hate preacher Mikaeel Ibrahim down to a house in Thamesmead, in South East London. Ibrahim is the muscular bodyguard of Anjem Choudary and other Islamist leaders and the man who threatened to behead me outside the Saudi Arabian Embassy. After we found out his address - using the usual cocktail of intelligence techniques - we descended on his house during the day, about ten of us. We noticed a 'Team Islam' sticker in the window. It was definitely his home address.

Unfortunately for us, he wasn't at home, but his gobby, mouthy mother was. She came out hurling abuse at us while we filmed a video outside his house. She called us 'Kuffar' and I remember laughing at her ridiculous statements. After she had finished fulminating and gesticulating at us, we went on our way. Within a few days, I began receiving calls from a man claiming to be a police officer from Plumstead police station. He assured me it was nothing to worry about, they just needed to take a short statement about the activity at Ibrahim's home address. I asked if a complaint had been made and I was told that up to that point, no complaint had been made. Unfortunately, Plumstead police station was a long drive away so I told them if they wanted to take a silly statement from me, they would have to travel to a station local to me. They agreed and a time and date was set. At that point, I did not suspect anything untoward was being planned.

When I arrived at Sittingbourne police station – which was very close to me – I entered the station and was led to an interview room. Or so I thought! The station officers took me into a large room where there was sitting about six professional looking officers in executive suits. I sat down quite confused when they quietly informed me I was under arrest for threatening to kill the mother of Mikaeel Ibrahim! I leant forward to the nearest officer and looked at the blurb on his lanyard. There it was, in black and white: SO15 Counter Terrorism Command! I had walked willingly into an ambush.

At the same time that I was being arrested, three carloads of SO15 officers were fast approaching my home address and our office, which they raided with maximum force. Our staff were taken completely by surprise and after an exhaustive search of my property, they confiscated every single electronic item in the house. Laptops, memory sticks, printers, keyboards, external hard-drives, everything. They stripped our offices bare. This caused massive problems regarding administration and keeping Britain First ticking over.

I was kept in a police cell for 24 hours until I was led to an interview room for questioning. There they were again, SO15 Counter Terrorism Command officers, the elite of Britain's anti-terrorism defences, about to question me about a minor offence that took place on the outskirts of London. Was I a terrorist? Was I a threat to national security? No, of course not, I was a politician, albeit a very controversial one.

Believe it or not, but the mother of Mikaeel Ibrahim had gone to the nearest police station and claimed that I had threatened to kill her, even though we had recorded the events outside her house. After a grilling by these elite coppers, I was released on bail. About three weeks later, I got a phone call from an SO15 officer who told me the case had been *dropped* – no further action. Shortly after my arrest and the raid on my home address, the penny dropped and I figured out why on earth SO15 were involved: They simply used this silly incident to gather up all of our computer equipment which they then subjected to forensic inspection. It was an intelligence gathering operation. They knew full well that I wouldn't be so stupid as to threaten to kill an Islamist's mother. They knew we were too careful and disciplined for that. They simply wanted an excuse and an opportunity to go through our laptops and hard drives, to see what we were up to. All they would have found is leaflets, word documents and emails talking about organising protests and days of action!

But they didn't know what they would find, so they seized the opportunity to stick their devious noses into our business. They found sweet nothing, but they could have found all sorts of incriminating material if we indeed had been far right extremists! This was the first time I had locked horns with SO15 Counter Terrorism Command, but it certainly wouldn't be the last.

I remember once a Britain First officer in our South East region was arrested. His name was Steve Lewis and he had been a member and activist since 2014. Steve was very active and came to every activity, most of the time hitching a ride with me. Steve was arrested for wearing a political 'uniform' contrary to the Public Order Act 1936 – yes, that nonsense again. All he was wearing was a Britain First fleece and polo shirt – all available to purchase from our online merchandise shop - nothing even coming close to being a 'uniform'. This didn't stop S015 arresting and interrogating him. They kept Steve in custody for over fifteen hours. Steve was relaxing at home when a large group of uniformed police officers banged on his door, arrested him and took him away. It was only at the station that SO15 made themselves known. For this very minor public order offence Steve was banned from the Greater London area and prohibited from attending all Britain First activities. A colossal over-reaction considering when I was convicted of the same thing I got a £100 fine!

Steve was kept for 15 hours but not charged. He was led from his cell and taken to an interview room, to be greeted by officers from

SO15, elite anti-terror cops who subjected him to an interrogation. Consider this for a moment. For something so minor that it would warrant a £100 fine, specialised anti-terrorism officers were leading the investigation. This is the kind of ridiculous nonsense that Britain First has been subjected to.

Somehow, SO15 found out that Steve was chosen to lead a Britain First day of action in London outside Regent's Park Mosque because I had to sign-on at Bromley police station on that day and was unable to lead the activity. So, to stop this activity going ahead, they arrested him on spurious grounds. Typical sabotage tactics that would happen repeatedly. Steve was formally interviewed regarding his 'crime' and then he was led back to his cell. A short while later, he was led back to the interview room and suspected something was wrong. This time there was no recording devices being used and it was very 'casual' to use Steve's words.

The SO15 officers then did their hardest to convince Steve that it would do him the world of good if he would let them know what Britain First's plans were on a regular basis. They obviously knew that Steve was close to me and thought it would be worth a try to try and 'turn' Steve and get him to became an informer. Steve was a 'regional commanding officer' and thus knew what our organisation plans were and attended leadership meetings on a regular basis. So, he was a good 'target' for SO15 to try and flip. Steve said they talked to him in 'no uncertain terms' that he should play ball. In other words, they used menacing tones during this dastardly deed. Here we had a government policing agency trying to recruit a political activist to spy on a legally registered political party. Thankfully Steve rang me *immediately* upon release to tell me of this approach by SO15.

SO15 would become our arch enemies, harassing us constantly. They would lead every investigation against us, even for silly offences. They would proclaim in court - in front of the media - that Britain

First was a 'threat to national security' – direct quote. They would meet and greet me upon my release from prison and escort us to hostels where we would be placed under tight surveillance. They should be out catching terrorists, but it seems SO15's big priority for the last four years has been harassing Britain First. I do not blame them, however. I blame their political masters in the Home Office.

To be a leader of a revolutionary patriotic resistance movement, you must be able to stand your ground against the security services, such as SO15. You must be very, very switched on when it comes to police efforts of infiltration and subversion. You must be impervious to the constant pressure and persecution. You must eat stress for breakfast, lunch and dinner. You must subsist on pure adrenaline. You must be able to endure the most horrendous inconveniences and losses and still be able to function as if the weather was beautiful. If you lose your way, the establishment wins. If you buckle under the pressure, the establishment wins. If you fold and surrender, your country is doomed. If you give up, millions of children do not have a future.

This chapter has outlined but a fraction of the hidden struggle that I have had to endure to sustain our movement over the last seven years. I have been literally tortured over the years by the scourge of dirty tricks and treachery that is always present. So far, after eight years, Britain First has survived, which in itself is a *miracle*, considering what the authorities have thrown at us.

I have been through three separate prisons including months in solitary confinement, faced prosecution over six times and been arrested nearly fifteen times. My home and our offices have been raided multiple times, including by anti-terrorism officers. Our computer equipment and hard drives have been confiscated. I have been through every rung of the court system, from the magistrates to the High Court. I have been arrested but then not charged – 'no further action' – about four times. I have faced injunctions, bail conditions, prison licence and post sentence supervision orders all designed to curtail my freedom. I am the first politician to be banned from an entire British town (more on that later).

Several times, CPS prosecutors have tried – but failed – to increase my prison sentences in court by claiming I have a long criminal record, which isn't true. These cretins actually used the criminal record of a completely different person in court to try and increase my sentence, falsely claiming that it was mine, a deliberate and malicious falsehood. This nonsense was thrown out by a switched-on judge. Sometimes the authorities simply issue an arrest warrant for me knowing I am not in the wrong, to stop me attending a public event. I have had police officers promise me they will not arrest me if I hand myself in to a police station at a given time and date, only to be raided and arrested shortly after. I have even had SO15 officers sit with me like they are my best friends while waiting to go into court.

When taken all together, the level of persecution I have endured over the last seven years is utterly horrendous. I have been treated like a mass murderer or terrorist, but have never done more than a few months in prison at a time. This is the price you pay for taking a stand against the establishment. It is very hard to endure at times, but if you dare to be a leader of men, you must grit your teeth and persevere. Surrender is not an option.

19. Luton

The town of Luton in Bedfordshire is a haven for Islamic extremists and terrorists. Areas such as Bury Park are completely dominated by the acolytes of Allah. Prominent Islamists such as Saiful Islam, Ibrahim Anderson and many others hail from Luton.

On the day of the 7/7 London attacks, the jihadists responsible had travelled to Luton by car and then boarded a train for the capital. The 7/7 bombers were captured at Luton train station on CCTV before their murderous attack.

Dozens of terrorist plots hatched in Luton have been foiled by the security services. Luton is also a base for international terrorism, with local Muslims involved in overseas attacks such as Taimour Abdulwahab al-Abdaly who attacked Stockholm, Sweden. Luton Muslims have provided plenty of recruits for both the Taliban and ISIS. For example, Afzal Munir and Aftab Manzoor - both Luton locals - died in an American bomb attack in Afghanistan having gone to fight for the Taliban.

Anjem Choudary's Islamist organisation, Al-Muhajiroun, had a strong following in Luton, led by a notorious Islamist called Shahed.

Shahed claimed to have over two hundred hardcore followers in Luton alone, all dedicated Islamic extremists and supporters of the Taliban and ISIS.

Perhaps the most famous of Luton's Islamists is Saiful Islam, the goon who previously got a visit from Britain First at his home in Kenilworth Road in the heart of Bury Park, just a stone's throw from the home ground of Luton FC. Saiful Islam has praised Osama bin Laden and Al Qaeda for their 'courage' in fighting against the 'dictatorship and oppression' of the West. Saiful also said, 'The blame of 9/11 belongs to no one but the American government. They are the terrorists. Sheikh Osama warned America numerous times, it was because of their own arrogance, because they thought they are a superpower and nobody could match them, that Sheikh Osama taught them a lesson – a lesson they still haven't learned.'

'Wake up. Withdraw. Listen to the warnings. Muslims will stand side to side, not just Al Qaeda. The actions of the British and Americans have given prominence to Al Qaeda. All of us have a part to play in stopping the violence or the next 9/11 will take place in Britain, the next 7/7 could take place locally,' he added at a meeting of Islamists in East London.

Saiful Islam was reported to have helped an Islamist group in Belgium, called 'Sharia4Belgium', to spread its poison and hate in that country. Perhaps the most famous video of Saiful Islam is when he approached a car driven by ex-EDL leader Tommy Robinson in Bury Park. After a short discussion, Saiful punched Tommy in the face – an assault that was caught on camera. He was not arrested, despite the video evidence going viral on social media, another fine example of the hideous double standards in force in politically correct Britain. Saiful Islam has attended many of the protests and marches organised by Anjem Choudary and has given speeches at meetings and press conferences organised by Al-Muhajiroun.

Another famous extremist from Luton is Ibrahim Anderson, a

white ginger convert to Islam who was sent to prison for distributing leaflets in Oxford Street in central London in support of ISIS along with Shah Jahan Khan, another Luton local. These brazen scoundrels had the temerity to try and drum up support for ISIS in the heart of our capital city. Again, Islamists such as these become brave and confident because of the lame, restrained reaction of the police authorities to their activities. It is not a stretch of the imagination to say that the lacklustre response of the authorities encourages and facilitates these barbarians as they spread hate and plot to kill us all.

Luton is a notorious hive for Islamic extremists. Many of the videos floating around on social media and YouTube show armies of Muslims slapping their chests in the town centre and Bury Park, shocking scenes that should worry everyone who cares about the future of our country. Because of the strength of the Islamists in Luton and the endless media headlines conveying yet another scandal involving extremists and terrorists, Luton was chosen as a 'target town' for the Britain First movement.

However, from the very start, the authorities came down on our movement like a tonne of bricks, leading to years of persecution, court dates, bail conditions, criminal charges and trials. The 'Powers That Be' did not want Britain First turning up and upsetting the apple cart! Luton, and in particular the Bury Park district, is the subject of constant investigations and security service operations. The last thing they wanted is Britain First turning up and locking horns with the local hardline Islamists. But turn up we did and our activities triggered the most unprecedented backlash from officialdom that this country has ever seen.

It all started when Britain First announced a protest march through the town in opposition to the growth and prominence of Islamic extremism. This was to be our first political activity in the town. Almost immediately the news of our forthcoming demonstration triggered a ferocious reaction in the town. Britain

First was condemned by local councillors, local 'faith leaders', the police and the media.

Whatever the reaction of the local establishment, Britain First was going to exercise its democratic right to protest in the town. Sometimes local liberal clergy or politicians appeal to Britain First to scrap our plans, vainly expecting us to cancel on the basis of 'community cohesion'. Dozens of times we have told these vainglorious, publicity seeking idiots to get stuffed. Britain First will go where it wants, when it wants and no amount of snivelling bilge from these self-publicising imbeciles will change that.

A good example of this was an appeal for a face-to-face meeting with the local 'Christian' leaders of Bury Park that came immediately after we announced our intention to march through Luton. I travelled to St Mary's Church in the heart of Luton to meet four of the town's Christian clergy leaders. We sat down in an old room within the confines of this church and we discussed the issues of extremism, terrorism and immigration with them.

Among them was the notorious self-publicist Peter Adams, supposedly a Christian but I suspect simply a limp-wristed liberal traitor who loves nothing more than cosying up to Muslims in the town. This self-appointed 'community leader' is the archetypal white, self-hating liberal clown who feeds off the praise and approval of ethnic minorities.

As we discussed the issues surrounding our proposed protest, I began to see a big difference between the participants who were white and the only black vicar present. This black vicar represented a church in Bury Park and in contrast to the seething contempt I felt towards the CofE clergy present, this black man was much more 'up my street' than the white vicars.

The white vicars simply engaged in endless self-loathing, self-condemning claptrap, whereas the black vicar, unrestrained by political correctness, was much more of a robust Christian. I discussed with him the possibility of spreading the Gospel in Bury Park and converting some of the Muslims from Islam to Christianity. The white vicars were visibly horrified. I had much more in common with this black man than with the cretins that hailed from my own racial background.

To be honest, the meeting was a chronic waste of our time. In the end, we simply confirmed to them that the protest would go ahead and nothing on earth would be able to stop it. Like it and lump it. Then we left, having wasted several hours of our lives we would never get back.

When we left St Mary's, rather than depart for home in Kent, we decided to drive around Bury Park and other parts of Luton to get a feel for the town. We headed straight for Bury Park and I showed those accompanying me the home address of extremist-in-chief, Saiful Islam. We then drove down the main road through the Bury Park district and the local Muslims recognised us immediately. Several of them walked straight up to our vehicle in the blistering heat and shouted abuse through the open windows.

We gave as good as we got. Traffic was moving very, very slow down the main highway and at one point, when we came to a stop, two Muslims in a car pulled up next to us. They immediately gave us a torrent of abuse, claiming that they, the Muslims, 'run the country', but, as usual, we hurled strong language back and when I told the fat Muslim in the passenger seat that he was embarrassing himself, he hurled a can at our vehicle that just missed my face.

The Muslims in the car followed us all the way through Bury Park up the hill towards Dunstable. When we reached a roundabout at the top of the hill, I decided to stop to see if the Muslims would get out of the car and approach us, which they did. The fat Muslim in a white tshirt got out of his car, walked straight up to my window and threw a punch at me that landed. It was an uncanny replica of the video where Saiful Islam punched Tommy Robinson through the window of his car. But, as we were well clear of Bury Park, I did not drive off but instead pulled the hand break up and offered him a fair fight. He spluttered some abuse towards Jayda, calling her a bitch, before he walked off. The skinny driver of the car then approached and I told him straight, 'Go back to the desert!'

Shortly after this incident, the fat Muslim was arrested for assault and I was informed of this by Bedfordshire Police. The video footage of the incident was uploaded to Facebook and YouTube and viewed hundreds of thousands of times, so I hardly needed to submit any evidence to bolster a prosecution! There it was, a Muslim punched me in the face, on camera, and about four weeks after the incident, Bedfordshire Police rang me to inform that the Muslim thug in question would receive a 'no further action'. Imagine if a white racist thug had punched a Muslim on camera. He would be prosecuted and sent to the dungeons for a hundred years! But thanks to Islamic appeasement and political correctness, he was not punished in any way whatsoever, despite the incontrovertible video evidence. Is it any wonder that our people complain that it is one rule for us and another for Muslims?

Shortly after the drive through Bury Park, a video appeared showing the local Muslim, Christian and political 'leaders' all scrambling to denounce Britain First. Joining them was a senior officer from Bedfordshire Police, Chief Superintendent David Boyle, who announced that they were taking the 'unprecedented' step to apply to the High Court in London to ban our march in Luton! The EDL had held multiple protest marches through the town, as had endless Islamist groups - but up to that point, applications to ban protest marches were unheard of. You may have seen the TV programme presented by Stacey Dooley where she tags along on an Islamist march – and gets called a 'slag'. The Muslims were shouting 'UK police go to hell!' According to Bedfordshire Police, that march was fine to go ahead, but Britain First must be prevented from exercising our democratic rights! It seems that Bedfordshire Police and the local establishment were utterly terrified of Britain First, like we were something super-horrific that had to be stopped at all costs, democracy and freedom of assembly be damned!

Please remember that at this point on the timeline Britain First was a legal, registered, Electoral Commission sanctioned political party. But here was a police service using taxpayer's cash to stop a political party from holding a legal procession through a British town. I do not know of any other examples of this happening in British political history. As the senior officer said on the video, it certainly was an 'unprecedented' step for a public authority to take.

The Royal Courts of Justice in London are Britain's highest courts of law, excluding the House of Lords itself. I knew that we had to defeat Bedfordshire Police in the High Court or police forces would simply apply to ban us from towns across the country on a regular basis. This wasn't just our proposed march in Luton on the line, this was the very right to protest that was being decided. Imagine if Bedfordshire Police had won in court! It would have ended free political protests in the UK.

Through our usual solicitors, we managed to obtain the services of an experienced QC, Ian Glen, who we met at some of the poshest offices in central London I have ever seen, at Kings Bench Walk. He was a leading barrister in all aspects of criminal law, commercial crime, serious & organised crime, terrorism and regulatory offences. I was deeply impressed with this man and his broad experience and knowledge. Fighting a one-day hearing in the High Court is very, very expensive, usually costing around £10,000. This we raised through our supporters.

When the day of the hearing came, the media were in a frenzy to cover this important and high profile case. The Chief Constable of Bedfordshire Police was seeking to obtain an injunction 'to prohibit Paul Golding and Jayda Fransen for a period of 1 year from:

-Entering the town of Luton in Bedfordshire and its surrounding areas as indicated in the attached plan,

-Entering any mosque or Islamic cultural centre or its grounds within England and Wales without prior written invitation,

-Publishing, distributing or displaying, or causing to be published, distributed or displayed, any words or images, whether electronically or otherwise, which with regard to all of the circumstances, are likely to stir up religious and/or racial hatred,

-Using threatening, abusive or insulting words or behaviour thereby causing harassment, alarm or distress to any person,

-That a power of arrest be attached to any of these.'

The hearing itself was a complete farce and I was stunned by the staggering ineptitude of the barrister that Bedfordshire Police had chosen to represent them. I cannot remember her name but judging from appearances she was a Muslim woman. The strategy of our QC was simple: Let the other side try to justify their outrageous attempt to stifle free assembly in Luton. Sometimes, the best tactic is to stay quiet and do as little as possible and let the other side bodge things up themselves. This strategy worked *brilliantly*.

The Muslim woman representing Bedfordshire Police began her presentation, which was painful to watch. Over and over again, she was reprimanded or corrected by Justice Robin Knowles and I had to fight with all the strength I could muster to prevent myself bursting into laughter every sixty seconds or so. It is probably accurate to say that we didn't win the hearing, but instead that Bedfordshire Police sabotaged themselves. The hearing ended with the judge simply throwing out the application to ban Britain First from Luton. The police were humiliated and demoralised, but they only had themselves to blame for choosing such incompetent legal representatives.

About a year later, we heard of the sad passing of Ian Glen QC. He was an amazing practitioner of law and politically neutral and impartial, as all legal representatives are supposed to be! I would like to thank Mr Glen posthumously for the sterling work he did in opposing the fascist plans of the British police. May he rest in peace in the presence of the Lord.

Faced with the defeat in the High Court, the police changed tactics. Now that the proposed protest had the support of the High Court and simply *had* to go ahead, the police used their public order powers to impose a whole myriad of *restrictions* on our march. Section 14 of the Public Order Act 1986 gives the police the power to order protesters to restrict their demonstration to a certain place or route, define the number of protesters and the start and finish times. It is an offence knowingly to fail to comply with one of the Section 14 conditions. You can be arrested and prosecuted if you fail to comply.

Despite the defeat in court, Bedfordshire Police simply slapped a whole range of restrictions on our proposed march. They changed the route so that we avoided the town centre and marched through quiet back streets and industrial estates outside the town centre. They capped the number of protesters and forced us to hold our rally not in the town centre, but in a car park on the outskirts! We simply did not have enough time to challenge these outrageous conditions, so we had to swallow them and plough ahead. The main thing is that we had fought them to a standstill and despite their 'unprecedented' legal action to sabotage our activities, we won the day and our protest went ahead.

It is not an understatement to say that Bedfordshire Police is perhaps the most politically correct police service in the country. The lengths they go to appease radical Islam are astonishing. While round one had gone to Britain First, this was not the end of our struggles with Bedfordshire Police. Within a short period of time, we would be engaged in another turbulent struggle with these establishment goons. This time they would pull out all the stops to prevent Britain First coming back to Luton, leading to months of persecution and hardship.

20. London

I consider London to be my hometown, even though I grew up in a Kent postcode on the outskirts. Bexley borough is a London district and I grew up in the town of Erith, on the banks of the River Thames. I spent many days during my youth exploring the historical sites of London, including Westminster Abbey, the Tower of London and St Paul's Cathedral. London is without doubt the greatest city in the world. I could easily provide anyone with a three-day guided tour of the historical sites.

London has been the powerhouse of the British Isles for a millennium. However, London has the dubious honour of becoming the first major British city where indigenous Britons are a minority. In 2012, it was revealed that - according to a recent demographic census - indigenous white Britons became outnumbered by immigrants or people of foreign origin. For the first time since Londinium was founded by the Romans in 43AD, the native inhabitants of the British Isles were outnumbered in their own capital city.

The population shift has been decisive in turning London into a Third World city. Statistics from the aforementioned census showed that 45% of the population of the capital described themselves as 'white British', down from 58% in 2001. This trend is accelerating. Delving into the stats even deeper, the census reveals that a whopping 37% of the population of London is born overseas. The London Evening Standard reported in 2011, 'Statisticians said the census figures showed that London was the most diverse part of the country and was leading the way as the number of ethnic minority and foreign born residents rose nationwide.'

Christianity is also on the decline in London, with some 48% of residents classing themselves as Christian, down from 58% in 2001. White Britons left London at three times the rate of minorities in a process called 'White Flight'. Indigenous Britons, fed up with the encroachment of multiculturalism and mass immigration on their local communities, moved out of the inner city and suburban areas and head for the coast and the countryside. Literally millions of indigenous Britons have fled London in this way.

I have personal experience of this process of 'White Flight'. My parents were both born and bred in inner city areas of South London, namely Brixton and Lambeth. They both grew up during the 60s and 70s, a period where Enoch Powell was warning of the 'Rivers of Blood' to come. During these important decades, London was being overrun by wave after wave of immigration, totally transforming the demographic landscape. My parents have explained to me many times that during the period of their early youth, South London was still overwhelmingly 'British' in character and population. By the time my mother fell pregnant with me, the Brixton and Lambeth areas had been completely transformed.

A short while before I was born, my parents took the same path as millions of others and moved to the suburbs of London, specifically the borough of Bexley. When I was enjoying my youth, during the late 80s to late 90s, Erith was overwhelmingly a 'British' area and immigrants were very, very rare indeed. When I return to Erith these days, it has, unfortunately, been completely overrun

(Above) Our first 'Britannia Ball' in Dartford. Britain First has always been based on Ulster loyalism.

(Above) Britain First protest march in Luton, which Bedfordshire Police tried so hard to stop in the High Court.

(Above) My finest moment! Turning my back on newly elected Mayor of London Sadiq Khan.

(Above) Our first protest march in Dudley against plans for a new mega mosque in the town.

(Above) Visibly displaying my usual mix of contempt and cynicism towards the Muslim Protection Squad.

(Above) Proudly lifting the full can of soda that was launched at my head outside Belfast City Hall by an Irish republican bigot.

(Above) The day before Remembrance Day I had to 'sign on' at Bromley Police Station as part of my bail conditions.

(Above) Opposing a Dawah stall in Nuneaton with my activists. These Islamists rang the police claiming we assaulted them.

(Above) The famous confrontation with Brusthom Ziamani, who was later arrested on his way to behead a British soldier.

(Above) One of our many protest marches, this one through Luton, a well known Islamist hotspot.

(Above) Another day, another arrest for confronting Islamists. (Left) A section of our protest in Birmingham.

(Above) A Britain First activist is arrested for confronting convicted terrorists and Islamists in London.

(Above) When we marched in Rochester, all hell broke loose when the police blocked our path and asked us to disperse.

(Above) The coward Abdullah Deen being protected from our activists by the police. He was forced to flee across the road.

(Above) The enormous hostile crowd of Islamists that besieged just twenty Britain First activists outside Regent's Park Mosque.

(Left) Outside Laganside Court in Belfast before my trial for 'Hate Speech'. I was found not guilty. (Right) A Britain First activist is tackled by the police for charging at Anjem Choudary.

(Left) Chasing Islamists Abdul Mahid and Mohammed Rahman down the Bayswater Road in London. Our confrontation of these Islamists forced the police to take action. (Right) Being harassed by the police again, this time outside the Old Bailey in London.

(Left) This is the moment Britain First took off like a rocket. Me and a handful of activists blocking the path of Anjem Choudary in East London.

(Right) A Britain First activist is wrestled to the ground by the Met Police for charging at Anjem Choudary and his cronies in London.

(Left) I will always remember being dragged away by the police for shouting threats at hate preacher Anjem Choudary in East London.

(Left) The day I was arrested in Leicester for breaking my bail conditions. This was a sneaky attempt to get our activists out of the town centre.

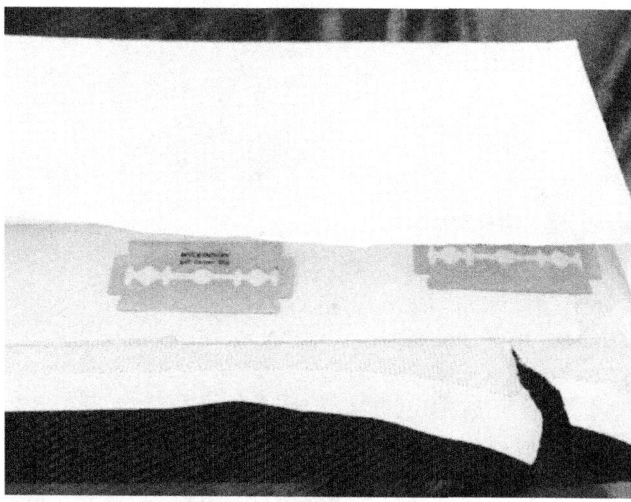

(Right) Just an average day in the office! These razor blades were some of many dangerous items posted to our head office PO Box.

(Left) Britain First has always attracted huge support among the British public. Despite the persecution from the state.

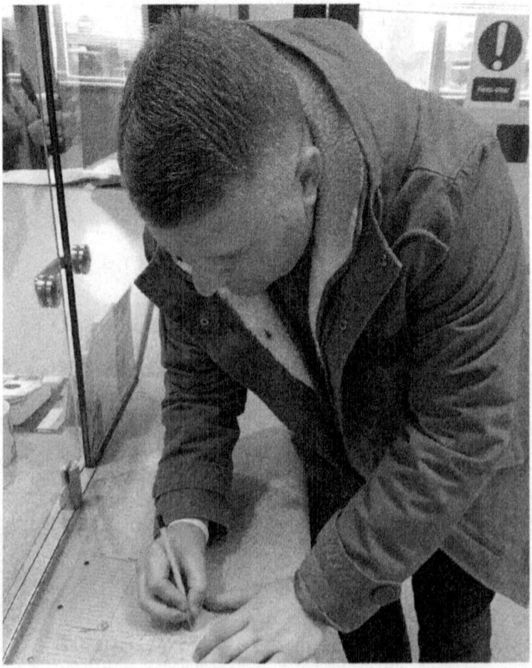

(Left) One method the police used continually to control my actions was to prosecute me for an offence and then apply oppressive bail conditions. Here I am forced to 'sign on' at Bromley Police Station. (Below) My bail sheet after my arrest by Bedfordshire Police with the restrictive bail conditions listed.

RESTRICTED

Kent Police

Custody Record No.	XY/XC/00465/16
Officer in Case.	SYSTEM TBA TO BE ALLOCATED
Date/time printed	15/02/2016 14:43

MG4A Conditional Bail Record

I certify that **PAUL ANTHONY GOLDING**
D.O.B. [redacted]
of [redacted] ,
has been granted bail, in connection with an offence of **WEARING UNIFORM WITH POLITICAL OBJECTIVE**

You are hereby bailed back to a Police Station in accordance with Police and Criminal Evidence Act 1984 S37(
Investigative bail and are required to surrender to custody
at **KENT POLICE, THAMES WAY, GRAVESEND**
on **30/05/2016 12:00 Hrs.**

The grant of bail is subject to the following conditions :-
NOT TO ENTER SPECIFIED LOCATION
NOT TO ENTER OR GO WITHIN THE LOCATION OF LUTON BEDFORDSHIRE FOR ANY REASON.

CONDITION OF RESIDENCE
TO LIVE AND SLEEP EACH NIGHT AT [redacted] AND MAKE YOURSEL
AVAILABLE TO ANY ATTENDING POLICE OFFICER WHO ATTENDS THAT ADDRESS TO MAKE CHECKS.

REPORTING CONDITIONS
TO REPORT TO BROMLEY POLICE STATION, HIGH STREET, BROMLEY, BR1 1ER EVERY SATURDAY BETWEE
1200 AND 1400

Reasons / Grounds:-
These conditions are imposed because they appear necessary to prevent the person named above from

(Above) Arrested outside the Indian Embassy in London for confronting Anjem Choudary and his minions. I was released shortly after, with a 'no further action'.
(Left) Arriving at Bromley Magistrate's Court for another trial, this time for breaching my probation. I was found not guilty on this occasion.

(Above) Britain First marches in London after the Westminster Attack. (Below) Being harassed by the police almost daily is part and parcel of being a patriot activist.

(Above) During our march in Dewsbury, the heavens opened and rain, snow and sleet poured down on us.

(Above) Candidates lined up in the GLA building in London. Being this close to Sadiq Khan was a nauseating experience.

(Left) Kent Police usually do not release mugshots for prisoners who serve under one year in prison. For me they made an exception. (Right) A photo taken outside Musgrave Police Station after my arrest for so-called 'Hate Speech' in Ballymena. (Below) The armoured Land Rover we proudly drove at the head of our 'Christian Patrols' in East London. The sight of this vehicle rolling down Brick Lane with our activists either side was incredible!

by an influx of migrants. The area is barely recognisable. All the old English families that once inhabited the streets of my youth have scarpered for the small towns and countryside of Kent. The houses that once played home to the families I grew up with are now occupied by migrants, Africans mainly.

The loss of London as a British city is an unmitigated disaster for our nation. Could you imagine the Japanese people becoming a minority in Tokyo? Could you imagine the Indian people becoming a minority in New Delhi? It would never happen, not in a trillion years. Unfortunately for the British people it is a catastrophic reality. Our ancestors have been betrayed. The streets that were bombed to smithereens by the Luftwaffe only 75 years ago are now strongholds of radical Islam. London is no longer a city that can be described as 'British'. Is it any wonder that millions of our people now refer to our capital city as Londonistan!

In late 2015, I discussed with our leadership team the immense benefits to our growing movement of contesting the London mayoral and assembly elections. This would be our greatest campaign yet. Not only was it a high profile democratic election, but the perks of standing a mayoral candidate were awesome. All mayoral candidates are entitled to a two-page spread in a booklet that is posted to every household within the Greater London area, population 8.2 million. Inclusion in this booklet cost £10,000, but it was worth it, not just for the enormous reach but because to be included among the 'big hitters' of UK politics was an obvious boost to our credibility as an upcoming political party.

I decided that I would be Britain First's mayoral candidate and Jayda would head our assembly list. Obviously, I had zero chance of being elected mayor of London, but Jayda had a slim chance of being elected as a member of the London assembly, needing only about 4.5% of the vote. The first mammoth task was to organise the paperwork and nominations across London. This was a gigantic logistical nightmare for a new party like Britain First. For me to stand as a Mayor of London candidate, we had to knock doors in every London borough and ask complete strangers to sign a form. We had to acquire ten of these 'nominations' in each and every London borough, including the Islamic dominated areas of East London. For a full week, we had teams of activists criss-crossing the metropolis knocking doors. It was an exhausting task. But we managed to complete the nomination forms and submitted them along with our £10,000 deposit. By this point, the campaign costs ran to nearly £25,000 and we hadn't even started campaigning yet.

Labour announced they were putting forward the poisonous weasel Sadiq Khan to be their candidate for Mayor of London, a man with a long history of links to Islamic extremism. I relished the chance to confront Sadiq Khan. I have stood for election many, many times and was elected as a councillor in 2009, an event that caused a media frenzy, so I had quite a lot of political experience.

Khan is a man that is mired with scandals and examples of extremism. The usually leftwing Spectator wrote of Khan: 'But you don't have to go back very far in Khan's past to find links with some pretty unsavoury characters....trying to get the UK to lift its ban on the American Nation of Islam leader Louis Farrakhan, who has described Jews as 'blood-suckers' and called Hitler 'a very great man', and speaking at the same conference as Sajeel Abu Ibrahim, a member of the now proscribed Islamist organisation that trained the 7/7 bomber Mohammad Sidique Khan.'

Sadiq Khan acted as legal representative for notorious 'Nation of Islam' leader Louis Farrakhan in the early 2000s who was trying to gain entry to the UK. Farrakhan has denounced white people as 'devils', described Jews as 'bloodsuckers' and called Hitler a 'very great man'. In 1990, Farrakhan claimed Jewish people controlled America 'like a radar controls the movement of a great ship in the waters' and said that Jews had 'got a stranglehold on the Congress'.

Reports from the time show that Khan played a very public and prominent role in the movement to get Farrakhan into the UK.

In 2004, Khan shared a platform with five Islamic extremists at a political meeting where women were told to use a separate entrance. Khan shared the stage with an activist who threatened 'fire throughout the world', a supporter of Palestinian terror movement Hamas, a preacher who called for an 'Islamic state' and a Muslim spokesman who called for attacks on the Royal Navy if it dared to stop arms being smuggled into Gaza.

Another speaker at this meeting was a man by the name of Ibrahim Hewitt, an extremist who called homosexuality a 'great sin' and called for adulterers to be stoned to death, as per Sharia Law. Hewitt is head of a charity called 'Interpal', which was designated as a global terrorist organisation by the US Treasury. According to Washington, Interpal funnels money to Hamas in Palestine. Another one of Khan's chums, Dr Azzam Tamimi, called for Israel to be destroyed and replaced by a caliphate (Islamic State). In 2006 Dr Azzam Tamimi spoke at a rally in London and told Sky News that 'fire will be throughout the world if they don't stop', referring to the Danish cartoons of the prophet Mohammed. Joining these inbred savages alongside Khan was an imam from Tooting, South London, Suliman Gani, who describes women as 'subservient'.

This is the man that Labour chose to be their London mayoral candidate. I positively despise Sadiq Khan. He's an obnoxious, self-important rodent with no charisma or talent. I was looking forward to getting on the campaign trail and promised myself that we would be causing Khan major irritation.

I started organising controversial activities in London, designed to trigger publicity and interest. We visited a halal slaughterhouse on the outskirts of East London and one sunny Saturday afternoon, thirty of us turned up and invaded the premises. We took them completely by surprise. The staff, mainly East Europeans, physically wrestled with our activists to stop us entering the precincts of the abattoir where the gruesome slaughter took place. We wandered throughout the premises and found large indoor pens where hundreds of sheep waited to have their throats slit while some Islamic barbarian recites a prayer to Allah. I felt physically sick, but I knew that if we pushed the boundaries of the law too far we'd all end up on charges. Halal slaughter is a barbaric and disgusting practise that needs to be outlawed immediately.

One of the perks of putting forth a candidate for Mayor of London is the free prime-time TV broadcasts you are entitled to. Producing a short broadcast that can be shown on TV channels is no mean feat. It is a brain-frazzling and complicated undertaking that stretched my limited video editing abilities and patience to the limit. Firstly, we had to film multiple activists that lived within Greater London for short segments to be included in the broadcast. These activists included an oriental woman from the Far East who lambasted radical Islam.

I visited the Cenotaph in London to film the beginning and end of the broadcast and I worked feverishly to produce the final edit. Then the finished product had to be submitted to the BBC, ITV and Channel 4 broadcast teams for approval. As predicted, these leftwing morons came back with a long list of changes and amendments, which we had no choice but to entertain. In the end, we had to edit three separate versions.

Then came the hard part. I had to travel for days on end to a professional video editing company in Soho in the West End to bring the quality up to broadcast level. Once in the professional studio, it turned out that several segments we filmed were of a low quality and had to be re-filmed. For days on end I worked with these experts to burn off dozens of DVDs that had to be couriered by motorbike to the TV networks as time was running out. The finished DVDs had to be in a certain format, at a certain resolution, at a certain aspect ratio and with a countdown clock at the beginning and so on. The whole project was a living nightmare, but we managed to pull it off despite our obvious ignorance of TV broadcast quality video production!

During the London campaign, we also decided to tackle the issue of the burgeoning number of Sharia Courts in London. Sharia Courts are an affront to our way of life and have featured in endless scandals involving mistreatment of Muslim women by their husbands etc. 'Sharia councils say they offer Muslim women a way out of religious marriage but critics argue this parallel legal system can leave vulnerable people trapped in abuse,' wrote the leftwing Guardian newspaper. Sharia Law is medieval and barbaric and has no place in Britain, under any circumstances. The rapidly increasing number of Sharia Courts demonstrates that vast numbers of Muslims are refusing to integrate into our British way of life. Instead, they are setting up a 'state within a state' where Islamic ideology reigns supreme.

In response to horror stories emerging from Sharia Courts, an inquiry was ordered by the then Home Secretary Theresa May. The Casey Review by Dame Louise Casey claimed that these Islamic courts 'supported the values of extremists, condoned wife-beating, ignored marital rape and allowed forced marriages'.

The biggest Sharia Court in London is in Leyton, on the outskirts of the East End. According to their website, 'The Islamic Sharia Council is a British organisation that provides legal rulings and advice to Muslims in accordance with its interpretation of Islamic Sharia...' This was too good to pass up on. I assembled a team and we headed straight for Francis Road in Leyton.

When we arrived, we found that the Sharia Court was housed in a normal residential building. On the side of the property in huge white letters was emblazoned, 'THE ISLAMIC SHARIA COUNCIL'. Sharia courts are regularly called 'Islamic councils' in order to confuse non-Muslims. Six of us burst through the front door and questioned the Muslim at the reception. On the walls were posters explaining the process for Islamic divorce etc.

After arguing with the receptionist, we simply decided to let ourselves into the other areas of the building and we started a room-by-room search. After a few seconds of searching, we actually found the room in which the court proceedings took place. There was a top table and in front of that, a table with seats for the parties in dispute. It resembled a miniature magistrates court. I tried to question another Muslim who came up out of the basement but he slammed a door in my face. Predictably, the operators of the Sharia Court described us to the media as 'ignorant', as if Sharia Law was some rosy blessing for mankind and we just didn't appreciate or understand it!

One major advantage that Britain First had going into these elections was our enormous support base on social media. We were able to upload a huge number of videos and target them at our supporters in London. Each of these videos had title bars emblazoned across them urging the viewers to vote Britain First and described the different colour ballot papers, one for the mayor and one for the assembly. We were able to pin-point our Facebook adverts specifically to those who 'Liked' our fan pages and who lived within the boundaries of Greater London, the voting area. I have no doubt that this social media strategy boosted our final vote enormously.

The London assembly building on the Southbank of the River Thames - opposite the ancient Tower of London - is a hideous post-modern architectural monstrosity. What an ugly addition to the London skyline. Within view you have the amazing Tower Bridge, the Tower of London and then you have this acorn-shaped abomination. Leftwing planning departments just love to wreck rustic British cities with Soviet-style, deformed edifices. One day, a patriotic government will smash the London Assembly building to the ground and replace it with a Greco-Roman or Gothic masterpiece.

When the day of the election arrived, we were predictably nervous. This was our first major high-profile election campaign and a paltry vote would embarrass our movement greatly in the prime gaze of the nation's mass media. This election took place at the height of UKIP's ascendancy. We expected them to steamroller us, but could we mobilise the hardline vote? I always enjoy these occasions, having stood as an election candidate many times. A plethora of famous politicians are in attendance and I enjoy the awkward moments in the elevators, café queues etc. when it's just me and them in close proximity. This happened with Nigel Farage and Boris Johnson. I do love being an 'extremist' sometimes!

The day of the count in the assembly building was eventful. The UKIP crowd were once again very, very supportive and many conversations were had were they expressed their admiration for our bravery in taking on Islamists. Despite the rank-and-file being warm and polite, the UKIP top team were predictably spineless. Nigel Farage especially always expends vast amounts of energy trying to avoid an innocent encounter with me or Britain First activists! I remember at the Rochester by-election count I crossed paths with him on a ramp and we locked eyes, just slightly. He immediately looked away and I simply said quietly, 'Hello Nige'. The lead candidate for UKIP was Peter Whittle, a homosexual who visibly despised Britain First. Towards the end of the day, he told all the UKIP candidates and activists present to avoid Britain First at all costs. Several of the UKIP team present told us this.

Nigel Farage actually owes Britain First a debt of gratitude. In March 2015, he was relaxing with his family in the Queen's Head pub in Downe, on the outskirts of South East London. Suddenly a gaggle of leftwing protesters entered the pub and harassed his family, causing them to be split up and forced to leave the area. The Telegraph said, 'Mr Farage said his children were so scared they had to hide from the protesters and criticised them for using force to make their point. The protestors, who dressed as migrants and breastfeeding mothers to express their opposition to UKIP, sent messages to journalists boasting of jumping on Mr Farage's car bonnet. The protesters claimed to have gone into the Queen's Head, chased the Farages out and then jumped on the UKIP leader's car bonnet as he drove away. Mr Farage is understood to have been with his wife and two younger children at the Queen's Head in Downe, Kent, when the incident took place.'

When I read the press reports, I was outraged. I had no particular love for Farage but this was a disgusting act of bullying that needed to be answered. I immediately ordered my intelligence team to find out everything they could about the leftwing protesters, who called themselves 'Beyond UKIP'. After some digging, we found that they were due to hold a planning meeting at a charity building in Old Street, in North London, the following Monday. This was to be an orgy of self-congratulations for harassing Farage and his family and traumatising his young children. Little did they know that twenty Britain First activists were poised to pounce on their little meeting.

This was a top-secret operation and information was kept very tight. Our activists did not have a clue what was going on until we were walking to the 'Beyond UKIP' meeting. When we arrived at the building, a few leftwing idiots were dotted about and they were in shock at our presence. We questioned them, asking them to reveal which room the 'Beyond UKIP' meeting was taking place in. They were all tight-lipped, so we searched the entire building. After an exhaustive search, we found them in a room on the ground floor. These brave socialist warriors had spotted us invading the building and while we were searching the rooms, they had barricaded themselves in!

We tried to force entry into the room and we could see the sheer terror in the faces of these gormless liberals. Not so brave now, were they! About ten of these spineless idiots were hanging onto the door handle trying desperately to stop us gaining entry to the room. For about half an hour we shouted challenge after challenge to these gutless morons to come out and face us. Harassing a lone politician and his children is one thing, facing an angry group of patriots is another. We stayed outside the door to their room for about half an hour trying to force entry. We shouted at them that our actions were in revenge for their harassment of Nigel Farage and his family. We could see through the glass that grown men were crying in fear and many of them were making frantic calls to the police. After a short while giving them a taste of their own medicine, we left the building.

We had struck terror into the hearts of this gang of cowards and shown the political Left that any similar harassment of patriots would be met with an identical reaction. The press went into a frenzy, calling us 'UKIP henchmen'. The 'Beyond UKIP' group vanished into thin air, never to be seen again. It was important that we demonstrated to the political Left - especially while they were celebrating victory by harassing Farage and his children - that the patriot movement could be equally as menacing. The difference being that we didn't harass children, whereas they did.

UKIP cleared up at this election winning multiple seats on the assembly. I asked several of the UKIP team that, with the poisonous Islamist dwarf, Sadiq Khan, on track to win, would they oppose radical Islam on their new platform. They replied that they would love to, but their leadership would not allow it! Both our team and the UKIP activists expressed disgust at this. I asked them, what was the point of standing, if they are not going to tear into Sadiq Khan and his Islamist background? Getting elected to the EU parliament is a good idea for Eurosceptic UKIP, but taking seats on the London assembly where their main job would be to oppose the Islamist mayor was a waste if they were not allowed to step up to the mark. Both the Britain First and UKIP activists agreed it was a sad situation.

When it came to revealing the results, all the mayoral candidates were ushered into a room and given the vote tallies in advance. I was but a few feet from the pocket-sized Sadiq Khan – not to mention the rest of the treacherous establishment candidates – and I positively despised breathing the same oxygen as these criminal scumbags. Sadiq Khan was shockingly short in height. He looked like he could barely see over a steering wheel in a car. The mood in the room was palpable. I was definitely the 'black sheep' of the room and proud of it. The rest of the candidates were chummy and talkative with each other. I just sat on my lonesome with a sneering face of conspicuous contempt!

Sadiq Khan easily won the election with 1.3 million votes, precisely the same number as the Muslim population of London! Funny that, I thought to myself. I was pleased to see that I had received some 105,000 votes, combining the first and second preference votes. 105,000 Londoners went out that day and put a cross for Britain First. A great result for our first major effort in London I thought, considering the demographic shift against us via 'White Flight' and the immigrant influx.

Then all the candidates were led to the top of the building separate from the party delegations. We were directed into the conference room and out onto a stage for the official declaration of the results. I was stood between the conservative candidate Zak Goldsmith and the Green candidate, Sian Berry. I was so infuriated that the toxic hobbit Sadiq Khan had won that I determined I would ruin his great moment of triumph - and I succeeded *marvellously*. The results were read out by the returning officer, candidate by candidate, and Khan was declared the victor. Khan stood forward and walked to the lectern, facing the media and the crowd. It was now or never.

As soon as Khan started speaking, I turned my back on him. Turning your back or leaving the room is a traditional political protest. Facing the bare glass walls of the building, I stood in silence. I could hear gasps and complaints from the crowd! The Labour delegates were furious and I could hear their whispered, mumbled protestations. I struggled not to smile, which would have taken the edge off the seriousness of my protest. I could hear the frantic clicking of the media camera lens shutters. I could tell that, despite Khan waffling away with his interminable acceptance speech, the attention of the moment was on me, not him. Mission accomplished!

That few minutes where I stood with my back to him seemed like an eternity. But it worked. By the time he had finished, I had thoroughly ruined his big moment! The media immediately went into overdrive. Story after story, TV report after TV report, all focussed on one thing: Me turning my back on Sadiq Khan! It really did take the edge off his victory! It couldn't have worked out better. London's first Islamic mayor had his glorious victory ruined at the zenith of the celebration by little old me.

The election of Sadiq Khan is a disaster for our nation. For the first time since the founding of London, thousands of years ago, it is no longer a European city, confirmed in the most horrid way imaginable. Khan used his position months later to pontificate about the election of Donald Trump as President of the United States. He would use his position to condemn both Britain First and Trump when the latter shared some of our videos on Twitter. When Brexit was in full swing, Khan would use his position to call for a separate trade deal with the EU for London. Under his watch, however, violent knife crime and murder rates have spiralled. Khan's London is a dangerous, crime-ridden Third World slum in decline.

21. Bury Park

In January 2016, I assembled a large team of Britain First activists at Toddington services on the M1 for a controversial and incendiary operation. We didn't know it at the time, but that day's activities were going to have major repercussions.

Security was kept very tight for this operation. We had a minibus at our disposal to transport our activists to the destination. The whole activity was organised like a military operation. I knew that if word of our intentions was leaked we would face serious danger. Considering our target area, a leak would end with us - most probably - being killed that day.

When everyone arrived at Toddington services, I briefed the assembled activists. Our destination was none other than Bury Park, the infamous nest of Islamic extremists and terrorists in the suburbs of Luton. We would march up and down the main high street giving out 'Christian Patrol' leaflets and Britain First newspapers and we braced ourselves for a ferocious reaction from the local Muslim population. We said a prayer and boarded the minibus.

We headed straight for Bury Park and arrived at the petrol

station at the beginning of the road where it meets Luton town centre. We quickly disembarked and broke into two teams, one for each side of the high street and started heading in the direction of Dunstable. We had achieved the element of surprise – the strict security around this operation had paid off.

Almost immediately the air was filled with the screeches emanating from a hostile white female convert to Islam in a hijab. This white Muslim convert immediately spotted our activists and launched into a frightful, blustering tirade. She pursued our activists as fast as she could. She was clearly the aggressor from the CCTV that would soon be disclosed in court.

Jayda heard the vicious condemnations from this woman and crossed the road to confront her. What followed was all captured on video - not that this helped in court. The woman in the hijab was with two small mixed-race children and it was obvious from observing that she had married a Muslim man and converted. This white convert then threw a barrage of verbal abuse at Jayda, calling her a 'slapper' for daring to be dressed in non-Muslim clothes.

For the record, it was a cold day and Jayda was covered head-to-toe with clothes – she even had a beanie hat on! The convert then stroked her own clothes while shouting 'decency', 'decency'. If Jayda had been walking about in a mini-skirt and high heels, I could have appreciated this woman's point. But the only flesh Jayda was displaying was her face. This exchange between Jayda and a white female Muslim convert does give a powerful insight into the mind-set of Islam vis-à-vis the way that culture expects women to cover up. Both women were essentially showing the same amount of 'skin' in public (just their faces) but Jayda was labelled a 'slapper' simply because she wasn't wearing an Islamic hijab.

Jayda retorted that the only reason Muslim women cover up is because Muslim men cannot control their urges. To be fair, it is part-and-parcel of Islamic culture that women must cover up so that men do not have impure thoughts. That is the situation, in a nutshell. Jayda was simply pointing this out. The white convert then denounced Jayda for parading herself in front of 'dirty men' even though Jayda was completely covered up head-to-toe. Jayda stood her ground and repeatedly stated that Britain was a Christian country. As the convert was being dragged away she lifted a clenched fist to Jayda's face. Anyone with an ounce of common sense could see that the Muslim convert woman was the aggressor and she was the instigator of the verbal exchange. The woman in the hijab followed our activists. She pursued us up the road. She called Jayda a 'slapper'. She raised her fist to Jayda. However, Bedfordshire police would soon convert her into a victim. Political correctness gone mad.

After this encounter ended, we progressed further up the high street and walked past a greengrocers. A Muslim man working in the store raised a hostile middle finger to me and shouted, 'Fuck you mate'. I replied, 'What did you say Sir?' To which he proclaimed, 'This is our country!' Jayda stepped forward and stated that Britain is a Christian country, to which this Muslim replied, 'It's not a Christian country. You jealous that we're taking over?' 'How are you taking over?' Jayda retorted, to which he said, 'We got it mate. We've taken over.' Jayda proceeded to explain that Britain First wasn't afraid of Muslim extremists. The whole exchange would sicken the hardest of patriots. To be fair, the Muslim was only telling the truth! Muslims are taking over this country – that's a demographic fact, not an opinion.

Very quickly the situation escalated. Teams of Muslim men started to surround our activists and the situation became very heated. We started to proceed back down the high street towards the minibus. As we made our progress at a slow pace, an elderly Muslim man launched an attack on one of our activists. The situation was close to exploding into violence. Aggressive Muslim men approached us asking, 'What are you doing here?' and, 'We hate you mother fuckers'.

Our activists acted with iron discipline to the torrent of abuse and threats. Simply walking slowly down the high street while surrounded on all sides by hostile Muslim men. Muslims screamed abuse from passing cars. Muslim men got right in the faces of our activists, foaming at the mouth while screaming expletives.

The police quickly arrived and tried their best to control the hordes of Muslim thugs. Eggs and missiles were criss-crossing in mid-air then landing on our activists. After being pursued for about three-hundred yards, we decided to halt and stand our ground. We were heavily outnumbered by a large crowd of Islamists. The police would not have been able to control either side had it degenerated into violence. But one thing was for certain: We were not being run out of the area. That's why we stood our ground. We made the choice as to when we would be leaving, not the Islamist aggressors. While we stood facing off against the other side, a young Muslim woman managed to get to within a few feet and shouted into the camera, 'The Muslims will take over, watch!' Appalling, yes, but she was speaking the truth.

Standing next to Jayda who was holding a big white Christian cross, I shouted, 'Reject the false prophet Mohammed and follow the true Saviour of the world, Jesus Christ our Lord!' The Muslim thugs threatened me not to insult their beloved Mohammed, but I simply kept repeating this line over and over. Loud shouts of 'Britain First, fighting back!' filled the air as the police pleaded with us to depart. After a short while, we walked at our own pace back to the minibus and left Luton.

As soon as I got back home, I immediately started to edit the full video report. There was a huge amount of footage to sift through, but once it was posted to the Britain First Facebook page, the video exploded and went viral. Within a few days, the video was seen a whopping 30 million times! It was huge news across the world. The video from our activity in Bury Park was the most successful video we ever uploaded. I remember sitting in astonishment watching as the numbers increased rapidly! One million. Two million. Ten million. It kept going and going and going until it petered out after a week or so at 30 million views on Facebook and around 2 million views on YouTube. I couldn't believe it. To say the video went viral would be a colossal understatement.

The huge furore around our march through Bury Park triggered a wave of publicity. On TV, radio, the tabloids, the broadsheets and online news websites. It was wall-to-wall coverage (all hostile to Britain First of course). The widespread coverage in the mass media helped the video to continue its viral circulation on social media.

Bedfordshire Police immediately swung into action. Detective Inspector Jackie Dadd said to various newspapers: 'We are urging members of the community to come forward and report any information they may have about Saturday's demonstration, so that we can continue to determine whether any offences were committed during the afternoon. At Bedfordshire Police we are committed to making the county's streets safe and protecting the public. We are keen to hear from anyone who witnessed this demonstration and collate all the evidence available to ensure that appropriate action is taken where needed.'

The Home Office even commented on our operation, saying the following in an official statement: 'The government condemns those who seek to spread hate by demonising British Muslims. Those who seek to divide us damage our country by stoking anti-Muslim hatred and deliberately raise community fears and tensions by bringing disorder and violence to our towns and cities.'

I then learned that a public meeting had been organised in Bury Park, where, incredibly, Bedfordshire Police made a pledge that - regardless of guilt or culpability - no local Muslims would be arrested - under any circumstances - following on from the events in

Bury Park. Assistant chief constable Mark Collins told the meeting: 'We are making three commitments, the first being an investigation which will leave no stone unturned, the second is that we will be seeking an injunction to prevent Britain First from returning to Luton and thirdly that no members of the local community will be arrested over the events of last Saturday.'

I was gobsmacked. Here was a police force, basically giving the Muslim thugs a free pass for any acts of criminality on that day. I am certain that if the majority of the British population knew of these police decisions, they would be outraged. But the fake news media will never bring them to the public's attention. Imagine if a police force had given a free pass to white youths who had hurled racial abuse at a group of Muslim political activists? It would be an international scandal of mind-boggling proportions.

A petition was launched calling for Britain First to be banned and was circulated widely among leftwing and pro-Islamist groups. A spectacular outpouring of phoney sympathy with the poor Muslims of Bury Park polluted the coverage of the incident. The liberal-Left and their politically correct, pro-Muslim cohorts went into overdrive. The aforementioned Luton 'Christian Leaders' came out in force and posed for endless photos with local imams. The whole turgid display was vomitous in the extreme.

Bedfordshire Police was determined to punish our movement for having the temerity to enter Bury Park. In my personal opinion, the fact that the video of the day's festivities went viral and was seen by tens of millions of people, meant that a public display of punishment had to be meted out to Britain First. A message had to be sent to the British public that such successful and illuminating incursions into Islamist strongholds - exposing their bigotry and intolerance - would not be tolerated.

Bedfordshire Police pursued a two-prong strategy to punish Britain First. Firstly, they applied to the High Court in London for an injunction that would prevent both Jayda and I from entering Bury Park and Luton town centre. Secondly, they would pursue the pair of us for criminal charges arising out of what happened that day in Bury Park. The dark hand of the intelligence services was all over this campaign to punish Britain First. Imagine if other patriot groups entered Islamist strongholds and captured footage of Muslims shouting that they were 'taking over' Britain. Patriots and nationalists had to be deterred from this kind of activity, hence the ferocious campaign of persecution directed at Britain First.

A few weeks after the Bury Park incident, I received a phone call from our solicitors who informed me that Bedfordshire Police sought to speak to both me and Jayda over the Bury Park incident. If we did not surrender ourselves voluntarily, we would be raided in the early hours and arrested. Many times in the past I have been stung after being invited in for a 'voluntary' police interview, only to be arrested and my office and home raided, Gestapo style. So, before we arrived at Ebbsfleet Police Station in north Kent, we made sure our office was emptied of hard-drives and laptops and our homes likewise.

The reason Bedfordshire Police wanted to interview us in Kent - rather than being summoned to the Bedfordshire area - as was normal practice - was simply because they did not want any of us coming anywhere near Luton again, so terrified were they of us coming near the town!

After announcing ourselves to the front desk of the police station, a team of plain clothes CID officers came out to greet us. A loathsome idiot by the name of DC Stone displayed his credentials then invited us in to be voluntarily interviewed. Jayda gave him a verbal grilling and I couldn't help myself when I called him an 'obnoxious little shit' following his threats to raid our homes 'in the early hours'. He gave me a stern look and instructed me not to swear.

'You need to be interviewed under caution, and if you don't

cooperate you will be arrested', said DC Stone. I replied with a simple, 'Go on then, arrest us!' If they wanted to speak to us, they would have to arrest us. DC Stone then walked off in a huff threatening to 'call his boss' on us. 'You're a bunch of jobsworth ambulance chasers' I hurled in the faces of the CID police idiots. 'I don't know why you don't go back to Luton and kiss some more Islamic backside, because that's what you're best at'. These Gestapo morons sometimes need to be told in plain, frank language what you think of them.

When DC Stone re-emerged some ten minutes later, he pulled me to one side and informed me that I was 'under arrest on suspicion of wearing a uniform with a political objective'. After weeks of 'investigating' the events at Bury Park, the best they could pin on me was that I was wearing a Britain First hoodie and beanie hat! The 1936 Public Order Act again, the law Parliament passed to scupper Oswald Mosely and the Blackshirts. Jayda was arrested at the same time for the same thing.

After giving 'no comment' interviews, we were released on police bail. Considering we had been charged with such a paltry and minor offence, the bail conditions were certainly extreme. The restrictions placed on us were clearly designed to sabotage our political activities. The restrictions were as follows:

1. Not to enter or go within the location of Luton Bedfordshire for any reason;

2. To live and sleep each night at [home address] and make yourself available to any attending police officer who attends that address to make checks;

3. To report to Bromley Police Station, High Street, Bromley, BR1 1ER every Saturday BETWEEN 1200 AND 1400.

For something as ridiculous as wearing Britain First merchandise contrary to the 1936 Public Order Act, these restrictions were disproportionate and over-the-top. When I had been convicted of the same offence in January 2015 I had received a £100 fine. Now we had to endure a form of house arrest and to sign-on every Saturday at a police station. The reporting condition in particular was specifically designed to stop any Britain First activities or days of action from taking place each Saturday. Most people work on weekdays and Sunday is a day of rest, so Saturday is traditionally the day for political activities.

For months on end we had to travel to Bromley Police station to sign a report card, completely preventing any possibility of organising activities. This was a deliberate plan to sabotage any Britain First activities and we had absolutely no choice but to comply. When we challenged these restrictions in Chatham Magistrate's Court the CPS prosecutor acting for Bedfordshire Police freely admitted – no shame whatsoever - that these conditions were intended to scupper any possibility of Jayda or I organising political activities. The CPS prosecutor didn't even attempt to sugar coat his demands. Reporting conditions are usually dished out to football hooligans, to prevent them attending football matches that take place at certain times. They have never been applied to political party leaders.

The 'condition of residence' to 'live and sleep each night at [home address] and make yourself available to any attending police officer who attends that address to make checks' was designed to stop us travelling around the country. It anchored us to a specific address in London. Again, a deliberate plan to sabotage any Britain First activities being organised, except in the South East of England. The CPS prosecutor acting for Bedfordshire Police listed certain towns in the North of England that they did not want Britain First to visit! Specifically those with 'Asian communities'.

This entire enterprise was obviously a deliberate and calculated plan to halt Britain First activities and to tie our leadership team down with restrictions. However, they underestimated our resolve and mettle. We welcomed their petty persecution and stood firm in the face of their devious and malevolent schemes.

22. Guilty

The only option we had in front of us was to challenge the oppressive bail conditions imposed on us by Bedfordshire Police in a court of law. We immediately applied to Chatham Magistrate's Court for a hearing and when the day came, the three magistrates simply decided that the restrictions would stay in place. More politically biased nonsense from the judiciary, as expected.

The lead magistrate actually tried to justify their decision by stating that, because 'Paul Golding had pleaded guilty to the same offence previously', the restrictions had to stay in place. For the record, I had never pleaded guilty to any offence up to that point, let alone wearing political uniforms. A total falsehood from a magistrate in a court of law.

The magistrates at Chatham did not even explain how they reached their decision, as they are expected to do, even after being asked to do so by our solicitor. They left the court room for a measly three minutes or less before returning to deliver their decision. These lefty-looking middle class magistrates had already made up their mind, even before they heard any evidence or argument.

Unfortunately, breaching court bail after being charged with a crime is not an option as repeated non-compliance with restrictions can lead to remand in prison. This is the situation we found ourselves in. Very soon though, I would break free of these restrictions by a crafty little manoeuvre that Bedfordshire Police were not expecting.

In fact, one of the sneaky tricks the CPS prosecutor used to guarantee that the magistrates would keep the restrictions in place was to promise that the restrictions would only be *temporary*. They promised the magistrates they would be in place until the end of March. So, the magistrates were more inclined to keep them in place, given the short time frames. However, when the end of March came, surprise surprise, the restrictions were not lifted by Bedfordshire Police. So, we simply tore them up and considered them done and dusted. If Bedfordshire Police arrested us, they would have to justify in a court of law why they *lied* in the previous court hearing. It was a calculated gamble that did not pay off!

During the period of these bail conditions, in May 2016, I organised a day of action in Leicester in the run-up to the EU referendum, a city we had never visited before. Around fifteen activists attended and we laid out a stall in the city centre, opposite an Islamic dawah stall. We campaigned for many hours for Britain to leave the EU until a rabble of scruffy leftists from the Socialist Worker's Party turned up hell-bent on causing trouble.

These clowns tried and failed to overturn our campaign stall, but ended up being launched across the high street themselves, their own table being mangled in the process. Soon, a pathetic looking 'Save the Badgers' march came tumbling along and bolstered the numbers of the leftwing opposition and very quickly a stand-off commenced. Several times some of the masked Antifa goons tried to attack our campaign stall but were repulsed with ease. It has never worked out well when leftwing troublemakers take on Britain First activists.

For several hours, some of the worst specimens of humanity tried their best to disrupt our day of action. I am talking about freaks with multi-coloured hair and piercings all over their faces, hippies, smelly soap-dodgers and masked students. The subsequent media reports described these trashy unwashed morons as the 'people of Leicester' and 'locals', but they were anything but. Once again, we enjoyed big support amongst the local English population but faced harassment and threats of 'Section 14' and 'Section 34' notices from the local Muslim Protection Squad.

Towards the end of the stand-off with the Marxist rabble, being a hot and sunny day I decided to take a bodyguard with me and slip off for a toilet break. I walked off in the direction of a nearby Burger King and managed to get approximately thirty feet away from our activists when police swooped from every direction and seized me. I was immediately arrested for breaching the bail conditions imposed on me by Bedfordshire Police. I was grabbed under both arms and frog-marched towards a nearby police van. I was driven to a local police station and booked into the custody suite. During my arrest, I slipped my bodyguard my mobile phone to stop the police taking it.

The police used my bail conditions simply to get me out of Leicester, as Britain First was standing its ground and refusing to leave because of the opposition from Antifa and the soap-dodgers. Once I was arrested and taken out of the equation, the police threatened all of our activists with immediate arrest and so they departed from Leicester in orderly fashion. Job done for the police. The media immediately reported that we had been run out of town by the 'locals'. Complete poppycock. For many hours, we stood our ground and did not budge. It took police chicanery to get rid of us, nothing else.

When I arrived at the custody suite, I was held in a tiny concrete cubicle for an hour and a half. The arresting officers and the custody sergeant did not know whether to book me in or release me. They rang Bedfordshire Police for clarification but they were reluctant to confirm anything as they had promised that the bail conditions finished at the end of March. It was incompetence at its worst. Why hadn't they carried out these checks about the validity of my bail conditions *before* they had arrested me? Simple, because they wanted me out of Leicester city centre at all costs, even if they were completely disorganised and confused about my bail conditions.

When I was finally booked in by the custody sergeant I was re-arrested, but this time on suspicion of assault! I pretty much laughed in his face and couldn't believe what I was hearing. Someone in the town centre had claimed that I punched them before being arrested. I may be many things, but I am not stupid enough to punch someone in the face in the middle of several hundred onlookers, CCTV cameras and police officers. I was then led into a boring cell with nothing but a Bible and a hard-blue plastic mattress and left to reflect on what the hell was going on.

I sat reading the New Testament for two hours until a police officer opened my cell and told me I was free to go. That was it, no interview, no statements taken, nothing. But arrested, held and released, no charges whatsoever. The custody sergeant informed me on my way out that the assault charge had been given a 'no further action' and I wasn't going to be charged regarding my bail conditions. As soon as I had been arrested, the police told our activists – who were planning on leaving the city centre and waiting for me to be released at the police station – that I was going to be held until the following Monday before being released, so they might as well go home rather than attempt to wait for me. Faced with this subterfuge, our activists decided it was best to depart Leicester entirely for home rather than go and wait for me.

The police knew full well that I was going to be released without any charges, but they did not want our activists hanging around in Leicester waiting for my release so they fed them a pack of lies to get them out of town. So, by the time of my release, I was the only Britain First activist left in Leicester and I did not have my phone! I did not have any numbers memorised either, as we rely on our mobile phones to store our contacts electronically these days. I quickly realised I had no wallet and thus no funds too, as I had handed everything to my bodyguard during my arrest to stop the police seizing it all.

So, there I was, stranded in Leicester on my own, with no numbers, no phone, no funds and no wallet. To make matters worse, I explained my dilemma to the police station staff and they simply told me to get lost. I had two choices: Stay in the police station until a miracle happened, or leave and walk the streets of Leicester with no money, no phone and no ID. Even if I chose to do the latter, then what? I was in a terrible predicament. Because of my notorious reputation and high profile, I couldn't walk around the streets of Leicester without security. I did not even know where I was or where to go.

The only hope I had was to ask the police station to call me a taxi and hope and pray a Muslim driver did not turn up. I could plead with them to take me to London and pay them at the other end. A longshot I know, but what other options did I have. The police station staff then refused to call me a taxi. Luckily, someone overheard me talking and offered to call me a taxi instead. I was thankful for that, but when the taxi arrived it was a Muslim driver and he immediately recognised me and refused to drive me anywhere. That plan had flopped and my desperation increased substantially.

Totally bewildered, I left the station front desk and headed out into Leicester. I walked for about a mile down roads and streets but I didn't have a clue where I was heading to. I was lost in the middle of suburbia. I quickly realised wondering the streets with no destination hoping for a miracle was a dead end and so headed back to the police station. I then had an idea. I got the number of the police front desk wrote it on a piece of paper. I then waited for about an hour for a member of the public to come into the police station. I immediately begged them to let me use their iPhone and explained my awful situation. Thankfully, they allowed me to use their iPhone and I logged into Facebook and messaged everyone I could a short message explaining the quandary I was in and included the phone number of the front desk. I then logged out and handed the phone back.

Within two minutes the front desk phone started to ring off the hook and within twenty minutes several nearby activists had arrived to sit with me until my father arrived to pick me and take me back to London. By the time he arrived I was physically and mentally exhausted.

It turned out the police had refused to give any information about my detention to my mother and father who had made enquiries about my wellbeing. This was a breach of police rules and it shows the lengths that Leicestershire Police went to – out of pure spitefulness - to sabotage our day of action and leave me stranded in a hopeless situation. I managed to extricate myself only by the skin of my teeth. It could have ended in disaster for me. This true story demonstrates how much aggravation and hassle these bail conditions can inflict on us. They are no joke. When they are imposed on us - to curtail our freedom and clamp down on our activities - they are difficult to overcome.

The next bombshell to drop on our heads was an application from Bedfordshire Police for an injunction in the High Court. But, before the battle over this injunction took place, we decided to organise a day of action in Luton town centre that would cause maximum annoyance to Bedfordshire Police despite the restrictions in place. Jayda and I were both banned from entering Luton *in person*, but Britain First wasn't! So, we organised for units from around the country to converge on Luton for a day of action. Jayda and I signed-on at Bromley Police Station at the required time and then headed for a conference room in a Bromley hotel. We had purchased special radios and other devices to allow us to control events as they happened *remotely*. It was a remote-controlled day of action that completely side-stepped the bail conditions that had locked us down. In the end, a very sneaky way of annoying Bedfordshire Police. During this town centre activity, our activists faced attack by local Muslims and at least one masked Muslim was arrested.

The proposed injunction was delivered to our solicitors via courier and – as expected – the terms were draconian. The bundle that had been compiled by some of the most expensive solicitors in the country - acting on behalf of Bedfordshire Police - was at least two inches thick. Both Jayda and I were prevented - either by ourselves or by instructing anyone others - from:

(a) Entering any Mosque or Islamic Cultural Centre or its private grounds within England and Wales without prior written invitation.

(b) Being within a designated exclusion zone in the Bury Park area save unless that person remains at all times within a railway carriage travelling along the railroad adjoining Luton railway station.

(c) Causing, permitting, encouraging or inciting any person to enter or remain in designated exclusion zone in the Bury Park area save unless that person remains at all times within a railway carriage travelling along the railroad adjoining Luton railway station.

(d) Publishing, broadcasting, distributing or displaying, or causing or encouraging to be published, broadcast, distributed or displayed, any images or films showing any person or event, on a date after the making of this order, within designated exclusion zones in the Bury Park and Town Centre areas.

(e) Entering a designated exclusion zone in the Town Centre area save in accordance with paragraph 1 (g).

(f) Causing, permitting, encouraging or inciting any person to

enter or remain in the designated exclusion zone in the Town Centre area save in accordance with paragraph 1 (g) below.

(g) The Respondents are permitted to enter a designated area in the Town Centre for the purposes of, and only for the purposes of, attending hearings at Luton Magistrates Court and Luton Crown Court at which they are required to attend as defendants in criminal proceedings. They are also permitted to instruct legal representatives to attend such hearings. The Respondents must give the Chief Constable of Bedfordshire Police advanced written notice of all such attendances by 5pm on the working day before the relevant hearing.

We hastily organised a meeting with our civil litigation solicitors and the sheer scale of fighting this injunction was laid bare. If we fought the injunction and lost, we would be liable to cover all of Bedfordshire Police's legal costs, which ran into the tens of thousands of pounds, even at this early stage.

I asked our solicitors for a conservative estimate of what the total cost of fighting the injunction to the bitter end would be, and if we lost the case. They estimated anywhere between £60-£100,000. I was horrified. Please remember that Bedfordshire Police is a taxpayer-funded organisation, so if they lost, only the taxpayer would foot the bill. If Britain First lost this case, we would face bankruptcy.

Bedfordshire Police also deployed a sneaky method of almost guaranteeing a win - even a partial win. They included in the terms of the injunction some *reasonable* demands, such as not entering any mosques in England and Wales. It was pointed out to us that we would lose miserably if we tried to fight this particular demand and thus even if a single term of the proposed injunction was imposed by the judge, we would be liable for costs. It was a no-win situation. If we continued to fight this injunction, we would lose somehow, someway and be liable for big sums of money.

So, I faced a hard choice, between fighting this attempt to ban us from mosques, Luton and Bury Park, risking total disaster and bankruptcy in the process, or simply agreeing to the injunction. Bedfordshire Police were using their vast financial resources to outgun us and force us to withdraw opposition to the injunction, lest we risk financial ruin.

A good army commander realises when he is outgunned and doomed to lose in the short term and so retreats and lives to fight another day. There was only one realistic option for me as leader of Britain First and that was to mitigate any costs that would result from agreeing to the injunction. We proposed to Bedfordshire Police that we would agree to the injunction on the basis that we paid no legal costs whatsoever. Within half an hour they came back to us and demanded that we paid £10,000 in costs otherwise it would go to court.

We stood our ground and told them to sod off. If we were to agree to the injunction, we would not tolerate paying any of Bedfordshire Police's legal costs. They went off in a huff to deliberate and a few hours later they came back to us and agreed that Britain First would not have to pay any of their gargantuan legal costs. It was a lucky escape, even though we had to agree to an unprecedented court order that banned an entire political party and its leaders from an entire British town. This was the first time this has happened in British political and legal history. It truly was *unprecedented.*

Very soon notices with my face on it were appearing in mosques all over the UK explaining to Muslim worshippers the terms of the injunction and asking them to be vigilant in case we invaded their mosques and breached the order! One of these notices read:

'In August 2016 Bedfordshire Police successfully applied for an injunction in relation to two members of Britain First. The police service argued that Britain First activists has caused community tensions with their activism in Luton. This notice is circulated to inform communities of the Order and to seek their help if it is breached.'

The notice continued, 'Paul Golding and Jayda Fransen, leaders of Britain First, are forbidden, by Order of a High Court injunction from the following: Entering any mosque or Islamic cultural centre or its grounds within England and Wales without prior written invitation. Police have the power of arrest if they have reasonable grounds to suspect either of them has breached this Order. Please call the police on 999 if you believe Paul Golding or Jayda Fransen to be breaching this Court Order. Even if the protests are outside the premises / grounds please still do make police aware.'

It was during this outrageous civil litigation in the High Court that Bedfordshire Police announced that Jayda was to face criminal charges for 'religiously motivated harassment' of the Muslim convert woman in Bury Park during our activity there. Yes, you read that correct. Even though Jayda did not instigate the exchange of words and it was Jayda that was called a 'slapper' and had a fist raised to her face, *she* was the one to be prosecuted. Political correctness gone absolutely bonkers. Bedfordshire Police were throwing everything except the kitchen sink at us to punish us for such a sterling job exposing Islamic extremism in Bury Park.

Both Jayda and I attended a preliminary hearing at Luton Magistrate's Court to organise the case management for our upcoming trials. It was at this hearing where we both had to enter pleas of guilty or not guilty to the charges of wearing political uniforms - for me and Jayda - and also for 'religiously motivated harassment', for Jayda only.

For several months, I had been tortured by signing on every Saturday and not being able to travel, as per our bail conditions. It occurred to me that I was enduring all of these restrictions for an offence that, if found guilty, I would probably receive a measly little fine. For purely *tactical* reasons I decided to enter a plea of 'guilty' for this minor offence! Bedfordshire Police were *horrified*. The judge gave me a fine of several hundred pounds and there and then, I was *free* of restrictions! Their plan to tie me down for months on end with bail conditions had been eviscerated by my unconventional tactics. They were *visibly* upset. I pleaded guilty purely to get rid of the restrictions. The restrictions were more horrid than the punishment I would receive for the crime itself! A sneaky little tactical move that outflanked Bedfordshire Police.

When Jayda and I and a bunch of our security volunteers were in Luton Magistrate's Court, a very polite young Muslim man came over to me and sparked up a conversation. He congratulated me on 'telling the truth' that Islam sought world domination and that jihad and spreading Islam - until it reigns supreme across the entire Earth - was the very essence of the religion. He said that it was true that Muslims like him are looking forward to the day when Britain becomes an Islamic caliphate. I was astonished. He said he respected me for opposing this process, being a native British Christian, but that Islam was unstoppable and it was only a matter of time before it dominated the West. I asked him to join me outside to film a short video and he agreed.

When we started filming, this polite young man said readily and freely said that I was right, Muslims do want Sharia Law in Britain. He said that Sharia Law will take over the whole world and that it was part of his religion. I asked him whether he believed that Britain would be an Islamic Sharia state, and he replied, 'One hundred billion percent!' I asked him, 'You want that to happen?' to which he replied, 'Definitely, more than anything'. He ended by saying, 'Just sit back and watch the show because it's gonna happen!' I was stunned by the refreshing honesty of this young Muslim man. But the video is *disturbing* and I urge all of those reading this book to go and find the video on our website and watch it.

After a month or two, Jayda faced trial at Luton Magistrate's Court for 'religiously motivated harassment' and also failing to surrender herself to Bedfordshire Police while on bail. The prosecutor acting for Bedfordshire Police was, once again, an inept buffoon that was constantly overruled by the sitting judge. Some of the evidence they presented against Jayda was thrown out by the judge and the trial descended into farce on several occasions.

At one point, the prosecutor called a local Christian vicar to give evidence, only for the judge to kick him out of the court for waffling and telling outrageous lies. His 'evidence' was disregarded. Then the prosecutor called a local Muslim to give evidence who had featured in several anti-Britain First TV documentaries. This miscreant was stopped mid-stream and asked to re-read the statement he had given to the police because the two did not correlate!

Then came the supreme village idiot, DC Stone, the same hapless goon that had arrested me at Ebbsfleet Police Station months before. This moron made such a hash of presenting his evidence that it resulted in the judge throwing out the charge of failing to surrender for bail. Nevertheless, the main plank of the trial was the religiously motivated harassment charge and this revolved around the angry exchange between Jayda and the white Muslim convert woman in Bury Park. This was a summary offence that carried a maximum sentence of a £2,000 fine. With the charge of failing to surrender for bail thrown out, the threat of prison was removed. A brilliant development in the course of the trial.

To be honest, we were fighting a losing battle from the beginning. The judge assigned to the trial had a track record of Islamic appeasement and leftwing views. District Judge Carolyn Mellanby is infamous for creating important judicial precedents during her tenure in the Luton courts. Mellanby was the judge hearing the case of the seven Muslim men accused of disrupting the homecoming parade of the Royal Anglian Regiment in Luton, an event that spawned the creation of the English Defence League by Tommy Robinson.

When the Royal Anglian Regiment case opened, the Islamists *refused* to stand for Mellanby, stating they would *only* stand for Allah. To accommodate these Islamists, Mellanby *changed* the rules of the court so that they did not have to stand for her because she came in first and the Islamists entered court after her. Failure to stand for the judge would usually be considered contempt of court, but not for radical Muslim extremists!

Mellanby described the white Muslim convert woman as 'eloquent' when giving her verbal evidence in court. When she retired to make a decision, we knew what was coming. When she re-entered the court, she pronounced Jayda guilty and fined her £2,000, the *maximum* she could impose. The circus did not end there. Mellanby tried to impose an unlawful restraining order on Jayda that would prevent her mentioning the name of the white Muslim convert woman. This, as was pointed out in court, was illegal and after many strained arguments back and forth this idea was abandoned by the judge. Mellanby more than once expressed her desire to 'protect' the white convert woman, an over-the-top and totally biased approach from a supposedly impartial judge.

The conviction of Jayda for religiously aggravated harassment ended the long running persecution of our movement by Bedfordshire Police. They excelled themselves in their campaign of hate against Britain First, all to appease the militant Muslims of Luton. Both Jayda and I ended up with extra criminal records, thousands in fines to pay and a High Court injunction that prevented us - as political party leaders - from entering an entire British town. Nothing like this has ever been seen before in our country. It is a truly unique and disturbing campaign of enmity from a supposedly neutral and impartial public service. The entire saga was funded from beginning to end using taxpayer money.

The Islamists of Luton must have been laughing their socks off at the Dhimmi stupidity of the mainly white British police officers and Labour councillors who pioneered this tragic affair. Luton has effectively become a 'No Go Zone' where Islamic blasphemy laws apply. The treatment meted out to Britain First sent a clear message to anyone else brave enough to attempt to campaign in Luton against radical Islam. The message was clear, you will be subjected to horrendous persecution if you dare. Luton is a Sharia town, end of. Stay away, patriot bigots!

That was the point of the entire exercise. But Britain First will be back, as soon as the current injunction ends in 2019. Then Britain First will be back with a vengeance and we will not respect any supposedly taboo areas of the town. We will go where we want and we will get our message across. If this triggers another bout of persecution, so be it.

23. Jo Cox

Thursday 16th June 2016 is a day I will never forget. At first it started as an ordinary day in the office, dealing with administration issues and video editing. Our staff were getting on with their duties, sipping from cups of tea. We were all completely unaware of what was about to unfold. Suddenly and without any warning, the phone started ringing off the hook. All hell broke loose. The main office phone line, plus our mobiles, starting to ring furiously. Very quickly we established that there had been an attack on a sitting female MP by – supposedly – a Britain First supporter.

I had been in this situation once before, when Neil Masterson attacked and hospitalised George Galloway. On that occasion it wasn't prime time news and Neil Masterson wasn't really attached to Britain First. However, when I learned that the female MP had died after the attack I realised that this was an apocalyptic situation and the full gravity of the situation hit me like a freight train. I perused the online newspaper websites and this attack was dominating the news agenda. It was wall-to-wall coverage on TV, radio and online. It was being shared frantically by millions of people on social media.

It was international news from San Fransisco to Tokyo. The story had one dominant feature: That it was a 'Britain First supporter' who carried out the attack. Worse still, this unknown attacker had shouted 'Britain First' during the attack.

This really was a *serious* situation. I knew that the establishment would grasp any opportunity to shut down Britain First and this had the potential to be the end of our movement. According to the newspapers, a popular female Member of Parliament had been butchered on the streets by a crazed Britain First far right extremist.

We sifted through the headlines and hastily prepared media articles searching for facts about the attack. What was the assailants name? What had he *actually* shouted during the attack? But for several hours, it was nothing but an international frenzy of blanket coverage and denunciations of Britain First. This story quickly assumed global proportions. On British, American, Canadian, European, Australian and Asian TV this attack was the number one headline. And right at the centre of this global storm was Britain First.

The attack took place in Birstall, West Yorkshire. After a while, a man called Thomas Alexander Mair was identified by the police as the attacker. He had shot and stabbed local Labour Party Member of Parliament for Batley and Spen, Jo Cox, multiple times as she was on her way to her MPs surgery. According to Wikipedia, 'The incident was the first killing of a sitting British MP since the death of Conservative MP Ian Gow, who was assassinated by the Provisional Irish Republican Army in 1990, and the first death of a politician during an attack since county councillor Andrew Pennington was killed in 2000.'

Thomas Mair was a 52-year-old unemployed gardener who had a long history of mental health problems. Whatever had been said about Mair's widely reported mental health issues, he was without doubt a far right extremist. But was he a member, activist or supporter of Britain First? Literally millions of online articles and rcports were published that fateful day all making the claim that Mair had shouted 'Britain First' during the attack. Thanks to this claim, Britain First was getting the blame for the entire attack and Jo Cox's death.

For the first twenty-four hours we were sitting nervously waiting for the inevitable police raids. Because the situation was so serious, we dared not hide our hard drives and laptops as we usually did when we were being persecuted for Mickey Mouse offences. No, this situation required complete and total transparency. When the name Thomas Mair was released by the media, I began frantically searching our email, activist and membership lists looking for his name. This was one of the most stressful few hours of my life as I knew that, God forbid, had his name popped up in one of our searches, we were doomed. After intensive, comprehensive and thorough searches of every list, database and spreadsheet we could fine, it dawned on us. Thomas Mair was *nothing* to do with Britain First.

Hundreds of thousands of people from around the world had signed petitions, signed-up for email updates, became members, donors and activists over many, many years, but not *once* had anyone by the name of Thomas Mair (or Tommy Mair, Tom Mair or in fact anyone called Mair) *ever* been involved in Britain First in the slightest way. We breathed a titanic sigh of relief. While we were engaged in these panicked searches we conducted dozens of media interviews, issued statements and prepared videos. The office was a mad house all day. We relaxed somewhat because we knew at this point that Thomas Mair was nothing to do with Britain first and we prepared a huge number of files for the police whenever they came knocking.

Mair was certainly a far-right extremist and an unhinged lunatic. Wikipedia claims the following:

'Mair had links to right-wing political groups including the National Front and the English Defence League; he had attended far-right gatherings and purchased far-right publications, to some of which he had sent letters. In his home were found Nazi regalia, far-right books, and information on the construction of bombs. He had searched the internet for information about the British National Party [BNP], apartheid, the Ku Klux Klan, prominent Jewish people, matricide, white supremacism, Nazism, Waffen SS, Israel, public shootings, serial killers, William Hague, Ian Gow (another assassinated MP), and Norwegian far-right terrorist Anders Behring Breivik (about whose case he collected newspaper clippings).' Not a single mention of Britain First there. The police later described Thomas Mair as a 'loner in the truest sense of the word ... who never held down a job, never had a girlfriend [and] never [had] any friends'.

One major fact most of the media reports forgot to include was that, the evening before Mair launched his attack on Jo Cox, he had visited a mental health centre asking for help because he was chronically depressed. He was sent away and told to return the next day! Imagine if the staff present had helped Mair when he was pleading for their assistance. Jo Cox may still be alive. This moronic act of negligence by the staff at the clinic in question certainly contributed to the ensuing attack. They had a chance there and then to help Mair before he flew off the handle, but they told him to bugger off because he didn't have an appointment. This inconvenient little fact was systematically hidden by the mass media during their frenzy of hate against Britain First.

On 18th June, Mair was asked to confirm his identify at Westminster Magistrates' Court and said, 'My name is death to traitors, freedom for Britain'. At his subsequent trial, at the Old Bailey, Mair made no attempt to defend himself whatsoever. Thomas Mair was quickly found guilty, given a long prison sentence, and the 'judge said he had no doubt Mair murdered Cox to advance a political, racial, and ideological cause - that of violent white supremacism and exclusive nationalism most associated with Nazism and its modern forms', according to Wikipedia.

Despite the distortions and falsehoods of the media, if Mair had shouted 'Britain First' during the attack I knew incontrovertible evidence of this would surface at his trial. However, this never happened because, as it turns out, he didn't shout 'Britain First' during the attack but instead had shouted 'This is for Britain', 'keep Britain independent', and 'Put Britain first'. All of these 'slogans' can be put into their proper context considering the attack on Jo Cox took place at the height of the EU referendum of that year.

The first tweet to appear online regarding Britain First involvement was from Labour MP Maria Eagle, who made the 'he shouted Britain First' claim. Maria Eagle later deleted this tweet. Why? Why would she take it down? LBC and several other outlets responsibly reported that no witness at the scene heard 'Britain First' being shouted. Even the leftwing lying rag, the Mirror, published a headline which threw doubt on our involvement: 'Eyewitness heard attacker shout Britain First or put Britain First'. Not really definitive, is it? But despite the lack of hard evidence, the 'he shouted Britain First' claim grew legs and went viral and dominated the narrative. The idea that a supposedly 'far-right' organisation was behind the attack was too juicy to pass up for the lying snakes that infest the mainstream media.

I remember that the attack caused such a political and media earthquake that campaigning during the referendum was suspended temporarily while the 'nation mourned'. Of course, the Remain campaign seized on Jo Cox's death to laud her pro-EU credentials. Absolutely shameless, but it never influenced the result of the referendum, thank heavens.

The establishment reaction to the death of Jo Cox was

indulgent in the extreme. Union flags on public buildings including parliament, Downing Street and Buckingham Palace flew at half-mast. An avalanche of tributes and eulogies dominated our screens and newspaper columns. A fund set up in her memory raised over a million pounds and part of this was given to an extreme leftwing organisation called 'Hope Not Hate'. There were public memorial events and songs released in the charts to commemorate her memory.

More recently, a public square in Brussels has been named after Jo Cox. Picnics, street parties and concerts have been organised to remember her. Barack Obama, Angela Merkel and dozens of other politically correct world leaders got in on the action. The Italian parliament even went as far as establishing the 'Cox Committee' on intolerance, xenophobia, racism, and hate crime, naming it in her honour. I could dedicate several chapters of this book to the memorial efforts and posturing that unfolded after her death. But hopefully you get the picture from these few examples.

Again, right at the centre of this global calamity was widespread acceptance that Britain First was somehow to blame. But, the fact remains: We had *nothing* whatsoever to do with her death. Nothing. In fact, long after her death a prime-time documentary appeared on TV and one of the detectives heavily involved in the investigation stated categorically that Thomas Mair had nothing to do with Britain First. No evidence of Britain First involvement appeared in court at his trial. This hasn't stopped the media and political establishment smearing our movement at every opportunity. We still endure leftwing hecklers screaming at Britain First on our activities that we killed Jo Cox, but the truth has nothing to do with the political Left, never has.

No one except the evil and twisted want to see a mother gunned down and stabbed in broad daylight. As a result, we condemned this attack in the strongest possible terms. If this country had a Britain

First government, Thomas Mair would have been executed long ago. There's a wider issue here, that our elected representatives are - and should always be - *sacrosanct*. Attacks on certain elected officials in Ancient Rome were punished with extra ferocity and savagery, as it was considered that, for example, 'tribunes of the people', needed to be given extra protection to enable their political system to function. Elected Members of Parliament should be considered in the same category. Once you are elected by the British people, you are part of the state, of our democracy and thus untouchable, under any circumstances. This includes assault by political activists. Any harassment or assault of a sitting MP should be mercilessly dealt with and the harshest punishment meted out to the assailant.

For weeks after the attack I waited nervously for police raids that I was convinced would happen. The whole world was blaming Britain First, so obviously I suspected that serious police units would be deployed to grab our computer equipment, hard-drives and databases to make comprehensive, forensic searches to see if Thomas Mair was connected to our movement. But, the police never showed up. They conducted no raids. I did not even get a phone call from the investigating officers asking for information.

There was no contact whatsoever between Britain First and the police regarding the murder of Jo Cox. Nothing. Again, I reiterate that on national TV the investigating officers stated categorically that they looked into a 'Britain First connection' and found nothing. They also conducted forensic searches of Thomas Mair's home and computer equipment and again, found no Britain First internet searches, publications etc. Nothing. For me, all of this speaks volumes. Despite the global witch-hunt against Britain First in the media, no hard evidence of any connection between our movement and Thomas Mair was found, at any time, by anyone. This immutable fact is ignored by the political Left, who still refer to Thomas Mair as a 'Britain First terrorist'.

Shortly after the attack, I remember a photo I had taken in Dewsbury surfaced and went viral on social media. It includes a number of our activists on a day of action in that town. A supporter of Britain First who randomly spotted us jumped in the photo with our activists, which was taken behind a Britain First banner. The political Left circulated this image far and wide and it went viral on social media. They claimed that the member of the public who jumped behind the banner was Thomas Mair. But even a cursory look at a photo of Thomas Mair and the gentleman in question in Dewsbury reveals this as a falsehood. They look nothing alike. Nevertheless, this shows how easily it is for a contrived falsehood to grow legs on social media. The political Left is not concerned with the truth, only by how much damage they can inflict on their opponents using deception and lies.

24. Cardiff

The al-Manar Centre is an extremist Salafi mosque in the Cathays area of Cardiff, Wales. It is actually just a residential house with an extension built on the back of the property to provide more room for worshippers. It is quite an inoffensive looking mosque, compared to the domed monstrosities that dot the skyline of the north of England.

The al-Manar Centre is famous for pumping out recruits for Islamic State (ISIS). Back in 2014, the mosque received widespread opprobrium when it emerged that several of its worshippers - Nasser Muthana and Reyaad Khan - appeared in an ISIS propaganda video. Of course, the al-Manar Centre denied that it had radicalised these ISIS fighters. They were later killed in military strikes in Syria.

This seems to be a repeating pattern across the United Kingdom. Mosques radicalise young impressionable Muslims and face no sanction whatsoever from law enforcement. No one is questioned or held accountable. The mosques themselves are not closed. There are no police raids. No arrests. It seems that, compared with virtually every other area of society, mosques are no-go zones for the authorities. I have heard rumours that police forces must give advanced warning of raids that involve police dog units. This is obviously counterproductive, giving any lawbreakers in these mosques time to ferret away any incriminating evidence. The authorities show no such 'cultural sensitivity' when dealing with any other section of society. Islam is - as I have always said - a 'protected species' in modern Britain.

One of the imams at this particularly nasty mosque goes by the name of Ali Hammuda. He was originally suspected of radicalising the young ISIS recruits. Nevertheless, he was not arrested, questioned or placed on restrictions. He carried on spewing his poison and bile to Islamic worshippers unimpeded. This particular mosque was on my radar but I never considered confronting it until Hammuda hit the headlines years later.

Hammuda was recorded by an undercover reporter telling young Muslims that it was permissible for them to keep sex slaves, simply because that was what the prophet Mohammed did as outlined in a Hadith (Islamic holy scripture). Part of Hammuda's duties at the mosque include organising Islamic study classes attended by children aged 13-18 years. It was during one of these classes that he made this shocking and revolting claim. He was also recorded telling these impressionable children that the 'world is close to the end of time'. It's obvious that Hammuda is a clerical nutcase and Islamist extremist, but he has never been touched by the police authorities.

Hammuda was born in Palestine, so could easily have been deported. Hammuda was secretly recorded by Daily Mail journalist Rizwan Syed while investigating hardline Islamist militants in the UK. Syed had harsh words to say about his time at the mosque: 'I saw books preaching brutal violence, sexism, homophobia, aggressive physical jihad, dismemberment and capital punishment implemented by the state. It reinforces the idea that what these militant groups are doing, what ISIS is doing, is legitimised by history.'

The extremist cleric Hammuda was quoted as saying during the secret recording: 'One of the interpretations as to what this means is that towards the end of time there will be many wars like what we are seeing today. And because of these wars women will be taken as captives, as slaves, yeah, women will be taken as slaves. And then her master has relations with her because this is permissible in Islam: it's permissible to have relations with a woman who is your slave or your wife.'

There you have it. Incontrovertible evidence proving - beyond a reasonable doubt - that this Cardiff mosque is preaching an extremist version of Islam that includes approval of kuffar sex slaves, violence, jihad, sexism and homophobia. Was anything done by the authorities despite this chronic extremism? Why of course not. Hammuda wasn't arrested. The mosque wasn't raided. Muslim organisations did not condemn the revelations. In fact, the Muslim Council of Wales supported Hammuda and published public messages of support, calling the media reports 'bizarre' and 'certainly unfounded'. Muslims certainly do stick together when criticised.

This ridiculous and frustrating level of appeasement and inaction from the authorities - whose job it is to protect us - propelled me into action. If the police wouldn't do anything about this Salafist mosque, then Britain First would. After the extraordinary sacrifice from millions of British heroes in innumerable wars and conflicts, I cannot in good conscience sit back and allow Islamist extremism on this scale go unanswered in one of the biggest cities in Britain. Something had to be done, so we swung into action.

I organised a team of activists and we headed for Cardiff. I drove all the way from Kent to lead this operation. This operation took place during the endless persecution inflicted on us from

Bedfordshire Police and about a month after we agreed to the civil injunction barring us from every mosque in England and Wales. Because of the prohibition placed on me by the High Court, I decided that I would not personally enter the mosque myself, but wait outside while the activists headed inside and confronted Hammuda.

We arrived at the mosque and did some cautious reconnaissance in the area. This particular area of Cardiff was well known as a student housing area and opposite the mosque are several campuses of the University of Cardiff. This complicated things, as students are notoriously leftwing and if it became common knowledge that Britain First was outside the mosque opposite then they would come out in droves – like they did in Leicester – to oppose us.

So, we kept our heads down and scouted out the area. We parked around the corner and walked to the entrance of the mosque, which was on the side of the building. We stayed put for quite a while and to our surprise, we spotted Hammuda walking into the building. It was now or never so we leapt into action.

At the front entrance, I halted and stayed outside the door for the duration of the operation. The activists entered the mosque, intent on confronting Hammuda and his extremist rabble. On all previous mosque invasions, I had proudly and unashamedly entered the precincts of the building to confront whoever needed confronting. I was gutted that I had to wait outside this time. I waited patiently outside, speaking pleasantly to several young Muslims who recognised me and stopped to chat.

Inside the mosque, our activists challenged another imam and several worshippers to produce Hammuda. They claimed he wasn't in the building, but we had seen him with our own eyes entering. Our activists asked the imam what he thought about Hammuda's comments about sex slaves. The imam waffled about an article Hammuda had written claiming that Muslims could not have sex slaves but he had clearly been caught on audio recording so it was never in dispute. The imam simply lied repeatedly claiming it was all falsehood from the media. His only argument was to blame the media for telling lies. But you can't argue with an audio recording, can you?

Our activists produced a printed photo of Hammuda and told the worshippers and the imam that we would find him no matter what and that we would be back to confront him. Hammuda the coward could hide in a cupboard all he wanted, but he couldn't evade us forever. Hammuda is a classic example of an imam who preaches the extremism of the Koran to young, impressionable Muslims who then go out and commit atrocities or travel overseas to join jihadi organisations like ISIS. I have never seen any evidence of the authorities tackling radical hate preachers like him. To the contrary, radical Islamists receive benefits, legal aid and free houses, all paid for by the taxpayer. Our country truly has its values system back to front.

When the activists re-emerged, I was still waiting patiently at the front door and we hopped in our motor and left Cardiff for Caerphilly. There we hooked up with our Welsh activists for lunch. I regret doing this now because shortly the CCTV from the establishment we dined at was to be used against us. Once I arrived home in London I edited and uploaded the video where it received hundreds of thousands of views across our social media network.

A BBC report published after the operation said: 'Police are investigating a complaint from a Cardiff mosque which received an uninvited visit from Britain First. The far-right group posted a video on YouTube showing members in the Al-Manar Islamic Centre in Cathays on 20 August. The visit followed claims made in national newspapers in July that Shaykh Ali Hammuda, an Imam at the mosque, was a radical preacher, which he strenuously denied.'

Several weeks passed during which our efforts and attention

were focussed on Jayda's 'trial' for religiously aggravated harassment in Luton. During one of the many court hearings in the run-up to the trial at Luton Magistrate's Court, several uniformed police officers approached me while I was hanging about inside the court waiting room and passed me a thick bundle of papers inside a folder. They informed me that paperwork relating to a breach of a High Court injunction had been served on me and quickly walked away leaving me very confused.

It quickly dawned on me that Bedfordshire Police were dragging me into the High Court over our operation in Cardiff against Hammuda. While I did not enter the mosque myself, they were claiming I still breached the order by sending an activist team inside in my stead. I was convinced that day I had side-stepped the terms of the order – that's why I waited outside. Nevertheless, what we had done was morally justified in trying to confront a hate preacher who was poisoning the minds of young people. And after all, this particular mosque was virtually an ISIS outpost and provided recruits for their barbaric activities in Syria and Iraq.

Rather than take decisive and highly justifiable action against Hammuda, once again the Muslim Protection Squad was attacking the political activists who were doing their job for them. Was confronting a radical Islamist hate preacher the crime of the millennium? For the Muslim Protection Squad, yes it was. This is yet another sterling example of the lopsided, haphazard approach the authorities take when dealing with radical Islam. Islamists are protected or left alone and patriots are harassed and persecuted. This is not an accident, it is a deliberate policy put in place by leftwing politicians when occupying offices of state.

Upon reading the legal bundle dumped on me by Bedfordshire Police it was clear they wanted me severely punished. The paperwork specifically referred to a 'committal to prison'. I immediately organised a meeting with our legal team and a barrister they had asked to represent me. After surveying the contents of the legal bundle, which included witness statements from worshippers at al-Manar Centre and their imams, CCTV disks and of course, our own activity videos downloaded from cyberspace, I was told to expect six months in prison. I was shocked upon receiving this advice. I was expecting to go to prison for confronting a radical Islamist who said it's okay for Muslims to keep sex slaves? It took a long while to sink in but eventually I was determined to fight this nonsense.

The Muslim Protection Squad had me backed into a corner, but I would go down fighting and I would fight them to the bitter end. The date of my forthcoming 'trial' for 'contempt' of a High Court injunction was set for Thursday 15th December 2016 and to prepare for the worst, I stepped down as leader of Britain First and placed Jayda in charge as Acting Leader until my release. Jayda and I prepared the movement for my absence, which included passing all my roles and duties over to Jayda and others, to make sure the wheels of our movement kept turning while I was incarcerated. I had never been to prison before, but I am not a shrinking violet and so I grit my teeth and put my fate in the hands of our Lord.

25. Pentonville

On 15th December 2016, I arrived at the Royal Courts of Justice on the Strand in central London. Presiding over my 'trial' for breaching a High Court injunction was Judge Moloney. Moloney is a judge at Crown Court level, and I sensed immediately that this was bad news. Crown Court judges preside over criminal trials and are used to banging people up.

My strategy for that day was simple: To apologise for breaching the injunction and hope for the best. I wasn't apologising for trying to confront a hate preacher who was caught saying it was okay for Muslims to keep sex slaves. I was apologising to the judge for not giving the exact terms of the injunction enough scrutiny. Nevertheless, when a defendant is apologetic and admits to the breach – especially if the breach was *accidental* - it is rare that they are committed to prison for a first breach. But, as leader of Britain First, I understand that normal rules of law and sentencing don't apply to me. I am to be given the harshest possible punishment because my political views are not those of the establishment.

The hearing went reasonably well. Bedfordshire Police and their barrister laid out their evidence, which I did not dispute. Then my barrister apologised on my behalf and outlined that I stayed outside the mosque in an attempt to observe the terms of the injunction. What threw me off was the judge's attitude to both sides. He was almost hostile in his probing and questions to Bedfordshire Police, but nice as pie to my barrister. This encouraged me that I would not be sent to prison. At half time, I ventured outside of the court to see our activists, who were told not to enter the court itself so as not to upset the judge. I told them that the judge seemed friendly to our side.

However, this was simply the judge being sneaky. By the time the hearing was concluded and the judge retired to make a decision, I was confident I would not be going to prison. I was told by my solicitor that if uniformed officers of the court did not arrive by the time the judge returned, I was safe. An eternity of tension and anxiety passed as we waited nervously for the judge to return to give his verdict.

Then, suddenly, two uniformed officers of the court made their way into the court, a sure sign that a custodial sentence was about to be dished out. I sat refusing to believe it. After being so 'nice' to our barrister and dismissive of Bedfordshire Police, surely he wouldn't send me to prison. I had apologised and it would be unusual – unless someone had been hurt in the process – to send someone to prison for a first breach. Then the judge returned and we all stood to our feet. What followed was one of the most craven politically correct judgements I have ever heard.

Judge Moloney said my actions were a 'deliberate and cynical defiance' of the injunction. Disregarding the reasons for my actions, i.e. confronting an abhorrent hate preacher, Moloney said our activity was an attack on all Muslims, not just those at the mosque! The Daily Mail stated: 'James Weston, counsel for the Chief Constable of Bedfordshire Police who brought the committal application, said that members of the mosque found the conduct provocative and unnerving and were concerned that it could have escalated if prayers had not been over.' No mention of the scandal about Islamic sex slaves. No mention of the ISIS fighters being pumped out by this mosque. No, I had been accused of hurting their feelings and thus I had to be chastised.

I remember Judge Moloney saying that the police needed to be 'backed up' in their efforts to keep Muslims safe. It became crystal clear why this particular judge had been dragged out of the Crown Court criminal trial circuit and had been drafted into the High Court that day. Here was a judge very experienced and used to banging up defendants. A few years previously, a normal civil law High Court judge had sided with Britain First when Bedfordshire Police tried to ban us from Luton. So, this time, they imported a judge from a criminal court who they knew would happily throw me into one of London's stinking prisons. It also dawned on me that Judge Moloney's horrid attitude to the police and his genial approach to my barrister was another piece of arse-covering theatre designed to avoid an appeal against his decision.

Coming into court that day I was told to prepare for six months, or longer, if I was committed to prison. So, when he said that I was to be sent immediately into custody, I panicked to some degree. But then the judge ordered that I serve just two months in prison. Because of the way sentencing works, I only had to actually serve half of that actually in prison. The rest would be on licence. Thankfully, I later learned that the state or police are unable to apply licence conditions to you when your offence is contempt of court. So, I only had to serve four weeks in prison, my first time.

My solicitor turned around to the court officers and asked them what prison I would be taken to, and they replied 'Pentonville'. Once again, I became agitated. I knew from general knowledge that HMP Pentonville in north London was a dangerous, Islamist and gang run hell-hole. It had a notorious and violent reputation and is one of the most famous prisons in the country. But, in these situations, you simply do not have a choice. I was going to Pentonville whether I liked it or not.

Our activists were outside the court room and I was led past them in handcuffs by the court officers. I locked eyes with them and stated, 'No surrender'. I was then led down a dozen corridors and ancient looking passageways to the underground cells. There I was searched and put in a tiny concentre cubicle on my own for many boring and tedious hours. Time drags infinitely when in these situations! After an eternity waiting nervously, I was taken out and placed inside a prison transport vehicle. I was sat down again in a tiny metal cubicle. The seat was rock solid plastic and the window was tiny. It hot and stuffy and uncomfortable and I was in a full two-piece suit.

In this dreary, cramped transport vehicle, I began to ponder my predicament. This was my first time in prison so I had no idea what to expect. I know from studying the issues surrounding radical Islam that most prisons are dominated by Islamist gangs. My anxiety levels were through the roof, wondering if I was going to be thrown into the general population wings or put in solitary confinement. To my surprise, the transport vehicle started heading towards East London. HMP Pentonville was in the opposite direction, I thought.

I started to worry if I was actually being taken to HMP Belmarsh instead. If I was, I was as good as dead. Would the state stitch me up and throw into a prison full of Islamic terrorists and jihadis? I looked restlessly out the tiny window and noticed we were in Whitechapel, scene of so many of our controversial activities. We passed the East London mosque. This was the most bizarre route to Pentonville imaginable! But then we pulled into a court in Stratford, picked up some extra prisoners and turned around, heading for north London. I was enormously relieved.

The prisoner in the cubicle in front of me started hollering to me, asking me what my name was. I obliged and asked what Pentonville was like. He replied that it was a' war zone', where stabbings happened daily and gang conflict was rife. My anxiety levels exploded. I prepared myself for the worst. That two hour journey in the prison transport vehicle was perhaps the most tense and unbearable of my life. Humans are programmed to fear the unknown, no matter how tough you are. I prayed repeatedly and thought to myself, if this is God's plan then just ride it out. My first prison sentence for a political 'crime' was about to begin.

When we arrived at HMP Pentonville, we drove into the grounds of the prison and one by one the prisoners were taken out of the vehicle and taken to reception. I had formulated a plan to ensure that I would be segregated, away from the general population. I was confronted by a young lady at reception who gazed at my paperwork, asking me some jovial and friendly questions. Then she hit me with it, 'Oh, are you a VIP, do you know who you are being segregated?' The relief washed over me like a tsunami. I asked her what she meant, and she replied that I was going to be isolated.

HMP Pentonville is a Victorian prison opened in 1842, making it nearly 180 years old. The whole place is rotten and infested with cockroaches. Pentonville is a remand prison, where defendants are kept awaiting their trials for serious offences. Pentonville used to be a site for executions. Many famous people have been incarcerated in Pentonville, including IRA terrorists and leaders such as Eamon de Valera, poet and playwright Oscar Wilde, Ulster footballer George Best and singer Boy George.

The International Business Times said during this time, 'The most recent prison inspection report, from 2015, found HMP Pentonville to be unsafe with levels of violence much higher than in similar prisons. It also struggled with gang-related issues, the report said, and left inmates suffering filthy cells and without access to daily showers, clean clothes or eating utensils.'

After being booked in I was led to a room with a TV to wait for the basic equipment they provide for you. Then a guard asked me if I wanted something to eat and led me around the corner to a small canteen. My worst fears were then confirmed, the entire prison was packed to the rafters with bearded Muslims. Muslims looked at me with confused expressions and I grabbed some food and was taken back to the waiting room. After a while, I was examined by a doctor and then when the wings were locked down for the night, I was led to 'F Wing'. F Wing is officially stated as the 'Detoxification Unit'. This wing of the prison is reserved for drug addicts and alcoholics. I was led to a filthy cell on the fourth floor, told to enter, the door was locked and I was alone.

Surveying my new home for the next four weeks, I was appalled. It was rancid. There were bits of old food, piles of dust and used dirty clothes on the floor. There were piles of dirty rubbish in the corners. Even though I was in despair, I pulled myself together and spent the next hour or so cleaning and tidying. What a shit hole. Dirty, disgusting, unclean and unhygienic. I wasn't expecting the Savoy, but I equally wasn't expecting a Siberian gulag.

F Wing was much quieter and more relaxed than the other wings. I had many, many conversations with the prison guards and they relayed a tale of woe every single day about the misery and carnage taking place on the general population wings. But F Wing wasn't immune from the gang warfare elsewhere in the prison. I kept a daily diary of everything that happened while I was languishing in my cell. This detailed account was being compiled for this very book, but upon my release the prison authorities confiscated everything.

I was kept in solitary confinement for the duration of the four weeks. I was permitted out of my cell only once a day for fifteen minutes to collect my dinner and some medication. That was it. The rest of the time I was banged up. Luckily, I suppose, my cell window faced towards central London, so had a great view. I was sent to Pentonville on 15th December, so I had to spend Christmas and New Year inside. A great source of annoyance. I remember watching the New Year firework display out of my window, a small pleasure in the midst of grinding boredom and lethargy.

While the fourth floor was part of the 'Detoxification Unit', the fifth floor above was home to the 'VPU', the Vulnerable Prisoners Unit. In other words, degenerate sex offenders and paedophiles. I was taken to this floor every day for my medication and had to endure the presence of some vile specimens of humanity. I did not know what these reprobates did specifically, but the fact they were all on the 'nonce wing' meant they were all lowlife scum. I did, however, remember one black man that was on the wing. Months later, I remember perusing the Daily Mail online and recognising his face. It turns out he was a sex attacker who had tortured and mutilated his girlfriend. If only I had known this fact when I was in his presence in Pentonville!

Life grinded on for an interminable period of time. Four weeks in solitary with limited entertainment seems like five years. For the first two weeks, I had no books whatsoever. Every time I go to prison, my book orders and food orders always take an eternity. Perhaps this is deliberate. The TV in my cell had a limited number of freeview channels, but had a screen the size of a laptop and it was secured to a cabinet on the other side of the room. This places a strain on your eyes. I missed my LCD widescreen!

For the duration of the four weeks, I had no visitors at all. When Jayda and my father were due to visit me, I simply got a letter pushed underneath my door stating that they had not turned up. I was furious, as you can expect. However, when I rang Jayda, she related a different narrative of events. It turns out that the prison had taken the unusual step of moving my visit to a Sunday, to avoid me being in the same room with the Muslims on the other wings.

That was fine by me. However, when Jayda and my father arrived for the planned visit, they were simply told to go away. Then they lied to me saying that they had not bothered to turn up. The photos they took outside the prison gates stated otherwise. I had been stitched up.

Almost every day there were fights and prisoners being stabbed, 'shanked' to use prison speak. I would be laying peacefully in my bed watching some soul-destroying day time TV programme, when it seemed like a riot had started outside my door. I could hear shouts, screams and gang members walking past shouting, 'Go get the shank, get the shank'. Even on F Wing, Pentonville was a battleground. About halfway through my sentence, it broke on the news that major rioting had broken out at prisons around the country. Birmingham prison was completely taken over and trashed by the inmates. HMP Swaleside on the Isle of Sheppey in Kent was affected too, with serious disturbances. I was waiting for Pentonville to erupt, but it never did, thankfully.

Not content with stitching me up over my one and only visit, the prison authorities decided to put me in danger during my release, due on 11th January 2017. The day finally came when I was to be released and I prepared the night before, packing up my belongings etc. Prisoners are discharged at approximately 10am, or thereabouts, on their release day. So, my security team arranged to be outside the gates at 8.30am to make sure they were there and ready to pick me up. Obviously, the prison authorities listened to my phone calls making the preparations for this and decided to sabotage me.

I was sleeping peacefully on my rock-solid bed when at 6am a group of prison officers burst into my cell. Obviously taking me completely by surprise, they informed me I had only a few minutes to get out of the cell. I jumped to my feet half naked and asked them for some privacy, but they would not leave my cell. I had to get dressed and washed at lightning speed in the close presence of these guards. They then led me to the reception, booked me out, confiscated my notes, as stated earlier, and kicked me out into the mean streets of north London in the pitch black with no phone and a huge plastic bag full of clothes and other belongings.

Thankfully, there was a café open on the other side of the road and I asked them if I could use their phone, which they graciously consented to. I rang my father and he alerted the security team – who were staying in a hotel nearby – that I had been kicked out much earlier than planned. The prison authorities did this out of pure spite, nothing else. I ordered myself a fry-up and sat down eating my first decent meal in four weeks, until my security team arrived to collect me.

Immediately after my release, I posted an incendiary video message to my supporters that attracted widespread condemnation from the media and the political Left. To quote verbatim from a well-known leftwing media outlet:

Campaign group Hope Not Hate, which fights the Far Right in Britain, warned the video was a 'chilling threat' from a group that was already 'volatile'. Wearing a suit and standing before a black backdrop, Golding says his stint behind bars left him 'even more angry, more determined and more bitter at the scum and criminals ruining my country than ever before'. He says he will use 'every fibre of my being' to confront 'every traitor in this country'.

Those who have spent 'their careers undermining our nation' will 'succumb to this movement eventually and endure a day of reckoning for your crimes', he says. He adds 'every lie, every act of treachery will be revisited on you ten fold'. 'I can promise you, from the very depths of my being, you will all meet your miserable ends at the hands of the Britain First movement. Every last one of you,' says Golding. 'This is without doubt, a chilling threat from an organisation that barely operates within the law already. An organisation that thrives on confrontation, fear and violence,' Hope Not Hate wrote.

This was not in any way, exaggeration. I was even more determined and driven to fight the enemies of my nation when I was released from HMP Pentonville than I had ever been. Every revolutionary that fights the established political orthodoxy will be sent to prison. History is littered with such examples. And rest assured, I am no ordinary politician. I live and breathe purely to fight for my country and I despise and hate every last politician and journalist who has contributed during their careers to the dismemberment of Britain. One day, the boot will be on the other foot and anyone who has committed treason will be punished according to the law.

My first stint in prison toughened me up and allowed me to rest and recuperate. It was long, boring and depressing but it was simply another chapter in the story of our movement. As a Christian, I consider persecution to be a badge of honour. Persecution is confirmation that you are on the right track. As Jesus said, 'If the world hates you, remember that it hated me first'. Christians have been horribly persecuted throughout history. My namesake, Saint Paul, suffered greatly. I am happy and glad to be attacked, demonised and persecuted for the cause of British survival and the resurrection of Christian civilisation. The Bible instructs all Christians to stand firm in the face of persecution. All British patriots should rejoice when the establishment and their evil minions launch their attacks on you. Always remember the immortal and immutable words of our Lord, 'Blessed are those who have been persecuted for righteousness' sake, for theirs is the Kingdom of Heaven'.

26. Audacity

Shortly after I was released from Pentonville, Britain First responded to the Muslim grooming scandal in the West Midlands town of Telford by organising a protest march. Hundreds of patriots turned up from around the country. We invited a Polish guest speaker to address the crowd at this event, a famous man from Poland called Jacek Miedlar. Jacek was the man giving rabble rousing speeches at the annual Independence Day marches in Warsaw. The video of this gigantic march has gone viral on social media in the UK several times. The Polish with their gargantuan, disciplined parades put us British to shame. It is impossible to mobilise huge crowds in the UK without the participation of the football firms. We British are simply not militant like the continental Europeans.

The day before the march was due to take place, Jacek flew into Gatwick airport but was arrested immediately by the Muslim Protection Squad. They kept him for hours before putting him on a plane back to Poland. He was deported simply because he was due to speak at an event organised by a registered British political party! You couldn't make it up. Many patriots from around the world have been blocked from entering the UK.

Meanwhile, Islamist hate preachers regularly fly into the UK from every corner of the world to spew Wahabbi hate and bile and the authorities do nothing. One example is Shaykh Hamza Sodagar, a hate preacher who has called for gay people to be beheaded or burned to death. This creep previously posted a video listing five ways in which gay people should be killed. I remember travelling to north London with an activist team to stake out the event this villain was due to speak at. Despite his extremism, Sodagar was allowed into the UK. He was not arrested at the airport, nor was he deported. Yet a Polish ex-priest who happens to love our country was treated like an international criminal by our corrupt and moronic border police. I absolutely despair with our country sometimes.

Shortly after Telford, the nation was rocked by another Islamic terror attack, this time in the heart of London. On 22nd March, Islamist Khalid Masood drove a car across Westminster Bridge on the pavement, killing four people and injuring nearly fifty. After crashing his car, he walked into the grounds of Parliament before stabbing to death a policeman, Keith Palmer. He was then shot dead by armed officers. In a final text message, Masood stated he was waging 'jihad' against the West. Masood was a lone operator, but he was, without doubt, motivated by the jihadist ideology of radical Islam. Britain First immediately announced a protest march in London, which took place a few weeks later.

The attack in London triggered another wave of anti-Islamist activities by Britain First. Shortly after, we tracked down a notorious Islamist in Birmingham by the name of Krissoni Henderson. This big-mouth brute is infamous for his aggressive rants while in Birmingham city centre that have gone viral on social media. This wannabe jihadist was previously found guilty of religiously aggravated threatening behaviour. Henderson was found guilty of abusing a woman in the street – who he called a prostitute -

over her skinny jeans. These medieval freaks are always happy with amputations, stonings and beheadings, but object to skinny jeans? Britain First narrowed down the search to a single road in Birmingham, then canvassed the local shops who confirmed they always see Henderson coming out of a certain block of flats. Shortly after the video of our activity was released, Henderson sent an email to HQ challenging me to a duel!

I then decided to go for the 'jugular' of Islamism in Birmingham, an area called Sparkbrook. This notorious area was deemed the 'Jihad capital of Britain' by the media. We decided to visit the area with an activist team and distribute anti-extremism leaflets. We walked through Sparkbrook holding huge white Christian crosses and the locals were outraged. We were pelted with eggs and subjected to verbal abuse. Muslims in cars followed our vehicles when we left the area. I could see why Sparkbrook was considered such a perilous and precarious area.

Our team then headed up the road to Alum Rock and invaded a notorious Islamic bookshop that had been caught selling publications encouraging Muslim parents to teach their children jihad. The Madina Book Centre was in the news at that time for encouraging parents to 'keep alive in the children the spirit of jihad'. Some of these books referred to Jews as 'evil-minded' and advocated the death penalty for adulterers and gays. This shop had to be confronted, so we turned up in a minibus with a team and gave them hell. Despite the overwhelmingly Muslim population of the local area, we rocked up, disembarked and entered the shop, staying for just long enough before large numbers of aggressive Islamists converged to oppose us.

Heading into Islamic strongholds with only a small team of activists has always been the Britain First forte. Every other patriot movement has been too reluctant to carry out these kind of activities. But whether it is Brick Lane, Bury Park or Sparkbrook,

Britain First will never recognise the existence of any 'No Go Zones'. We go wherever we want, regardless of threats, intimidation or overwhelming odds. This approach also puts the local Islamists on their toes and makes them realise that - regardless of the limp-wristed treatment they receive at the hands of our PC police forces – at least some British citizens will confront them for their vile deeds.

This period of hyper activity was also notable for our annual opposition to the communist march through London on UN anti-racism day, held on Thursday 21st March. Once again, Britain First was hideously outnumbered, this time by some 10,000 communists to only 25 Britain First. We love these odds, they never deter us. Our activists formed up on the statue in Piccadilly Circus and waited patiently for the giant procession of liberals, socialists and hardcore communists to make its way down Regent Street. This annual march has to be the biggest freak show on earth, a mixture of hippies, sexual degenerates, hardline Soviet style Marxists with a sprinkling of famous politicians and celebrities.

This year, the hardliners knew we were coming and were prepared for us. The communist group, Antifa, turned up in force before the parade reached us and attacked wearing masks while hurling purple smoke bombs at us. All hell broke loose. Nevertheless, our team stood our ground and refused to budge, goading these blockheads to remove their masks and fight us like real men. The air was thick with purple smoke and the police struggled to keep our opposing lines apart. Imagine the uproar if a gang of far-right extremists turned up in London wearing masks and hurled smoke bombs at political opponents!

Soviet communist flags were openly displayed on this procession, with no reprimand by the organisers. Very quickly the huge procession made its way to Piccadilly Circus and our tiny presence managed to draw away thousands of these mutants from the march itself. These leftists were particularly agitated by the sight of our 'No more mosques!' banner. We were hemmed in by enormous crowds of leftwing oddballs, a truly epic 'Rorke's Dift' moment. The police struggled for hours to keep the Bolshevik hordes from overrunning our positions. But we would not budge, not even a few feet to safety.

It's hard to articulate the delight we take in confronting thousands of traitors with just a handful of patriots. Over and over, throughout our short history, Britain First emulated the spirit of the three hundred Spartans and their stand at Thermopylae against frightful odds. We truly see ourselves as the defenders of Western, Christian civilisation against the barbarian hordes. At this point on the timeline in the early 21st Century, we find ourselves once again in as much peril – perhaps even greater peril – than we faced at the Gates of Vienna in 1683. Only the same selfless and fearless conduct shown by the likes of Sobieski and the other heroes of Europe will save our civilisation from subjugation. To date, no one has proved their mettle and gallantry in this regard except Britain First.

27. Ramsgate

In September of 2016, a young English girl, who had been enjoying a night out, walked past a pizza shop on Northwood Road in Ramsgate, Kent, while on the phone to a friend. She was drunk and this had caused her to become disorientated and unable to find her way home. Suddenly, the owners and workers of the '555 Pizza' shop - a group of Muslim migrants from Afghanistan - taking note of her drunken state, seized her and dragged her upstairs into a dingy flat. There, they flung her down on a 'grubby' mattress and proceeded to rape her repeatedly, taking turns while laughing.

After taking turns raping this girl - who is too young to be named - they halted the ordeal and she ran out into the street screaming and crying until she was found by a random woman who took her home. The young girl called 999 and the recording was later played in court. DNA from all four migrants was found during forensic tests. The young English girl was described as being 'passed around like an entertainment device' during the attack.

Prosecutor Simon Taylor said, 'Every single orifice had been penetrated by the group of men, while others watched, laughed and joined in themselves.' Mr Taylor also added: 'There was much laughter in that room where she was being subjected to the ordeal.' Amazingly, despite the DNA evidence and the horrific nature of the crime, all four of the perpetrators were given bail and carried on running the '555 Pizza' shop where the attack took place. This showed a complete lack of concern by the judge for other vulnerable women in the locality. One of the attackers then fled the country and was apprehended in Italy, then brought back to the UK to stand trial.

This heinous attack shocked the people of Ramsgate and caused a big furore in this corner of Kent. Because the attackers were given bail and allowed to mingle with the public, when the trial started Britain First decided to take action. It was simply disgusting and unforgivable that – despite iron-clad DNA evidence – immigrant gang rapists should have been given bail. Not only that, but they were allowed to carry on – business as usual – working at their sordid little pizza shop. I am absolutely certain that if this gang of paedophile rapists were from a white English background, they would have been remanded to prison until their trial. Thanks to political correctness and its paralysing effect on common sense, these monsters were free to roam the streets.

Their high-profile trial for rape started in early May 2017 and it immediately started to make national headlines. What made us sick was that the offenders had been granted bail and they were repeatedly pictured standing outside of the Canterbury Crown Court building smoking and chatting, seemingly not a care in the world and certainly showing no signs of strain or remorse. Despite all being foreigners who had come to this country as guests, they decided to abuse our hospitality, break the law and subject one of our children to a vile gang rape. Could you imagine going to a different country and behaving in such a fashion? It is truly barbaric and they should have been kept in custody until a jury had decided on their guilt, not released into the wild putting other children at risk. Once a dirty gang rapist, always a dirty gang rapist in my eyes. When one of the offenders fled the country, the remaining culprits should have had their bail immediately rescinded.

Britain First immediately swung into action, prompted by emails arriving at HQ from Ramsgate locals asking for us to expose the whereabouts of these vile sexual predators. A team of us drove up to Ramsgate and we tried to confront the rapists who were hiding inside of the '555 Pizza' shop. I filmed while Jayda banged on the glass and hurled challenge after challenge to the men inside to come out and face us. We could clearly see them inside pointing their mobile phones at us recording our every word and movement. The migrants inside the shop later claimed in court that they were 'terrified' of the Britain First contingent. Their children, especially, we very fearful of our presence, they claimed. However, when one of the recordings taken from inside the shop was played in court, you can hear the children and the adults laughing and joking. Hardly paralysed with fear and dread.

After we left the vicinity of the pizza shop, we travelled to Canterbury Crown Court where the trial was taking place. We spotted a group of males standing with a barrister immediately outside the entrance. We were convinced it was the rapists and their legal representative. We immediately walked up to them and Jayda proceeded to interrogate them about who they were. They claimed they were in court for a driving offence. One of the males finished his cigarette and went back into the court building. The barrister followed. One of the males, clearly a foreigner, then responded, preaching to us that Islam is 'perfect' but humans were not. He obviously took offence to Jayda using the term 'Muslim paedo bastards'. However, for a moment we considered the possibility that these males were not who we were looking for.

So, we entered the court, leaving our camera with reception, proceeding through security and then checking specifically what court the trial was actually taking place. We proceeded to the correct court, only to find the same males sitting waiting for their trial to recommence. The bastards had lied, but now we knew their faces. We moved upstairs to the public gallery and waited for the trial to re-start. Then we were approached by officers of the court who told us the judge had banned our presence! We had to leave immediately or face arrest for contempt of court. The judge would not re-start the trial unless we left, which we very prudently did.

We uploaded the video report to our enormous social media pages which triggered a wave of emails congratulating us on doing something to expose the migrant rapists. Some of these emails from locals contained the home addresses of the offenders. These addresses were in Ramsgate and Canterbury, and we immediately visited them to ascertain whether they were false flags or the true home addresses of the rapists. By speaking to neighbours, we were able to verify these addresses. Campaign leaflets for distribution to the rapists' neighbours were immediately drafted. One by one, these addresses were visited and our activists gave out leaflets to everyone in the immediate vicinity warning them about the monsters they had in their midst.

Why did we do this? Wouldn't *you* like to know if one of your neighbours was a paedophile gang rapist? Would that knowledge unsettle you and make you think about your children's safety? In our opinion, the neighbours of these villains had every right to be informed. Some leftwing elements posted on social media during that time that, 'Everyone is innocent until proven guilty'. That is true, however, DNA evidence from these migrant paedophiles had been found after extensive forensic tests. The likelihood of them being found 'not guilty' was negligible. Likewise, one of them had already fled the country trying to escape justice, pretty much confirming their collective guilt. The fact they had been granted bail, in our eyes, justified us blowing the whistle on their whereabouts. Our duty is to defend our people, not to worry about the 'rights' and anonymity of migrant paedophiles.

The videos from this campaign were uploaded to our social media channels and received millions of views. Our activities raised the general awareness of the trial and the crime considerably. Hundreds of thousands of ordinary British citizens heaped praise upon Britain First for warning the local residents about the presence of these criminal paedophile rapists. However, unknown to us, the Muslim Protection Squad were busy behind the scenes preparing their latest assault on our movement.

On a quiet Wednesday evening in Kent, both Jayda and I were traveling down a country road when the traffic in front of us came to a sudden halt. We were completely unaware of what was going on and considered it to be a simple traffic jam. In fact, a police van had blocked the road up ahead and before we knew what was happening, around half a dozen police cars ambushed us from every direction. This was the closest thing I had ever seen to being a SWAT team or SAS ambush. They came out of nowhere from every direction to block us in. Within seconds our car was surrounded by uniformed officers, who ordered us to get out. The police cuffed us and carted us off to the nearest police station. They immediately seized our mobile phones, sat-navs and laptops.

Simultaneously, the Muslim Protection Squad raided our offices and homes, grabbing every memory stick, USB device, laptop and PC they could find. Thankfully, it is standard policy for us to host everything of value online, in secure, encrypted cloud servers. Our hard drives have military level encryption too. Nevertheless, the police usually take everything electrical they can lay their hands on, including devices that do not even store information, like laser printers. This unnecessary thoroughness in seizing equipment is designed purely to shut down our day to day administration. It causes a big temporary headache, but is never fatal.

At Tonbridge police station, both Jayda and I were informed we had been arrested for offences contrary to the Public Order Act 1986, specifically inciting religious hatred. This particular charge carries a maximum sentence of seven years in prison. We were kept in custody for the next eleven hours until we were released on bail at 6am in the morning with no phones or money. During our interrogations, we were questioned by officers that appeared to us to be plain local CID. It later turned out that this entire investigation was instigated and carried through by none other than 'SO15 Counter Terrorism Command'. I presumed that terror police existed to combat terrorism, not investigate acts of low-level harassment. More on that later. Just to be spiteful, the date we were ordered to return to the police station was the 3rd June, the well-publicised date of our forthcoming protest march in Birmingham! The police are not subtle in their blatant sabotage of our legal activities. Our protest march had to be postponed.

Naturally, the Muslim Protection Squad slapped both of us with repressive bail conditions prohibiting us from even mentioning the reason why we had been arrested. We were warned in no uncertain terms that should we mention the circumstances of our arrest – i.e. the campaign against the migrant paedos in Ramsgate – we would be re-arrested and possibly remanded to prison until our trial. I remember thinking, 'Hold on a moment, how comes the migrant paedophiles are given bail but me and Jayda are threatened with remand if we even mention the very reason why we were arrested?' Other conditions prevented us from holding any political activities in the county of Kent and banned Jayda and I from entering the town of Ramsgate. We also had to 'sign on' again every Saturday at Bromley police station at 3pm.

This squalid saga was the latest confirmation that the police authorities will react with fury against anyone who dares to shine a light on issues relating to Islamism and migrants. Even when the object of your campaign is a gang of discredited paedophile child rapists, if they are Muslim, migrants or both, the police will rush to shield them from any exposure. The offenders in Ramsgate had perpetrated an act of unspeakable horror on an English child. One of them tried to flee the country. DNA evidence linking them to the felony that took place at '555 Pizza' was being used to convict them. Yet despite all of this, the police spared no expense in launching a well organised and slick SAS style ambush on two politicians who had the temerity to warn local residents about the criminals living close by. You couldn't make it up.

I cannot comprehend what goes through the minds of those who order actions like this. How can this possibly be justified by a sane person? A decent, moral and healthy society would probably have given us medals for our actions. But in politically correct Britain – a country afflicted by social Marxism – we are hounded, ambushed, prosecuted and punished. How many times have you heard someone, somewhere, say that 'this country has gone mad'. It is true, as a nation we are a diseased, rotten, sickly mental patient. Political correctness has completely subverted our value system, to the point where criminals are victims and victims are criminals. I didn't realise it at the time, but this particular bout of persecution was going to last a long time and come very close to destroying Britain First.

28. Trump

By mid 2017, Britain First had grown to prodigious size on social media. We had shortly before hit 2 million followers on Facebook alone. We were reaching the usual 50 million people every week with our daily videos and posts. We were reaching more people organically every week than the BBC. I knew from dependable sources that this situation was freaking out the establishment, who were putting stupendous pressure on Facebook to close us down. Facebook weathered the storm and kept our pages online.

They came under more pressure in mid 2017. On 3rd June, a group of Islamists used a vehicle to launch an attack on pedestrians on London Bridge. They then entered the nearby Borough Market and started to attack revellers with knives. Eight innocent civilians were killed in the Islamist attack. In retaliation, on 19th June, a man by the name of Darren Osbourne drove a van into worshippers outside the notorious Finsbury Park mosque, injuring eight people. A few months later, on 23rd January 2018, it was alleged that Osbourne had had 'contact' with 'far-right groups' including 'Britain First'.

The basis of this was that Osbourne received a direct message from our deputy leader Jayda Fransen on Twitter. This claim was carried internationally by the fake news media. The truth was radically different, however. During this period, all Britain First Twitter accounts used a system called Crowdfire. This system allowed an autoresponder – a private message using a template - to be sent *automatically* to all new followers. Osbourne had simply followed Jayda on Twitter and then received an automated message.

That did not stop the media blaming Britain First for the attack on Finsbury Park mosque, just like they did when the MP Jo Cox was killed. Never let the truth get in the way of a fake news story! The media are desperate to falsely tie groups like Britain First to terrorist outrages in the hope of getting us proscribed. As with the investigation into the murder of MP Jo Cox, Britain First never received even a single phone call from the investigating officers during their enquiry into the Finsbury Park attack. They knew full well it had nothing to do with Britain First, but that did not stop the dishonest media trying to drag our movement through the gutter, again.

In November 2017, I visited Jayda at her home address and spent a few hours with her. During this visit, Jayda received a random call from a journalist and I could see the colour drain from her face. When she ended the call, she looked at me ashen faced and said, 'President Donald Trump has retweeted me on Twitter'. Both of us were stunned. The gravity of the situation took some time to process. Could the President of the United States have really retweeted posts from one of our Twitter accounts? My brain was fried within thirty seconds thinking about the implications of this. If true, it would be global news and would thrust Britain First into the international limelight. Trump is a notorious Twitter addict and uses his account to literally run the government of the United States. If our little movement had been retweeted by the most powerful man in the world, we knew the consequences would be cataclysmic.

Nervously, I opened the Twitter app on my iPhone and typed 'Trump' in the search box. To my absolute amazement, it was true. Trump had shared no less than three separate videos from Jayda's account. A period of surreal mental confusion followed, as we tried to grapple with this titanic and monumental situation. Within 24 hours, Jayda's Twitter account had tripled in size to 100,000 followers. Britain First was international news. Our Facebook pages started burgeoning in size. My phone was ringing off the hook with media interview requests. This really was D-Day for us. Thankfully, I had over a decade of experience handling the hostile media. I swung into action immediately.

I quickly booked a nice conference room in a hotel at the Dartford Bridge, easily accessible for the London based media teams. Once we arrived I started to direct the dozens of TV channels, journalists and presenters to the hotel. Like the Mongol hordes an endless deluge of media hacks started to arrive. We literally had a queue of the highest profile media outlets in the world. Reuters, Press Association, BBC, ITV, C4, RT, CNN and many others all took turns interviewing Jayda. Some of the poorer quality outlets, like Vice TV, had their interviews terminated and they were told to leave. While this was happening, I fed an endless conveyor belt of short videos and posts to our vast social media empire. I could have dropped dead from exhaustion by the end of it.

While we enjoyed ourselves riding a high of international fame and attention, in reality Trump retweeting us brought serious danger and damage in its wake. It propelled Britain First onto the global stage and for many days, nothing else came close to rivalling this story across the entire world. The reaction from the liberal-Left establishments across the Western world was hysterical. An entire book could be written about this period. It was absolutely crazy, and seemed like Jayda and I were temporarily on a par of importance with the likes of Trump, Putin, Theresa may and Angela Merkel.

The condemnations were many and widespread. Trump's retweets - and Britain First - were condemned by Labour leader Jeremy Corbyn and the rest of the Labour Party, TV personality Piers Morgan, Prime Minister Theresa May, the Archbishop of Canterbury Justin Welby, Mayor of London Sadiq Khan, Parliament, the EU Parliament, the EU and many, many others.

A major discussion was triggered - including debates in Parliament - on whether to ban President Donald Trump from coming to the UK. Media presenters and TV channels across the West pressured Trump to remove the retweets and apologise. He stood firm and refused. But by far my favourite reaction was the endless media reports that accused Britain First of literally 'destroying' the age-old 'Special Relationship' between the UK and the United States! Trump's retweets caused a major diplomatic row, with strong and vociferous protests from the UK government being rebuffed by Trump himself and the US State Department. We simply could not absorb that we had caused a major diplomatic incident between the UK and the USA!

Theresa May lambasted Britain First during Prime Minister's Questions in the House of Commons, saying that we spread 'hateful narratives which peddle lies and stoke tensions'. The Archbishop of Canterbury said in an official release, 'Britain First seeks to divide communities and intimidate minorities, especially our Muslim friends and neighbours. Britain First does not share our values of tolerance and solidarity. God calls us as Christians to love our neighbour and seek the flourishing of all in our communities, societies and nations. I join the urgent call of faith groups and others for President Trump not just to remove these tweets, but to make clear his opposition to racism and hatred in all forms.'

Hindsight is a wonderful thing and for a while, we simply embraced the colossal focus on our movement and our international infamy. However, the Trump retweets were to trigger a chain of events that would lead to the violent censorship of Britain First. Thanks to Trump, we simply got too prominent in the eyes of the establishment. Only three weeks after the Trump retweets, Twitter suspended the Britain First, Paul Golding and Jayda Fransen accounts. These accounts were verified with the blue symbol. Nevertheless, Twitter simply wiped us out. Unfortunately, Trump did not condemn this act of naked censorship. We expected him to comment, but he never did.

At the same time, YouTube placed restrictions on every video on our official channel, pretty much destroying its reach. But Facebook did not follow suit and take us down, so we breathed a sigh of relief. We could still reach tens of millions of people every week, just on Facebook. However, Facebook imposed what is called 'Shadow Banning' on all our official pages. This means that posts do not get served to everyone who has 'liked' our pages, just a small percentage. This is censorship by the backdoor. We started getting hundreds of emails at HQ complaining that they no longer saw Britain First content in their newsfeeds. Our organic reach dropped steadily from 50 million people reached every week to only 5-8 million. Again, with hindsight, rather than just take us down, Facebook were cutting us down to size before they made their move.

In January 2018, Donald Trump was interviewed by TV personality Piers Morgan for the popular morning show 'Good Morning Britain'. Piers badgered Trump to apologise for the retweets. Instead, Trump said, 'If you are telling me they're horrible people, horrible, racist people, I would certainly apologise if you'd like me to do that.' Not exactly a direct apology, but that did not stop the world's media from launching into a frenzy of 'Trump finally apologises' stories. Trump knew *exactly* who Britain First were and why he retweeted Jayda *specifically*. He did not retweet posts from the Britain First account, or mine. He chose Jayda specifically and for a very good reason.

As mentioned in the previous chapter, during this period both Jayda and I had to 'sign on' every Saturday at Bromley police station in South East London. We had both recently travelled to Belfast as guests of an elected city councillor to give speeches at an anti-terrorism rally. This rally was held in the wake of the terrible nail-bomb attack on children at Manchester Arena. Other speakers included Paul Rimmer from Liverpool, and John Banks from Yorkshire. During this rally, a can hurled into the air by an IRA supporter nearly hit me in the head, without a doubt causing me serious damage if it had landed. Luckily, I saw it flying through the air and managed to bat it out of the way. Our speeches contained nothing but strong condemnations of radical Islam.

When me and Jayda made our way to Bromley police station to sign on, as we were leaving the station a contingent of suited officers with funny accents approached us and arrested Jayda. They took her through a door into the guts of the police station and left me outside with a bodyguard. An officer emerged shortly after informing me they were taking her all the way to Belfast! We were told that this was due to an offence committed while making a speech a month earlier in Belfast. At this point, only Jayda had been arrested. Britain First obviously made a huge fuss about Jayda's arrest and the videos were viewed all around the world. Jayda was only exercising her right to freedom of speech, but this did not stop her being arrested.

It is my view that the news of this outrageous arrest and the impact it would have on freedom of speech in the UK somehow made its way to the desk of President Donald Trump. As a way of poking Theresa May in the eye for what was happening, Trump retweeted some of Jayda's videos. This would draw attention to Jayda's plight and simultaneously embarrass the UK government. There is simply no other explanation for why Trump would go out of his way to do what he did. Some have claimed he acted impulsively. That could have been considered as a possibility, except for the fact that

Trump retweeted no less than *three* of Jayda's videos. No, this wasn't an act of random and impulsive social media sharing. This was a deliberate way of prodding the UK Prime Minister over the abuse of free speech in her country. Unfortunately, Trump's intervention on behalf of free speech had the opposite effect. The UK establishment came after Britain First with apocalyptic ferocity.

The number of arrests, prosecutions and restrictions aimed at Britain First proliferated rapidly. 'S015 Counter Terrorism Command' led the charge, along with the Home Office and No 10 putting social media – especially Facebook – under enormous pressure to silence our movement once and for all. While Trump's retweets boosted our profile among the peoples of the Western world, it backfired spectacularly when the establishment came down on us like a tonne of bricks. Britain First had been condemned by entire governments, parliaments, world leaders, the EU and the entire global media. The establishment must have panicked when the retweets happened, but their determination to bring us down was massively bolstered. Over the next year, they would nearly succeed.

29. Registration

The Electoral Commission is supposedly an independent body set up by the UK Parliament to regulate democratic elections. This includes political party registration, finances, election spending and sanctions against rule breakers. The Electoral Commission is supposed to be an impartial and neutral regulator, devoid of bias and partisanship in favour of any shade of political belief. The Electoral Commission is the custodian of democracy in Britain. Unfortunately, however, the Electoral Commission has become, in recent years, a biased, tendentious and partisan institution, displaying blatant favouritism for the political Left and placing every obstacle in the way of patriots and conservatives.

Britain First was first registered as a political party in early 2014. The registration process was completed within a few short weeks. Britain First enjoyed the status of being a formal political party until November 2017. We submitted accounts every year and as a registered political party, we fought parliamentary by-elections, European Parliament elections and I stood for Mayor of London. Every year, every political party has to fill out a form and re-register, for a small fee.

In November 2017, for reasons explained in a later chapter, I missed the re-registration deadline by a few hours and the supposedly neutral Electoral Commission refused to accept the re-registration. I was informed that Britain First would be de-registered as a political party and there was nothing I could do about it. I was told I would have to re-apply and start from scratch. This unnecessary and spiteful de-registration was deliberate, the leftwing bigots running the Electoral Commission hoping to remove any protection given to Britain First by the status of being a registered political party. They could have just accepted our re-registration documents, even though they were a few hours late, but they refused to budge. If I had been the leader of a leftwing, socialist or communist party, I have no doubt that they would have given us a bit of leeway.

I had no choice but to apply from scratch to register Britain First as a political party. But at that point, I had no idea of the tremendous obstruction, delay and sabotage that the Electoral Commission would subject us to. At the time of writing, the battle to register Britain First as a political party again has been raging for nearly two years and we have submitted to less than *seven* fresh applications, each one rejected on the most ludicrous grounds.

Even though Britain First was de-registered in November 2017, the process of blatant and politically motivated obstruction began before that, in April 2017. The UK is divided into two separate political jurisdictions, Great Britain and Northern Ireland. Britain First was registered from 2014 until 2017 in Great Britain, which includes England, Scotland and Wales. In April 2017, I submitted an application to register Britain First in Northern Ireland for the first time.

What followed was almost two years of ridiculous obfuscation, procrastination and deferral. The simple process of registration takes around thirty days. When Britain First was first registered as a political party in 2014, the process only took a few weeks. It is my view that at some point in 2017, the Electoral Commission decided to throw off any pretence of being politically neutral and became a nakedly partisan organisation. A decision was made within the institution to wage war on anyone holding patriotic or conservative views, to block, delay and obstruct them with every trick in the book. The Electoral Commission was transformed into a wing of leftist politics with no care or interest in political neutrality.

To give a taste of the outrageous and scandalous delaying tactics the Electoral Commission deployed against Britain First, please read the following legal letter which was sent after the refusal of our first application to register in Northern Ireland:

Dear Electoral Commission,

Our clients lodged an application with the Electoral Commission to register a party in Northern Ireland in April 2017.

Our client received an email response from Registration Officer, Josh Dunne, stating 'We will shortly be publishing the details of your party name, description and emblem on our 'Current Applications' page of our website for public comment.'

Mr. Dunne asked a series of questions about the party's submitted Constitution to which Mr. Golding replied that he was happy to make any amendments that were required.

On the 19th of April, Mr. Golding submitted an updated Constitution as per the recommendations of Mr. Dunne.

Mr. Dunne did not reply or acknowledge receipt.

On the 20th of April, Mr. Golding sent another email to Mr. Dunne asking for an update on the new submitted Constitution that was provided.

On the 2nd of May, a reply was finally received from a Mr. Craig Wakeford, which stated 'During our assessment we identified an issue with your financial scheme and constitution that must be resolved before the application can be taken further.'

The same day, 2nd May, Mr. Golding replied stating, 'Please explain in detail any issues that need to be rectified regarding our application and we will make the necessary changes.'

Later that same day, Mr. Golding received a reply from Craig Wakeford, stating the following: 'Thank you for that clarification, we will likely be back in contact with you later in May or early June to discuss the issues in your application.'

On the 22nd of May, Mr. Golding sent an email to the Party Registration team asking when the new Northern Ireland party would be registered.

On 15th June, Mr. Dunne replied asking for further amendments to our Constitution and Financial Scheme.

Less than two hours later, Mr. Golding emailed back with both the Constitution having made the requested changes.

On the 27th June, Mr. Dunne acknowledged receipt of the amended Constitution.

On 3rd of July, Mr. Golding sent an email containing the newly amended Financial Scheme.

Weeks later, on 21st July, Mr. Dunne finally responded and asked for more amendments to the Financial Scheme.

On the 26th, Mr. Dunne emailed Mr. Golding asking him to make the changes to the Financial Scheme urgently.

Two days later, on the 28th July, Mr. Golding emailed Mr. Dunne with the amended Financial Scheme he had requested.

The Electoral Commission then fell silent for a whole month until the 23rd August, when Mr. Golding and the Treasurer [redacted] received an email from Li Zhao (Party Registration) stating that the application to register a party in Northern Ireland had been rejected.

It is our view that the Electoral Commission deliberately hindered our client's application for a period of almost six months, continually asking for new revisions to their application whilst dragging out the process for as long as possible before finally rejecting it, despite the continual cooperation of our clients.

On the 13th November, Paul Golding once again submitted an application to register a political party in the jurisdictions of Great Britain and Northern Ireland.

On the 16th November, Mr. Dunne once again emailed Mr. Golding asking for a series of changes to the applications. On the 22nd November, Mr. Golding replied to Mr. Dunne with the revised Constitutions as requested, along with other information regarding officers' home addresses etc. On the 30th November, Mr. Dunne replied asking for the other office bearers to authorise the changes to the constitutions.

The same day, Mr. Golding replied with the relevant information. On the 13th December, our Treasurer, [redacted], received a letter (via email) from a Louise Edwards, Head of Regulation at the Electoral Commission.

The letter contained a fresh set of demands for further information and also a request for a formal meeting at the Commission's office in London. Our clients feel that the Electoral Commission is deliberately hindering our client's application to register political parties in Great Britain and Northern Ireland.

What should be a smooth 30-day process, is being obstructed and dragged out to inordinate lengths of time to frustrate our client's legitimate political activities.

Considering the May elections are fast approaching, our client is determined to get registered in time to stand candidates, as per their political rights. Our clients have consistently used the official Electoral Commission templates for its financial scheme, so rejection of this calls into question the veracity of these templates.

Our clients request that their applications are processed within 30 days and are not subjected to undue time wasting and obstruction.

Yours sincerely,

[redacted]

This legal letter did not have any impact on the political bias of the Electoral Commission. Starting in April 2017, Britain First has submitted no less than seven applications to register as a political party. Each application has been dragged out, delayed and sabotaged. Each rejection has been justified on the flimsiest of grounds, some reasons being given in areas where the Electoral Commission has absolutely no legal jurisdiction, such as party policy.

For example, one application was delivered to the Electoral Commission in early July 2018 and it was published on their website under 'Current Applications' on the 26th of July. The Electoral Commission kept Britain First waiting - deliberating delaying the process - for five months until they finally rejected our application on the most ridiculous grounds imaginable. The reasons given for their politically-motivated refusal were as follows:

- Britain First has policies which include a ban on the Burka, which could discriminate against Muslims.

- Britain First leaders have certain criminal convictions, such as harassing migrant rapists, which could discriminate against Muslims.

- A previous incarnation of Britain First was fined a small amount for a late annual return.

- The Election Commission doesn't 'believe' that the Britain First constitution is reflective of how the organisation is run day to day.

Let's examine these 'reasons' and you will see how utterly ridiculous this political sabotage by the Electoral Commission really is. The Electoral Commission was created by the 'Political Parties Elections And Referendums Act 2000' and it is this legislation alone which determines its legal powers and remit. Reason number one is that Britain First has policies which could discriminate against Muslims - such as banning the burka and niqab. Under the 'Political Parties Elections And Referendums Act 2000' the Electoral Commission has no powers whatsoever to interfere in - or reference - the *policies* of applicant parties when making decisions. The

Electoral Commission actually acknowledge this in their refusal letter.

Reason number two - referring to the politically motivated convictions Britain First's leaders - is again another area in which the Electoral Commission has no authority whatsoever. Some party leaders - such as Gerry Adams of Sinn Fein - have convictions for terrorism but this has never stopped them being registered. Under the 'Political Parties Elections And Referendums Act 2000' the Electoral Commission has no powers at all to refuse applications based on criminal records.

Reason number three, a reference to a small fine that was applied to Britain First several years ago, is another ridiculous example of purely political motives on the part of the Electoral Commission. Dozens of registered political parties are fined on a regular basis but never face any problems re-registering on an annual basis. The 'Political Parties Elections And Referendums Act 2000' gives the Electoral Commission no powers whatsoever to reject new applications based on previous fines. The three main parties - Conservative, Labour and Lib Dems - have all been fined tens of thousands of pounds by the Electoral Commission but have never faced problems re-registering. Britain First has never been fined more than £500.

The last reason given - that the Electoral Commission dismisses our current Constitution - is the final example of purely political motives at work during this process. The 'Political Parties Elections And Referendums Act 2000' does not give the Electoral Commission the authority to meddle in a party's constitution. The 'Political Parties Elections And Referendums Act 2000' gives the Electoral Commission powers that refer only to the *finances* of political parties, such as annual accounts and spending during elections and referendums.

Thus, the Electoral Commission - by rejecting this particular application by citing the reasons above - are meddling in areas where they have *no legal authority*. It is noteworthy that the Electoral Commission did not mention any financial matters that led to the rejection of this particular application.

In August 2018, elections officer George Whale and I visited the offices of the Electoral Commission in central London and showcased our financial, accounting and bookkeeping systems and these more than adequately satisfied the requirements of the 'Political Parties Elections And Referendums Act 2000'. The Electoral Commission simply took a collective decision to refuse Britain First regardless of any legislation or submissions we make. They are probably working hand-in-glove with the political Home Office to obstruct and hinder Britain First at every opportunity.

The specific reasons given for refusal of every fresh application border on the absurd. For example, the ban on face-coverings. This prohibition was implemented to prevent activists turning up at our events and activities with EDL-style masks. In our opinion, the only activists who insist on wearing face coverings, masks or balaclavas etc. are those intent on stirring up trouble. In any case, wearing a face covering provides a level of anonymity which can encourage a lapse into aggression or violence. It also makes it impossible for us to identify these activists and expel or discipline them. We want to avoid this kind of reputation destroying nonsense at our activities. Hence, we ban face coverings in Britain First, primarily because of an inclination to avoid the EDL experience. However, the Electoral Commission decided this is not allowed, because Muslims may join Britain First and they won't be allowed to wear their burkas and niqabs at our events! To quote them, 'This may indirectly discriminate against those who wear headscarves or face-coverings for religious reasons.'

As explained in an earlier chapter, I was banned from entering all mosques and their private grounds in England and Wales, by order of a High Court injunction. I was also prohibited from directing or ordering anyone else involved in Britain First from entering all mosques and their private grounds in England and Wales. I was sent to HMP Pentonville for breaching this injunction. Because of this, I inserted into our official Code of Conduct the following passage:

All Britain First groups, members, officials and supporters must refrain from entering any Mosque or Islamic Cultural Centre or its private grounds within England and Wales without prior written invitation.

This was simply because I was trying to observe the terms of the injunction. Nothing else. However, the Electoral Commission took issue with this as it would prevent Muslim members of Britain First from entering mosques! They said, 'Muslim members of the party would be at a disadvantage compared with non-Muslims, as they would be more likely to enter a mosque to practice their faith.' You simply can't win with the Electoral Commission. You are damned if you do and damned if you don't.

Another nonsensical reason for refusal was a party 'description' we applied for, 'Britain First, Taking our country back!' According to the Electoral Commission, this slogan was *racist*:

The use of the words 'taking' and 'our' in the proposed description, as well as the exclamation mark, conveys an aggressive call for action that also implies some ethnic groups or communities would be the subject of an exclusionary policy. We consider it likely that certain voters would find that offensive...

Britain First wants to take our country back, from the EU, corrupt politicians, the fake news media, and so on. Where does race feature in any of that? The Electoral Commission came up with endless reasons for refusing our applications, the vast majority of which were silly, irrational and incongruous.

The Electoral Commission is not a neutral and impartial body that oversees democracy in the UK, but a politically biased organisation that actively hampers and stonewalls certain points of view and political beliefs. The establishment simply does not want Britain First standing in elections - so they are doing all they can to prevent it, even if by doing so, they are effectively interfering in the democratic process.

Since April 2017, Britain First has submitted *seven* applications to register as a political party. All seven applications have been *refused*. While our leaders grandstand on the world stage waffling about 'democracy', political freedom in the UK is being gerrymandered and subverted by the political Left. Millions of our ancestors who fought for democracy are being betrayed and ominous moves are being made to transform Britain into a leftwing oligarchy. The Electoral Commission is the custodian of democracy in Britain, and they have chosen to destroy it. Shame on them. One day they will answer for their crimes.

30. Fugitive

While on bail awaiting trial for the Ramsgate campaign against the migrant gang rapists, my bail conditions forced me to 'sign on' every Saturday at Bromley Police Station in South East London. This was deliberately timed to prevent me from attending Britain First activities around the country. It tied me down, preventing me from making long journeys every Saturday. During the Summer of 2017, four police officers suddenly appeared at an address in Bromley that I was living in at the time. This police visit happened at around midnight. Luckily, I wasn't in, but the poor Britain First activist who was said that the police came 'mob handed' looking to arrest me.

At this point in my career, I am so used to being arrested it is just 'another day in the office'. But the police never provide details about the nature of the arrest or the offence that I had committed to trigger the attempted arrest. My solicitors made enquiries via the phone but these turned up a blank. So, two days later I headed to Bromley Police Station to hand myself in. I had absolutely no idea why the police were looking for me. I announced myself to the desk officers and explained the situation. They promptly headed into the interior of the station to make enquiries.

When they returned, they informed me I was not going to be arrested and that the investigating officer was making 'enquiries and gathering evidence'. I asked them what the offence was and they replied it was related to an incident outside East London Mosque. I managed to read some of the text on a piece of paper that the desk officer was clutching and it said something like, 'racial hatred and the distribution of material'. The desk officer told me it was a Public Order Act offence relating to stirring up racial hatred. The attempted arrest at my house was ordered by Tower Hamlets police station, the desk officer said.

I left the station and went home. I never heard another thing about this bizarre episode. But nevertheless, on this occasion, the police had the attitude of 'arrest first, drop charges later'. The police did not visit my home address at midnight looking for a cup of tea! They turned up to arrest me. There is no other scenario that makes sense. In the end, nothing happened. But this farcical episode demonstrates the lengths the police will go to badger, harass and intimidate patriots. They hope to grind down our willpower to resist, trying to wear us down and force us to give up. Most humans would buckle under this type of relentless pressure. You have to be hard as nails if you want to lead a serious British resistance movement and there are a few individuals out there who fit this bill. Not a lot, but some.

I have already mentioned how Jayda was arrested for giving a speech outside City Hall in Belfast. On her first bail back date, I attended court with her along with a Britain First contingent and before she was due to enter court, our group was approached by two smartly dressed gentlemen who looked 'official'. They walked straight up to me and placed me under arrest. I was very confused, asking why I was being arrested, to which they replied, 'In relation to giving a speech outside Belfast City Hall in August'. I couldn't believe it. I had said absolutely nothing wrong whatsoever during that speech, nothing that could be construed as 'hate speech'.

Shortly after, the other speakers, John Banks and Paul Rimmer, were also tracked down and arrested, taken to Belfast and charged with 'using insulting words in public contrary to the Public Order (Northern Ireland) Order 1986'. On this particular case, there were now four defendants. Obviously concerned about the situation, I re-watched the speeches given that day and they were, in my opinion, all completely *legal*. Only Jayda sailed 'close to the wind' with a few comments, but in the grand scheme of things, nothing that was said by any of the four defendants was, in my own personal opinion, illegal. Islamist hate preachers say far worse on a daily basis and are left alone. For example, isn't 'UK go to hell!' offensive? At the time, I thought that the PSNI was simply trying to tie us all down with bail conditions so we couldn't operate in Northern Ireland. Nevertheless, all four defendants would be on bail awaiting trial for over a year and a half. More on that trial later.

Around this time, I took the decision to book a much-needed holiday. After years of prison, upheaval, persecution and threats to my life, I needed a break. I hadn't been on holiday for many, many years and a break was long overdue. So, I booked for me, Jayda and two of our closest security to head to Lanzarote for a relaxing one week break. The only problem was that I had to 'sign on' every Saturday, so our solicitors wrote to the investigating officer at Margate police station to ask if we could be excused from this particular bail condition for one week only. The mistake I made was that I booked the holiday before I even applied for a one-off suspension of the bail condition. I should have waited until I had received permission.

In early September, we took off from Gatwick airport and landed in Lanzarote in the Canary Islands. For the next few days, we enjoyed a relaxing time in the sun. It was exactly what was needed after years of intense political struggle. However, the email from the investigating officer in Margate never came. I phoned our solicitors daily to ask for updates, only to be informed that no confirmation email had been received. Our solicitor chased the officer up via phone and email, but could not pin him down. When Saturday came and we had to sign on, we were obviously on a beach hundreds of miles away. We missed the opportunity to sign on, tanning ourselves on a beach sipping cocktails. Naturally, an arrest warrant was issued for Jayda and me.

While we were soaking up the sun and relaxing, back home we were wanted by the police. We effectively became fugitives from the law, but there was bugger all we could do except carry on with our holiday. What was the point in coming home early? We either immediately headed home, cutting our holiday short and got arrested. Or, we finished our holiday and then got arrested. We decided to stay put and enjoy the rest of our holiday. The rotten police would have to wait! However, I immediately instructed our solicitors to apply to a magistrate's court for the suspension of the arrest warrant, but this would take about a week to come to fruition and we only had a few days left in Lanzarote.

By the final day of our holiday, we faced a dilemma. Go home and be arrested, or somehow stay out of the UK until the issue could be appealed in a magistrate's court. After much discussion, we decided, effectively, to go 'on the run' until we had exhausted our legal options. What had started out as a harmless and much-needed holiday had ended with being unable to return to our homeland. What I feared upon return to the UK was being arrested and remanded in prison until our trial, which would take place many months later. Because of this, we had to apply to the magistrate's court for relief. If our plan worked, the magistrates would take pity on us and suspend the arrest warrant. Worst case scenario, we would end up exactly where we already where, on the run facing arrest.

Another problem was what to do until we could safely return

to the UK. We couldn't stay in Lanzarote, so instead we got in touch with contacts in France and decided to go on the run in Europe. I booked a flight for Basel, in Switzerland, and instead of flying home we headed to this historic city. We chose Switzerland because of the 'European arrest warrant'. We did not dare fly to France itself, lest we be arrested by the gendarmes and extradited back to the UK. Switzerland allowed us to touch down on continental soil and from there we could take advantage of open borders to travel freely. We made plans with our contact in France to pick us up after a few days, as he lived near to Strasbourg up the road from Basel. For a few days, we did the tourist thing in Basel while waiting to be picked up. We were also waiting for our hearing to take place back in England to get our arrest warrant suspended.

When the hearing took place, the magistrates took the side of the police and refused to suspend our arrest warrants. We were in a serious predicament. If we returned home, we would be arrested and flung in prison, with serious consequences for our movement. Our only option was to stay on the run and raise the stakes. I instructed our solicitors to apply to the crown court, the only option left. The crown court sits above the magistrates in order of importance and sentencing powers. But, lodging a new appeal would take another few weeks to get before a judge. We were literally stranded on mainland Europe, on the run from the police and unable to return home. A crazy situation had developed from a simple one week break in the sun! We found ourselves in a ridiculous predicament.

Finally, we were picked up in Basel and taken to Thionville, near the border with Belgium. From here we had no option but to wait it out and make good use of our time on the continent. We decided to use this opportunity to forge links and friendships with our friends across Europe. We were taken to Paris to a nationalist rally where we met French legend Jean Marie Le Pen, father of Marine Le Pen. To my surprise, we were the ones receiving much acclaim from French patriots who knew who we were and who admired what we had achieved in Britain. One of our security volunteers, Andrew Edge, was even made an honorary 'Musketeer'. The Musketeers were a long standing and famous group of French patriot bodyguards to the Le Pen family. We were all chuffed by Andrew's induction into this legendary French team. Vive la France!

We spent two days in Paris meeting French patriots, some of whom were very important and high profile. We visited the sites, including the Eifel Tower, which was inundated with migrants. Then we returned to eastern France meeting nationalists in Luxembourg and Luneville. We then headed for the European Parliament at Strasbourg - a horrible Soviet style building - to meet with an assortment of patriot MEPs and nationalist representatives. We travelled to Brussels to meet with Belgian MPs and political party leaders and also to Amsterdam.

While in Brussels, we made a visit to the infamous Islamist area of Molenbeek. We stopped in a square in the area and found around one hundred Shia Muslims engaging in the Ashura, a barbaric ritual where they slap and cut themselves. We walked in and among these Islamists without a care in the world while they shouted the familiar 'Allahu Akbar' and so on. They knew who we were. We could see them looking at us and whispering to each other. Nevertheless, we quickly did a live video on Facebook. Our small team were surrounded by dozens of these Muslims, chanting and slapping themselves. One of them even came up to us and told us to leave. I said, 'Do you know who we are?' He replied in a Belgian accent, 'Britain First'. Then suddenly a group of armed police approached us and ordered us to leave the area immediately or they would arrest us. Our thoughts moved to the 'European arrest warrant' and we quickly left, not because of the potential for trouble, but because we did not want to get arrested by the Belgian police and extradited back to Blighty. We then headed to Munich to meet with German patriots. All in all, we visited some seven different countries and met with MEPs, MPs, party leaders and prominent activists.

While we were busy travelling Europe, unable to return home, our appeal to the crown court took place but once again it failed to overturn the arrest warrant. We got dropped off in the beautiful Belgian town of Bruges to consider our options, which were bleak. An innocuous one week holiday had escalated into a major legal nightmare. If we returned home, we would be arrested and possibly remanded to prison for breaching our bail in the most blatant manner. The only other option was living in Europe indefinitely, which wasn't really an option at all. I got my thinking cap on and came up with a cheeky little plan.

Having spent a lot of time in Northern Ireland, I remembered that there are no physical border checks between the Republic and Ulster. Likewise, the Republic is not part of the United Kingdom and they would be completely unaware of any live arrest warrants for UK citizens. Here was a way of getting back into the United Kingdom without being arrested! I immediately booked flights from Brussels to Dublin. When we arrived in Dublin, two large Irish men recognised us and told us to leave Ireland immediately. I imagine they were IRA supporters. We then hired a vehicle and drove north, crossing the border and to keep out the way, we stayed for a few days in the small seaside town of Donaghadee to work out our next move.

Our next problem was the Irish Sea. This was, obviously, a big physical obstacle. Being in Northern Ireland was only half the battle. We needed to get back to *England* to make preparations for being remanded to prison. However, I soon realised that we were within the territory of the United Kingdom and any flight or ferry crossing of the Irish Sea would not require identification. We had run out of time and options, we had to chance our luck and get back to the mainland somehow. So, I booked our little group onto a ferry from Belfast to Stranraer and prayed for an uneventful crossing. However, on our way to Belfast ferry port, I suddenly noticed a whole convey of flashing lights in the rear-view mirror. At first, I did not think they were speeding up the motorway for us. But, when they got closer, they moved directly behind our vehicle and ordered us to pull over. That was game over, as far as I was concerned. After all, a total of four police vehicles wouldn't pull anyone over for a silly traffic offence.

I got out of the vehicle and the police officers informed me that our rented vehicle had pinged on the APNR cameras because it was reported stolen! I explained it was a rented vehicle, and they kept me waiting on the side of the duel-carriageway opposite Belfast City Airport for around an hour as they made checks. Jayda and our security waited in the hire vehicle. Unbelievably, the arrest warrant on the mainland hadn't reached the 'Police National Computer' (PNC) yet. I later discovered it takes around two weeks for arrest warrants to be sent from the mainland PNC to the police computers in Northern Ireland. After an hour or so of checking, the police let us go. I could not believe our luck. We then carried on to the ferry port and embarked to Stranraer.

Completely expecting to get arrested as soon as we docked in Scotland, the crossing was tense. But our anxiety was unjustified. When we docked in Stranraer, we kept a distance away from each other and nervously made our way off the ferry and towards the exit which was saturated with security. One by one, we walked straight past the multitude of security officers out to the waiting Britain First team I had asked to collect us. We did not receive as much as a passing glance.

I could not believe our luck. We had been 'on the run' for over a month and had travelled through eight different countries but now we were back on home soil. We were driven from Scotland to Sunderland in the North East of England. A local girl called

Chelsey had been gang raped by a group of migrants and despite DNA evidence, the Crown Prosecution Service had refused to press charges. Chelsey had been running a high profile and successful awareness campaign with multiple protest marches in the city. When we were in Northern Ireland, we had been invited to give speeches at the next 'Justice for Chelsey' rally, if we could get back to the mainland.

We laid low in Sunderland for a day or two until the rally took place and when the day came, we were facing another predicament. If we attended the rally, we would both be arrested and possibly remanded to prison. We were undecided what the best course of action was. In the end, because the campaign in Sunderland involved a sexual crime against a woman, we decided – with her agreement – that Jayda would go to the rally and I would stay hidden away. If Jayda was arrested, then I was better placed to get the word out, via email bulletins, website posts, social media, press releases etc.

Jayda and the Britain First team managed to hide away in a town centre pub and infiltrate the protest march itself as it passed by on the road outside. While the team moved with pace out the front door of the pub and into the road, they were spotted by the police who tried in vain to push their way into the crowd to arrest Jayda. One of our security was a stoutly built Polish activist, who was almost arrested because they confused him with me. He had to show them identification to get them to back off. The crowd marching through the city centre shielded Jayda from the police and they were unable to arrest her. All hell would have broken loose had they used aggressive tactics and the crowd made the police aware that any violent attempt to get to Jayda would be repulsed. Nevertheless, the police stalked Jayda but had to watch helplessly because she was so well guarded.

When the procession arrived at the rally point, speeches were given, including one from Jayda. The police watched on but unable to do anything. Once the speeches ended, the police refused to let the march proceed on the route back because of the presence of Jayda. A Mexican stand-off took place, with both the police refusing to allow the march to continue until Jayda was arrested and the huge crowd of local men refusing to hand her over! About fifty local men made a human chain around her and refused to budge. I was back at a local hotel watching the exciting events unfold live on Facebook. Suddenly, after a long while in a stand-off, I saw Jayda's red hair emerge from the crowd on a live stream and the police arrested her. I was told afterward that the police had threatened the crowd with CS gas unless they allowed them to arrest her. Jayda did not want anyone getting hurt, so she handed herself in. Even while she was being marched away, the crowd went wild and followed the large gang of officers hurling verbal abuse at them. Shortly after, the protest dispersed.

Some of the protesters then called me and told me they overheard some of the police officers whispering that a 'city-wide search' of all hotels was about to be launched to find me. If I stayed in Sunderland, I would most probably get nicked and end up in the cell next to Jayda. I got my security, packed my belongings and jumped on the M1 heading south as quickly as possible. I drove all the way to rural Worcester to ensure I wasn't arrested and stayed for a few nights, safely out of harm's way. Jayda was arrested on a Saturday, so was kept in the police station until Monday morning. On the Monday morning Jayda was taken straight to the local magistrate's court, so I headed back up the motorway to Sunderland.

What happened next was astonishing. I had arranged for our solicitor in the north of England to represent Jayda in court and I booked into a castle-style hotel just outside of Sunderland in the small town of Chester-le-Street to await events. I had Britain First activists at the magistrates court feeding me information. The next thing I heard, was that Jayda had been re-bailed and freed, no punishment whatsoever! I couldn't believe it. I was stunned. The three local magistrates simply gave Jayda a slap on the wrist and released her with the same bail conditions. This meant that I was off the hook too. We had to be treated equally by the judiciary and, as co-defendants, I was effectively re-bailed as well. Jayda was driven to the hotel I was based in and we gave thanks to God for our good luck.

It was because of the erratic criss-crossing of Europe and the British Isles that we missed the Electoral Commission deadline to re-register our party by a few hours. As outlined in a previous chapter, the Electoral Commission de-registered our party and then rejected application after application, throwing obstacle after obstacle in our face to stop us being able to contest elections. Utterly corrupt and politically biased, but unfortunately this kind of leftwing bigotry is now the norm in communist Britain.

About a week after the miracle in Sunderland, Jayda and I were due to be in court in Kent for the Ramsgate charges. The police, as expected, submitted an application to have us remanded to prison. When our solicitor explained to the judge - and to the police legal reps - that Jayda had been arrested and re-bailed, they were absolutely horrified. They were rubbing their hands with the thought that we could be put in prison for our expedition around Europe. But thanks to the magistrates court in Sunderland, we were untouchable. The police were visibly deflated.

Our five-week odyssey from Lanzarote to Sunderland through eight countries had come to an end with the both of us being given a slap on the wrist. I doubt very much the magistrates in Sunderland understood the gravity of the situation confronting them and because of this, they acted with unknowing leniency. This was a stroke of luck that got us off the hook for one of the most blatant acts of disrespect to the courts I have ever seen. It was not as though we were hiding our fugitive adventure around Europe evading the authorities. On literally every twist and turn of our epic journey we posted photos, videos and updates to our vast social media platform. Our voyage across the continent was seen by millions and our supporters were gripped by it.

It ended in a stupendous anti-climax in the court room in Sunderland. After that, we drove down to the M1 to home in Kent. What a surreal and hypnagogic period of my life. For five weeks, I had been an international fugitive of sorts. By sheer luck and good fortune, I managed to return home without suffering harsh consequences.

31. Folkestone

As 2018 dawned, Britain First faced its toughest test yet. Starting on January 30th, both deputy leader Jayda and I were due to face trial for the campaign of 'harassment' in Ramsgate. Jayda had more charges than me because she was the one who took the lead on the videos of the campaign. I was effectively just the cameraman. However, because of the 'joint enterprise' principle in law, I was culpable in many ways. With hindsight, this preposterous prosecution for harassing a gang of migrant rapists was actually a well-orchestrated establishment operation to destroy Britain First once and for all. It came close to succeeding, but more on that later.

Even though we were awaiting trial on bail, I was expecting the charges to be dropped when the gang of Afghan migrant rapists were convicted of their heinous crimes. At first, our charge sheets included the names of the rapists. Obviously, we uploaded videos to social media displaying this and shortly after the police amended the charge sheets and removed the names of the rapists who had recently been found guilty. Now we were being charged with 'harassing' their wives and girlfriends. You couldn't make this nonsense up. It was obviously a very bad PR exercise to charge the leaders of a political party with 'harassing' a gang of paedophile sex offenders. So, the police moved the emphasis onto the wives and girlfriends who, unbelievably, despite the conviction of the gang, all remained hitched and loyal to them. Disgusting creatures, all of them. The rapists were given fourteen years each in prison. It was wildly publicised but nevertheless, the police kept coming for us.

As the day of the trial loomed, I organised activists from around the country to escort us into the court. I was very nervous about this trial because our legal representatives told us we faced a very high possibility of prison. They also advised us that Jayda was far more likely to be sent to prison because she was the person speaking in all the videos. Because of my personality, I always err on the side of optimism. Even up to the verdict, I expected a suspended sentence or at the very worst, Jayda would be sent to prison but not me. This naiveté was to have serious consequences for Britain First. When I was sent to HMP Pentonville, Jayda as deputy leader was able to run Britain First in my stead. The main thing was that one of us had to be out of prison to run the movement. If we both were sent to prison simultaneously, it would spell big trouble and the establishment knew it.

When it comes to the judiciary, it really is a lottery when it comes to getting the right judge. Unfortunately for us, we were allotted district judge, Justin Barron, who we could see had a strong dislike for us in pre-trial hearings. Sometimes when it comes to trials, getting the right judge can make the difference between acquittal and prison.

This particular judge tried to move the trial up to the crown court, to avoid presiding over it himself. He clearly wanted nothing to do with it, because it would be a very high profile trial. It seemed to me like he didn't want the scrutiny. We opposed this move however, preferring to keep this trial with the magistrates court. If the trial had been transferred to the crown court, it would be a jury, not the judge, who decided our guilt. We would face a greater chance of being treated fairly in the crown court in front of a jury, but the sentencing powers are far higher in the event of a guilty verdict. In the magistrate's court, the maximum was six months, doing half of that in jail and half on licence. In the crown court, the sentence would be two years, again with half in custody and half on licence. We opted for the magistrate's court, to minimise the prison terms that were available to a judge if we were convicted.

Our trial took place over two days at Folkestone Magistrate's Court starting on January 30th. The trial itself was an absolute joke. The prosecution always opens with their case and Jayda and I took our seats in the dock. The first witness was one of the women who had been present in the notorious '555 Pizza' shop when me and Jayda arrived. There were men inside too, but they were not called as witnesses. I wonder why, cowards. The foreign woman spoke to the court through an interpreter, describing how she was terrified of me and Jayda at the window. However, when a video was then played to the court, taken by one of the children inside, you can hear laughing in the background. It was so obvious that she was playing for sympathy, exaggerating their so-called 'ordeal'.

The next 'witness' to be called was the man who talked to us outside Canterbury Crown Court when we turned up. This was the man who told us that Islam was 'perfect' but that humans were not. It turned out he was the cousin of one of the rapists. He was there to give him moral support. This snivelling weasel once again exaggerated his treatment by Jayda, claiming he was afraid and shaken by the words she used. During our cross examination, our solicitor asked him if, despite his claims of rampant hostility from both Jayda and me, he in fact shook my hand at the entrance of the court. This made him look silly. He claimed he was panic-stricken, but then we produced a video to be played in court that the prosecution had not seen and it clearly showed Jayda talking to him in a civil manner. He was talking absolute rubbish.

Next up was a slippery little foreigner who could not speak a word of English, using an interpreter to communicate to the court. He was a resident of an address in Hepburn Close, in Canterbury, home to one of the rapists. He falsely claimed in court that the rapist had recently moved out and that because of this, we had erroneously targeted him by mistake. Total, unadulterated bullshit. If only every witness who appeared in court had to take a lie detector test! I hope they introduce this one day.

The next witness called by the prosecution was a white English woman from Ramsgate, best friend of the girlfriend of the main rapist. This hideous beast would not look out of place on an episode of the Jeremy Kyle show. She kept staring menacingly at me and Jayda while we sat in the dock. We gave a cynical smile back which infuriated her further. Unbelievably, the main Afghan rapist had a wife *and* a girlfriend, who both knew about each other. The wife was a fellow Afghan and the girlfriend was white English.

It was at the home of the girlfriend that Britain First visited and leafleted the neighbours. The neighbours our activists spoke to confirmed that the rapist did indeed live at and visit this address almost every day. Further investigation at the time found that the rapist ferreted between the '555 Pizza' shop with his Afghan wife and his English girlfriend a few streets away. What a revolting setup. At the time of our visit, this vile woman was pregnant by the rapist. The best friend of this critter, who was a witness against Britain First at our trial, caused a furore by claiming that our visit to the house in May had caused the girlfriend of the rapist to miscarry her baby nearly six months later. This outrageous claim was blasted across the mass media, with headlines like, 'Britain First's Jayda Fransen blamed for baby's death'. Our solicitor protested at this claim in court and the judge ordered that it was suppressed from evidence.

Nevertheless, the media went into overdrive publishing story after story claiming that Britain First was responsible for the death of a baby.

This was complete hogwash, however. The girlfriend of the rapist miscarried her baby only a week or so after he was sent to prison for fourteen years. What is more likely, that she miscarried because of the stress of seeing her boyfriend sent to prison for fourteen years, or that our activists attended her house some six months previously? This did not stop them trying to misuse her tragedy to help get me and Jayda convicted. Absolute vermin the lot of them, bunch of paedophile, rapist lowlife scum. The fact remains, the miscarriage was not caused by us but by the imprisonment of the woman's dirty rapist boyfriend. Even after he was convicted, this scumbag of a woman stayed in a relationship with the rapist, even though he had an Afghan wife around the corner. Some people are just trash, pure and simple.

The final witness for the prosecution was the police CID officer who led the investigation. He was questioned by both side about matters relating to evidence, the arrests, the interrogations and so on. Our solicitor then probed him on his role within his department. He was hesitant to answer and did not confirm the unit he worked in. Our solicitor, who has a very sharp mind, actually asked the judge if he could approach and ask permission to ask his next question in an open court. The judge replied that he could not allow anything to be subject to secrecy in the middle of a public trial.

Our solicitor was obviously conflicted and sitting in the dock, I had no idea what was going on. Because the judge refused have any questions confirmed in secrecy, our solicitor had no choice but to put the question to the officer. 'Do you work for anti-terrorism?' he said. The officer replied in a fidgety fashion that he was in fact an officer from 'S015 Counter Terrorism Command', my old friends. I was stunned, and so was everyone else in the court room!

This entire drama had been engineered by the UK's top anti-terrorism police. Our solicitor then asked the officer - in a sarcastic fashion – if acts of low-level harassment outside pizza shops were their usual domain. The officer then gave the game away. 'Britain First is a matter of nation security,' he retorted! A matter of national security? A political party? This is part of the reason why so many terror attacks succeed, because the leftwing jobsworths of our anti-terror police units are busy harassing British politicians who love their country. What a mockery of police priorities.

After the prosecution finished presenting their case, the first day of the trial was over and I felt very optimistic about a positive outcome, due mainly to the balderdash spouted by the prosecution 'witnesses'. Surely if this came down to the evidence and the testimony of the witnesses, we would be acquitted. But, unfortunately, Britain is at a point where our judiciary is utterly corrupted and political.

On the second day of the trial, it was our turn to present our defence, which did not take long. Our defence was simple. We felt compelled to warn the local residents in the vicinity of the rapists who were residing in their midst. If there was any 'harassment', it was only directed against the rapists, no one else. Both Jayda and I were called to take the stand and give evidence. Then it was time for closing statements and after that the judge announced he needed time to give a written verdict.

He adjourned the case for five weeks, to early March. To be honest I was quite relieved. I thought the judge would give his verdict there and then and so we braced ourselves for the worst. This extra five weeks breathing space was very welcome as it allowed us time to prepare for possible imprisonment. We did not object when the judge asked us if we were okay with his request. Then the trial was over, finished. We left the court and gave a few TV interviews before departing.

What we could only just glimpse at the time, was that this entire saga was an establishment attempt to bring down our vast social media platform. What we did not know until late in the day, was that this case had actually gone all the way up the judiciary to the Attorney General. The Attorney General is the government's chief legal adviser and is a political appointee, appointed by the Prime Minister. I have mentioned previously how I came to know of meetings in the Home Office between the then Home Secretary, Theresa May, and an assortment of leftwing organisations to discuss how to combat the rise of Britain First. Now Theresa May was Prime Minister, and the Attorney General she had appointed was taking part in a low-level harassment trial on the fringes of Kent. The hand of Big Government was all over this case. If you combine Theresa May, her Attorney General and the leading role 'SO15 Counter Terrorism Command' took in the whole narrative, it is clear we were doomed from the word go. But at this point on the timeline, I did not know what the overall plan was. It was to be revealed to me when I was only four days into a new prison sentence.

The five weeks between the trial and sentencing passed quickly. Preparations were made for the possibility of both Jayda and I being imprisoned at the same time. But, with hindsight, nowhere near enough preparation was made. I was still positively optimistic that we would escape a custodial sentence and be fined or given a suspended sentence instead. I had no idea of the nightmare that was about to unfold.

On the 7th March, we returned to Folkestone Magistrate's Court for the verdict. We had a large team with us, including family members. After a long, nervous wait, the court settled down and judge Barron entered. He had with him a thick bundle of papers. Because this case was so high profile, the press gallery was packed. The judge began to read his statement, which dragged on for an eternity. He examined every aspect of the case and his rambling was interminable. Standing in the dock, we watched in horror as the judge came down on us like a tonne of bricks. No surprise there, to be honest. If the Attorney General was involved, then this was a big government enterprise. Of course we would be found guilty. The question was, would he send us to prison.

The judge rejected every single one of our arguments and castigated us for our actions. Barron said that our words and actions, 'Demonstrated hostility towards Muslims.' He continued: 'I have no doubt it was their joint intention to use the facts of the case in Canterbury for their own political ends. It was a campaign to draw attention to the race, religion and immigrant background of the defendants.' The judge said our campaign deliberately targeted the victims, which was nonsense since we specifically targeted the rapists, not their wives and girlfriends. A total, politically-motivated stitch-up. Jaswant Narwal, the chief crown prosecutor in the South East, said: 'The victims suffered the distress of the abuse followed by additional stress when the footage was uploaded to the internet.'

This was the 'spin' the establishment was putting on a campaign of confrontation against a gang of convicted migrant paedophile gang rapists. The rapists were transformed into 'victims', just to mislead people into thinking that Britain First were criminals and that we had broken the law. The media machine roared into top gear painting Jayda and I as horrible bigots and 'white supremacists' – to quote one newspaper – and the paedophile rapists as the poor, abused, brown victims of unspeakable acts of racism. The fact that these savages had kidnapped and gang-raped an underage English girl did not matter. Finding us both guilty as charged, the judge ordered a short break for a pre-sentence interview by the Probation Service, which both Jayda and I had to endure. During the break, my solicitor said to me that the statement that was delivered by judge Barron was, in his opinion, far too polished and detailed to have been written by him. My solicitor suggested that the statement was in fact written by someone 'higher up'.

After about an hour, we were summoned back into the court room for sentencing. The 'moment of truth' we had been waiting for for almost a year had arrived. It dawned on me later that the trial, the verdict and the sentencing were mere legal formalities that had to be observed. This entire situation had been decided by Prime Minister Theresa May and her Attorney General long ago. This was not the judiciary dispensing justice in the normal way, but a criminal bodge job that went to the highest levels of government. Why else would the Attorney General of the United Kingdom be involved in a low-key harassment trial in a seaside town? There was an agenda at work. Everything was pre-arranged and pre-decided. The trial, evidence and witnesses all amounted to nothing. We were guilty and going to prison from the moment we were both arrested. It is actually quite scary to think that the justice system in my country operates in this way.

After the Probation Service delivered their statements, the judge announced to the court that an immediate custodial sentence was needed to punish us both. Jayda was charged with four counts of religiously aggravated harassment and was found guilty of three. I was charged with three counts of the same offence, but only found guilty of one. I was sentenced to eighteen weeks and Jayda to thirty-six weeks.

What happened next was pantomime. While Jayda and I were led out of dock and down into the cells, awaiting transportation to our respective prisons, our supporters started going wild. According to reports, judge Barron had to flee the court room and the security officers desperately pleaded with our supporters to calm down. These security officers were actually very friendly towards us, and informed some of our supporters that the judge had to be escorted out of the building under heavy guard. Meanwhile, down in the cells, our solicitor came to see us and we were allowed a final, brief meeting until I was led to a prison transport vehicle. Whether I liked it or not, I was going to be out of action for the four and a half months.

The official sentencing guidance for the specific Public Order Act offence we committed is a maximum of only three months' in prison. This is the *maximum* of the sentence range, according to the judiciary's own guidelines. So, if the judge followed the rules, we should have been sentenced to three months for each offence.

I was found guilty of only one offence, so I should have been sentenced to three months, which would mean six weeks in prison. The judge, however, increased this sentence because he claimed it was 'religiously aggravated'. However, the religious angle was *already* incorporated into the offence itself. The offence was officially named, 'Religiously aggravated harassment' and thus he should not have increased the sentence past the three-month guideline, but he did. This was grounds for an appeal. But I decided against appealing because it would be sent 'upstairs' to the crown court, which, if my appeal failed, could impose a longer sentence. I did not want to take that risk, so I took it on the chin. Very dishonest of the judge, and very corrupt.

Meanwhile, the corrupt leftist goons of Kent Police were breaking their own rules in an attempt to embarrass both Jayda and I. The usual rules stipulate that mugshots of criminals are only released to the media for those who are sentenced to *longer* than one year in prison. Kent Police decided to break these rules, 'because of the effect their [Britain First's] hate crimes had on the local community.' I would submit that the ordinary British people of Ramsgate applauded our campaign of exposing paedophile gang rapists! The Independent newspaper reported: 'Kent Police's rules stipulate that mugshots are normally released for convicts jailed for a year or more, but a spokesperson said Paul Golding and Jayda Fransen were an exception. Due to the nature of the offences committed and the impact they had on the wider community, we believe it is in the public interest to make these available.'

The story of our arrest, prosecution and imprisonment outlined in this chapter is a scary one. All the big players are involved, the Home Office, the Prime Minister, the Attorney General and counter terror police. All of this ended with me serving a miniscule nine weeks in prison for a minor offence. This episode proves that the criminal justice system can be subverted by the British government to rid itself of political rivals. This rivals anything happening on a daily basis in Zimbabwe, North Korea or any other corrupt dictatorship or oligarchy. I was on my way to prison, but my woes were only just beginning. My inner strength and determination was about to be tested to the limit.

32. Elmley

After being bundled into a tiny cubicle in a prison transport vehicle, I began my cramped, humid journey to my new home, HMP Elmley on the Isle of Sheppey in North Kent. HMP Elmley was part of a cluster of prisons on the southern side of this island, along with HMP Swaleside - for serious offenders and those serving life sentences - and HMP Standford Hill, which was an open prison for low risk prisoners.

HMP Elmley is a category C prison for average criminals. There are several prisoners serving life sentences, but HMP Elmley is generally home to your average 'run of the mill' prisoners, about 1,300 in total. A prison at the site had first been opened in 1562, during the reign of Elizabeth I. The modern prison was built in 1997, so it was a relatively new prison compared to, for example, the Victorian dungeon HMP Pentonville.

When you are on your way to an unfamiliar prison, tucked neatly inside a tiny, uncomfortable plastic box in a transport vehicle, you are naturally anxious. It is more a fear of the unknown. However, as this prison was on the fringes of Kent, I didn't expect it to be an

Islamist-run slum like HMP Birmingham, for example. I hoped and prayed that it would be populated mainly by local Kent prisoners, and it was. When I arrived, I breathed a sigh of relief when I was led out of the tiny hot box and into the fresh air. I was led into the reception and processing area, fully suited and booted. There I engaged the prison officers in conversation to try and figure out if I was being put into isolation again. The answer was no, I was being put into general population this time.

My situation wasn't helped by the fact that my imprisonment was the main news on TVs throughout the prison. My imprisonment was top of the news bulletins on media outlets such as the BBC, ITV and Channel 4, all across the South East region. Everyone in the prison knew I was on my way in. I was given some basic prison utilities and clothes, my suit being packed away along with my other belongings. I was led through prison gangways to 'House Block 1', which contained the 'Induction Wing', where all prisoners spent their first two days.

To my total surprise, I was greeted like a hero when I arrived on House Block 1. A multitude of prisoners approached me to shake my hand and wish me well. Next, I was sat down with the 'SO', the Supervising Officer, and he explained the basics of routine, rights, entitlements and so on. This was my chance. I told him straight that if I was put into the general population, I would recruit an army and take over the entire block. He knew who I was and a few minutes later, the head of prison security joined us in the little office. I repeated my threat, that if I was thrown to the dogs on the ordinary wings, I would do everything within my considerably ability to recruit followers in order to protect myself and anyone else being bullied by Muslim gangs. I told the governor and the SO that they can expect 'speeches and upheaval' if they did not isolate me, and I meant it. The SO turned to the head of security and said that, in his opinion - judging by the reception I had received so far - I wouldn't have any trouble recruiting a following!

Both the head of security and the SO knew that I wasn't messing around, and they both agreed that I would instead be left in my own cell on the 'Induction Wing'. I was fine with this as the Induction Wing had a high turnover of prisoners coming and going. New prisoners only stayed on the Induction Wing for two days, then they were transferred to the normal wings. This meant that no gangs could form on the Induction Wing and there I would be safest. To be honest, I don't think for one second that the prison authorities considered my safety in their calculations. But as one of Britain's top 'far-right' rabble rousers, I had the ability - in their eyes - to cause major disruption and trouble.

After this initial meeting, I was led around the corner to 'A Spur', which hosted the Induction Wing. There I was shown to my cell, which was dirty and disgusting. I settled in and started cleaning it, making it habitable, just like I did in Pentonville. Again, to my surprise, all the prisoners gave me a warm welcome the next morning and I obviously relaxed. There weren't any Muslims at all on this wing of the prison. I just wanted to do my nine weeks and then go home. I did not want any upheaval or trouble.

Every time I get sent to prison, I realise just how burned out and exhausted I really am. Tiredness hits me like a freight train. For the first week in Pentonville, I slept some fourteen hours a day. It was the same in Elmley, I slept and then slept some more, and took advantage of the fact I had no mobile phone, no social media and no laptop. I literally went into hibernation to recharge my batteries. All of the 'Insiders' and wing reps on my block were very supportive and they helped me at every opportunity. I really owe these guys a debt of gratitude for their support and help, especially Rob. I did not find anyone who was hostile or opposed to me. The situation was, as far as prisons go for high-profile 'far-right extremists', perfect.

Then, about three days in, a pair of bearded Muslims were put into cells on the Induction Wing. I immediately sensed trouble. For a short while, these Muslims did not interact with each other. But when I came face to face with one of them, he said to me, 'Alright Paul how you doing?' I replied in a civil fashion but I knew he was hostile by the smirk on his face. A few hours later, I spotted this particular Muslim - who was a skinny little runt - talking feverishly with the other bearded Muslim, who was a far more stoutly built specimen.

Then came dinner time and I queued up with the other prisoners waiting to go to the canteen. These Muslims then came out of a cell on the ground floor and stood very close to me. I could have cut the tension in the air with a knife. They were eyeing me up and down and displaying visible hostility. I gritted my teeth and waited for the situation to explode. Then the door opened and everyone piled out to get their dinners.

I was absolutely determined to avoid any kind of conflagration with Muslims. I did not want my short prison sentence increased because of violent incidents. Because of rampant political correctness, it could end up with me being prosecuted for being attacked. Our PC approach to prosecutions is so back-to-front that even if I was the victim, I could end up getting prosecuted. It wouldn't be the first time this has happened!

So, I immediately reported this escalating situation to the SO and told him I wanted to avoid conflict at all costs. Unfortunately, whether by design or incompetence, I was ignored. Over the next day or so, I kept catching these Muslims watching me and whispering to each other. I am not an idiot and could see things were about to go nuclear. I told the SO again that there was a serious threat of possible violence on the horizon, but my warnings were ignored. I started to sense a stitch-up when these Muslims were kept on the Induction Wing way past the standard two days. Why weren't they transferred to the normal wings as is standard practise after two days? Why were my warnings being ignored?

I was in my cell the next day watching TV and eating my lunch, when suddenly a loud bang startled me. I turned my head to the left and found that the two Muslims had entered my cell and slammed the door. My immediate focus was on the smaller, skinny Muslim to the left who was holding a pen in his hand ready to stab me. Before I could react to the situation, the bigger Muslim on the right punched me square on the nose. Blood came out of my nose in torrents and I was completely disorientated. This sneak attack was so sudden and unexpected that I was in complete shock.

Within the blink of an eye they opened the door and left my cell. I was left covered in blood and desperately trying to steady myself and make sense of the situation. The rapid switch from peaceful eating to being assaulted and covered in blood was so extreme that it took me longer than usual to come to my senses. I stood to my feet and walked outside the cell. The Muslims had scarpered and were nowhere to be seen. A prison guard noticed me and the blood on my clothing and within thirty seconds a whole multitude of them had secured me in my cell. A doctor was summoned and cleaned me up. My nose was very swollen and the bleeding took an age to stop. A prison official then arrived with a small digital camera and took photos of my injuries. The Muslims in question were put on lockdown in their cells and shortly after transferred to the 'block', the punishment wing where prisoners were kept in splendid isolation and boredom.

The media widely reported that I had my nose broken during the attack. That claim was absolute rubbish. Pure media fake news. It then transpired that one of the attackers was Nasir Muhsen, an Iraqi asylum seeker. He had been jailed years earlier for taking part in looting during the infamous London riots. He was also serving a second sentence for a brutal attack on a prison officer in Elmley a few months before I arrived. He was notorious in the prison for being a bit of a nutjob.

The next day I was again watching TV and eating my lunch. Daytime TV is so mind-numbing that I was forced to watch Prime Minister's Questions which takes place live every Wednesday. I sat peacefully eating my paltry prison food and enduring the interminable screechy voice of Theresa May when a Labour MP, Bridget Phillipson, MP for Houghton and Sunderland South, jumped to her feet and announced that, 'Just a few minutes ago Facebook announced that it would be taking down several pages associated with the extremist group Britain First. [Loud applause] Does the Prime Minister join me in welcoming that. But does she also accept that there needs to be a clear role provided by government to give guidance to social media companies on how they operate in our democracy. [Loud applause]'

I must admit I nearly spat my food across my cell. I was stunned. After five years of building up our pages and reaching the astronomical following of nearly three million patriots worldwide, Facebook had taken the decision to close them down. No appeal process, no warning, they were just yanked down and deleted. You can imagine the volcanic frustration and anger I had to deal with while completely neutralised in my little cell.

The Prime Minister, Theresa May, then replied that she welcomed the decision by Facebook and thanked her 'Right Honourable friend the Home Secretary' for working with Facebook to get our pages taken down. She congratulated Facebook on their decision and expressed hope that other platforms would follow suit. This was the exact moment that democratic free speech in Britain truly perished.

Here was the highest democratic institution in the United Kingdom applauding the censorship of the most widely supported political movement in the United Kingdom. Freedom of speech, expression, liberty and democracy be damned. The political Left

- which includes the modern liberal Conservative Party - was applauding this act of naked fascist censorship. Britain First lost three million followers by this act of repression. The decision by Facebook was international news.

What has been termed the 'Great Purge' had begun and our movement was the first to be silenced. Many others would follow. I had no option but to endure this devastating news in my cell. It was the most frustrating day of my life. I could not do anything, except watch more TV and quietly fume. The leftwing organisation, Hope Not Hate, posted on their website that the removal of our enormous Facebook pages heralded the end of our movement.

The recent catalogue of persecution relating to the Ramsgate rapists now made perfect sense. The idea was to prosecute us for *anything*, find us guilty, then run to Facebook and demand that they close our pages. 'Look, these two individuals are guilty of anti-Muslim hate crimes and are now in prison, you have to take them down, they are horrible racists and criminals!', or something along those lines. If we had been found 'not guilty', I doubt Facebook would have taken the plunge and deleted our pages. But the conviction provided the perfect excuse for removing our enormous pages from their platform. An insidious and devious plan indeed, and it worked.

A few days after our Facebook fan pages were deleted, our online payment system was closed down too and our movement collapsed into a hideous mess. Finances quickly dried up and we were unable to pay bills and running costs. Our administration ground to a halt. The morons I left in charge outside sat on their hands and did bugger all. All activities had ceased, finances had dried up, our social media had been censored and I had just endured an attack by a Muslim prison gang. To say I was depressed would be an understatement. The worst part of this horrid situation was that I could not do anything about it. I just had to watch boring daytime TV in my cell and suck it up.

I was completely demoralised. My moral was shattered. Usually in such circumstances I would swing into action and deal with the problem decisively. But in my cell on twenty-three-hour lockdown with nothing but a small TV, I could not organise anything. The situation was made worse by the fact that the prison authorities took almost two weeks to provide me with my 'PIN' (Personal Identification Number) so I could make a phone call. For two weeks, I had no communication with the outside world. It was a bleak and demoralising situation.

This was perhaps the lowest point I had ever been in during my life. Then, a group of guards came to my cell and told me I was about to be moved to another wing. I pleaded with them to let me stay, but they were adamant. They were moving me next door to 'B Spur' where I would be among the general prison population. I packed my stuff and let them escort me to my new cell. Thankfully, I had a cell to myself. But almost immediately I was approached over and over again by the prisoners who pledged their support and promised me I would not be attacked again by Muslim inmates. A Muslim prisoner came up to me and expressed his fear that I would target him! I assured him that nothing like that would ever happen and that, if he needed anything, he should come and see me and I would do all I could to help him. He expressed his shock and thanked me for my kind offer. This was obviously media demonization and lies at work. To Muslims, I must be Satan himself.

The big welcome I received among the English prisoners was noticed by the prison guards and I could see them all chatting among each other. I was only on the new wing for about an hour, when one of the 'Insiders' - a big black man - came over to me when I was talking to a prison guard. He quickly warned me, 'You do realise the Muslim lifers are already plotting an attack on you upstairs? I just heard them.' I could have easily mobilised half a dozen of the English prisoners to ward off this new threat, but the prison guard immediately reported this to the SO. I was then approached by several guards and ordered into my new cell and the door was locked.

Then, 'association' finished and the wing went very quiet. I waited for about an hour until two large prison guards opened my door. One of the officers then ordered me to pack my things, again. He would not reveal where I was being taken. He was a snotty jobsworth and I instantly disliked him. He said to me in a condescending voice, 'You're stupid being a racist and getting sent to prison aren't ya', to which I replied, 'If confronting paedo rapists makes me a racist, then so be it!' The officers led me to the other side of the prison to the punishment block. I was told this was a precaution, 'for my safety'. I told them I was fine with that, but I obviously wasn't there to be punished and still wanted access to a TV. I was told that this would be provided soon but at the moment the prison needed time to figure out what to do with me.

So, I was placed into a repulsive, manky cell and left to rot in perfect isolation. The cells 'down the block' were the worst in any prison. The toilet was rotted and disgusting. The bed and desk and every wall was covered in what looked like the remains of excrement. The smell was appalling. All I had was a few books and a few sheets of paper to write letters. For the next eight days, I was denied a TV. I was going completely out of my mind with extreme boredom. To make matters worse, the Muslims who attacked me were my neighbours and they shouted abuse at me non-stop. I had to put up with their threats and vile language day after day. All I could do was read and soak up their endless abuse and taunts.

After eight days of this revolting existence, I had my first 'review'. I pleaded with the prison governor to allow me a TV. After all, I wasn't down the block as a punishment, but supposedly for my own 'safety'. Thankfully, they agreed, but it would take a few days as only one cell down the block had TV aerials installed. These prisoners had to be moved first. I could endure the isolation of solitary confinement as long as I had a TV. Without one, I would soon lose my marbles. A few days later I was moved to a cell with a TV aerial, but unfortunately this cell backed onto the small exercise yard for prisoners down the block. This meant that almost every day the Muslims that attacked me shouted up at my window and lobbed stones through the gap. This was an irritation rather than a worry.

While I was down the block, a detective from a nearby police station came to visit me. He was investigating the attack on me by the Muslim gang. I gave him a detailed statement and he assured me he was investigating the incident. He confirmed there was CCTV clearly showing the Muslims entering my cell and then leaving, followed by me covered in blood. He said he would be in touch once the enquiry had been concluded, but it might take a while.

Life down the block was boring and monotonous. I would wake up, have my breakfast, watch TV and read books until dinner, then watch evening TV, then go to sleep. It wasn't until I was down the block that I was able to make a phone call. I managed to get hold of my mother, who explained to me that Britain First was in absolute meltdown. No funds, no social media, no activities. The bastards I left in charge were doing absolutely nothing to keep the movement afloat. Everything had ground to a complete halt. This increased my frustration and demoralisation even further, but I was totally helpless.

While I was down the block, I wrote a letter to Jayda who was in HMP Bronzefield serving her much longer sentence. Several days later, a letter was passed under my door. Upon inspection, I learned I was going to be prosecuted for breaking a 'contact order'! I was informed this could lead to extra days being added to my sentence. I was furious. Without telling me, the prison authorities had put in place an order banning any contact between me and Jayda. This was done to 'safeguard the public', allegedly.

A few days later, I was put on trial within the prison for breaching this order. I explained to the prison governor that I was not informed at any time about the contact order and thus could not be held accountable for breaching it. The prison governor ordered her assistants to check a database on a computer in the room and confirm whether or not I was made aware of this order. To my great satisfaction, the computer confirmed I was not informed of the order. I was given a caution and dismissed. This was a blatant stitch-up by the prison authorities to add extra days to my sentence. Our establishment is so unbelievably corrupt!

I stayed 'down the block' in complete isolation for five weeks, the first week being endured without a TV. It might not sound like a long time, but being locked in a cell with nothing but a few books for over a week really does cause psychological trauma. With hindsight, I am absolutely amazed I did not catch hepatitis from the noxious and rancid cells. After five weeks down the block, I was content to stay put for the rest of my sentence. But the prison authorities had other ideas.

33. Liverpool

After five weeks of supreme boredom down the block in solitary confinement, I was in a routine. Then, at 7am, while I was fast asleep, a group of guards burst into my cell and informed me I had five minutes to get up and get packed. Still half asleep, I asked what the hell was going on. They told me I was being transferred to another prison. Again, I pleaded in vain to be allowed to stay in my little routine for the next three weeks until my sentence expired, but they refused. I had no choice but to drag myself out of bed and get washed and packed in lightning speed.

I was taken back through processing and informed I was being transferred to a prison in the *north* of England. I was shocked. Why was I being taken all the way from my home area, hundreds of miles away to a region where it would be very, very difficult for my family to come and visit me? More specifically, I was told I was being taken to HMP Liverpool, located in the Walton area of the city. In Elmley, I was literally twenty minutes' drive from my family and Britain First staff members. I braced myself for a horrific journey in a prison transport vehicle, in the tiny plastic cubicles I mentioned earlier. Thankfully though, I was put in handcuffs and placed into a regular civilian car with four prison officers who for the next six hours would be my escort.

I was relieved to be able to go for a long drive in the fresh air, but quite anxious about being taken out of my comfort zone to a new prison where I would have to start settling in from scratch. In prison, you become attached to your cell after a few weeks. After cleaning it and arranging your belongings, it becomes your home. Disruption to this is always unwelcome when you are 'inside'.

On the way up to Liverpool, I asked the prison guards questions about the nature of HMP Liverpool. They informed me it was a war zone. A rough prison with relentless violence and stabbings where prison gangs reigned supreme. This made me very anxious indeed. Hopefully I would be put into isolation again, but who knows.

After about two hours of driving, everyone in the vehicle was in urgent need of a toilet break, including me. So, we pulled into Oxford Services on the M40 and, still handcuffed, I was led into the services. This was a surreal experience being led like a chained slave through crowds of people all staring at us in amazement. Certainly, I had never witnessed such a scene before at a motorway services! As you can imagine, I was immensely embarrassed. We have all seen such scenes before in films. A group of stoutly built prison guards escorting a chained prisoner, but this time it was in a motorway services in public! It was one of the most bizarre and tense situations I have ever been in. Is this normal practice when transporting a prisoner? Or did they do it deliberately to embarrass and humiliate me?

Finally, after a long and boring six-hour drive, I arrived at HMP Liverpool. I was taken into the grounds of the prison and booked into reception. The first question I asked was whether or not I was being put into isolation. The guard said he had no knowledge of anything like that, and that I was going to be placed in general population. I explained the events that had occurred in Elmley and again I told them I would enjoy rabble rousing to gain support in the prison. The guard then assured me that HMP Liverpool had literally zero Muslims in the whole prison. Nevertheless, I braced myself for more carnage.

I was taken to the 'Induction Wing' and placed in a cell that absolutely stank of urine. I complained about the strong smell of piss but they told me to put up and shut up. I went through the same routine again of cleaning and organising my basic belongings and settled in. After a few days on the Induction Wing, I began to realise exactly why I had been transferred all the way from Kent to Liverpool. HMP Liverpool must be the tamest prison in the whole of Britain and with the highest percentage of white English prisoners. The prison was very quiet, compared to Pentonville and Elmley.

In fact, it was half empty. The total capacity of the prison is around 1,300, the same as Elmley. But at the time I arrived, it was home to only 650 prisoners. This prison was built around the same time as Pentonville, in the mid 1800s. This 170-year-old prison was rotting and disgusting, but quiet. The prison was so old and manky that cockroaches roamed freely, and were regularly killed in my cell. I am happy to say that I am a proud mass murderer of cockroaches.

My remaining three weeks in HMP Liverpool were very uneventful. There's not much really to say about these final weeks. I had my own cell, I visited the library regularly, did some English and maths tests, watched TV and kept my head down. I was looking forward to being released in early May. One thing did happen while in Liverpool that needs to be mentioned. I had a visit from my new probation officers who had travelled up from London. These officers were not your ordinary probation, but officers from the 'Probation Extremism Unit'. This important division of the National Probation Service had a remit for terrorism, extremism and violent gangs.

I was led from my cell and taken to the visitation centre.

There I met a black guy from a Jamaican background with cockney accent and a gormless white woman. They were about to drop an atom bomb squarely on my forehead. When I was released from HMP Pentonville, I had to do the second half of my sentence on licence. This licence period came with no conditions or restrictions. I expected the same treatment upon my release this time too. I later learned that when released from a prison sentence incurred from a contempt of court offence, it is the law that there are no licence conditions. This time though, I wasn't serving a sentence for contempt of court, but for religiously aggravated harassment.

The purpose of this visit from the Probation Extremism Unit was to serve me with my licence conditions, which would last for another nine weeks starting the day I was released. These conditions, as you can imagine, were restrictive in the extreme. The specific conditions are heavily worded and lengthy, so I am summarising them here:

- *Not to use the internet in any way*
- *Not to contact Jayda Fransen*
- *Not to engage in any political activities*
- *Not to leave his home address for nine hours per day*
- *Not to contact or associate with anyone in Britain First*
- *To surrender his passport to the police*
- *To provide details of his phone and car to the police*
- *Not to speak to the media*

As you can see, these 'conditions' made any political endeavours impossible. The jobsworths of the Probation Extremism Unit intended to extend my misery for as long as possible. Britain First had all but collapsed outside and I was looking forward to being able to fire into action to save it. Instead, for the nine weeks after my release I was going to be on lockdown with restrictions. If I breached these conditions, I would be recalled back to HMP Liverpool. The process of being recalled back to prison did not even need a judge or a court hearing. My probation officer could simply flip a switch and I would be back inside. I had to tread carefully.

The day of my release finally came after nine weeks' incarceration. I was very excited to finally go home. I had been exposed to Muslim thugs, assaulted, slung in isolation, moved around and transferred. The prison had tried to stitch me up to increase my sentence. It had been a short sentence in the grand scheme of things, but it was still a difficult ordeal. But the establishment was not done with me yet. They still had one more trick to pull on me before my nightmare was over.

When I awoke on the day of my release, I was like a child at Christmas. I was taken from my cell around 9am and taken through the prison interior to the processing area. Here I was given all my belongings and checked out of the prison. But, to my horror, I was handed some paperwork by an official which gave me my new address: Ealing Probation Hostel, 2 Corfton Road, London, W5 2HS. In total confusion, I asked what the hell was going on. Surely I had served half my sentence and could now go home on licence? Things went from bad to worse when I was informed that there were two car loads of police officers waiting at the gates to transport me to the probation hostel. I was escorted to the gates and to my surprise, there were two car loads of plain clothes officers waiting to greet me.

The excitement of being released had lapsed into massive frustration at this new stitch-up. I was placed in one of the cars and our convey headed down the M6 to London. I had a very bad idea in my head of what a 'probation hostel' would be like, full of drug addicts and violent criminal hoods. Pretty much, just like a prison wing! I was assured by the plain clothes officers escorting me that this wasn't the case.

After about an hour on the road, I began to get suspicious about the plain clothes officers that I was surrounded by. Surely there wasn't a need for two car loads of ordinary police to be in plain clothes just to taxi me to a hostel in West London? Something didn't add up. Then I had a light bulb moment! I asked them straight, 'Hold on a minute guys, are you lot from SO15 Counter Terrorism Command?' Reluctantly, and mainly due to my persistence, they confirmed they were. I was astonished. Talk about a total, unbelievable waste of police resources. During a time when the official Home Office terror threat is at the highest level – 'attack imminent' – here were two car loads of anti-terror police ferrying a politician down a motorway!

I asked them the million-dollar question, why? They didn't have an answer. I kept saying, 'Surely you should be out on the streets catching and investigating terrorists?' No wonder so many terror attacks escape the attention of our security services when they are carrying out such mundane tasks as providing taxi services for politicians. With an estimated – and widely reported – twenty-three thousand wannabe jihadists wandering our streets, surely the time and resources of SO15 would be better spent investigating the many Islamist networks flourishing in Britain. Obviously, someone at the Home Office disagrees.

34. Probation

After being released from HMP Liverpool, I was taken under escort to the Ealing Probation Hostel. Thankfully, it was nowhere near as bad as I had expected. The hostel was in fact a huge house in a leafy area about a mile from Ealing Broadway. For some reason, I expected Ealing to be a multicultural slum. Because of this, I doubted whether I would be able to go out in public and carry out rudimentary tasks, like food shopping. Ealing was in fact a very nice area, as far as areas of West London go! Yes, it was very liberal, trendy and leftwing, but it wasn't a rough council estate.

To further turn the screw on me, 'SO15 Counter Terrorism Command' and the Probation Extremism Unit insisted I had to 'sign on' at the hostel reception at 11am and 5pm on the dot every single day. I also had to be inside the grounds of the hostel between 11pm and, every day. In other words, I had to sleep there. All of this was designed to curtail my freedom. For security reasons, I had a family member pick me up from the hostel every day at 11am after I had signed on. It had to be a family member because I was banned from associated with anyone from Britain First. I was then able to go to local parks or shopping centres and relax a bit until I had to return to sign on at 5pm. My family then left me and I spent the evenings in the hostel watching TV or reading. I would also go out for early evening jogs in the warm summer weather when the sun was setting. Luckily, the hostel had a pool table which I took full advantage of.

The fact remains though, that all the other residents of the hostel were serious criminals who had served *years* in prison. Some of the other residents had been in the hostel for over a year. What the hell was I doing there? I had served only nine weeks inside for a minor offence. After speaking to the other prisoners in the hostel, it was patently obvious that - rather than let me go home - here was another method of extending my ordeal. Because of my bail conditions, I could not do anything political. I could not even go online to use the internet. I could not associate with anyone from Britain First. I was watched relentlessly in the hostel or in the back garden. Once I made a phone call in the back garden and wandered off to the area near the back fence. I then received a phone call from my probation officer asking me who I was speaking to! It was obvious to me that they were watching me like a hawk.

When SO15 first dropped me off at the hostel, they forced me to use a pay-as-you-go cheap mobile that, I am sure, was bugged to high heaven with recording and GPS devices. I was told if I was caught with an internet-enabled mobile, like my iPhone, I would be recalled to prison. The hostel itself was covered with CCTV cameras like a child is covered by chicken pox. I had no privacy whatsoever.

A few weeks into my stay at the hostel, there was a murder directly outside. The police swarmed the area and police cars were in abundance. I was shocked that a murder had taken place only about twenty feet from where I was sleeping. It reminded me to be careful. Meanwhile, Britain First was in extreme crisis. IT systems were being shut down for lack of payment. No funds had flowed into HQ for over a month. Our solicitors were on strike. Staff wages could not be paid and they had to be temporarily laid off. There had been no activities, publicity or social media for over two months. Britain First had disintegrated. Urgent action was needed, but I just had to sit back and take it on the chin.

After five weeks, I was allowed to return home to Dartford. My stay in the hostel was simply another way of prolonging my anguish and keeping an eye on me. It was completely unnecessary to place me in a hostel, which is supposed to be used for serious criminals who have nowhere else to go. I had a home that I could have been returned to, but half of the game with S015 is to cause as much annoyance and aggravation as possible. If they can inconvenience you, they will. I was relieved to be back home, finally. It had been a long and irritating journey of upheaval, boredom and worry. Although I had a short while to go before my licence expired, I could now relax in the comfort of my own home. After passing through four different cells in two prisons, nothing beats going home to familiar surroundings.

Shortly before my 'licence' was due to expire, I had a meeting with my probation officer. For a year or two previously, all prisoners who spend time inside are subject to 'Post Sentence Supervision' (PSS) upon release. This is a new tactic of the state to control citizens. The idea behind it is to continue a level of oversight over released prisoners to prevent re-offending. Post Sentence Supervision lasts for a full year after release and contains a standard set of requirements that you must follow. I was given a sheet of paper by my probation officer and he explained what would be required of me for the next twelve months. The exact requirements of PSS are reproduced here:

- To be of good behaviour and not behave in a way that undermines the rehabilitative purpose of the supervision period;

- Not to commit any offence;

- To keep in touch with your supervisor in accordance with

instructions given by your supervisor;

- To receive visits from your supervisor in accordance with instructions given by your supervisor;

- To reside permanently at an address approved by your supervisor and obtain the prior permission of the supervisor for any stay of one or more nights at a different address;

- Not to undertake work, or a particular type of work, unless it is approved by your supervisor and to notify your supervisor in advance of any proposal to undertake work or a particular type of work;

- Not to travel outside the United Kingdom and Islands except with the prior permission of your supervisor or in order to comply with a legal obligation (whether or not arising under the law of any part of the United Kingdom and Islands);

- To participate in activities in accordance with any instructions given by your supervisor.

Here was another nightmare about to start. My probation officer – and his superiors in the Probation Extremism Unit – were going to breath down my neck for the next twelve months, dictating where I could and could not sleep and travel. Every meeting I had with my probation officer was practically an interrogation about every facet of my life, political and personal. This was obviously an intelligence gathering exercise. My battle against their interference and sabotage was about to start and would end in total humiliation for them.

Finally, my licence was about to expire and I would be able to resume political activities. I was waiting for the exact moment to swing into action as Britain First was in a horrible mess. I was like an athlete runner bending down on the starting line waiting for the shot to fire so he could sprint forward at maximum speed and ferocity. When the day came, I was ecstatic and ready for action. Luckily, the end of my release coincided with the 12th of July loyalist celebration in Northern Ireland and I booked flights to go over only two days after the expiration of my licence period. I had to email my probation officer and inform him of my plans as I was required by PSS to do so. Quite unexpectedly, he vanished and went quiet.

I didn't think anything of it until - while training at a local boxing gym - I got a frantic phone call from my mother. She informed me that a police riot van full of officers had turned up at her house to arrest me. Luckily, I wasn't there, but the CCTV captured footage of the officers walking into the front garden. I tried to contact my probation officer but could not get hold of him. Then, I got a phone call from my friends in 'SO15 Counter Terrorism Command' informing me that my probation officer had secured an arrest warrant for me because I supposedly had breached my PSS. I told the officer I had followed it to the letter, but he said I'd have to explain that in court. So, I told him not to come back and arrest me, I would hand myself in the next morning nice and early. He directed me to hand myself in to Bromley police station, my second home.

The next morning, I travelled to Bromley station and handed myself in. I explained the sequence of events to the desk officer and she waddled out of sight to make enquiries. When she returned, she informed me that I wasn't wanted! I asked her to check over and over again but she was adamant: She had checked the systems, spoken to the station inspector and there was no live arrest warrant for Paul Golding. As you can imagine, I was very bemused. I asked them why a van full of police had come to my mother's house to arrest me, but they said they could find no information about the incident and that the arrest warrant must have been rescinded. I even showed them the CCTV of the incident.

I knew exactly what had happened. The 12th of July celebration in Ulster that year had been particularly troublesome. The police were coming down heavy-handed on the loyalist people, forcibly removing bonfires which prompted violence on the streets. The last thing the establishment wanted was for me and my merry band of extremists to roll into town. So, they issued an arrest warrant and tried to have me arrested on the verge of the 12th. By the time I would be taken to court and then released, the celebration would have passed. Job done, the establishment must have thought. But, unknown to the police and probation, I had actually refrained from travelling to Belfast because of the conflict on the streets there. I was in a position of being arrested for something I hadn't even done!

I filmed a short video outside the station explaining the situation and returned home. Then, to my total surprise, I got another call from SO15 and they informed me that I *did* have an arrest warrant out for me! I explained that I had visited Bromley police station to hand myself in but they told me the opposite and let me go. The SO15 officer did not believe me. He said he would make enquiries to ascertain the truth of the situation. A few hours later, he called back and confirmed that I was telling the truth but that I would need to hand myself back in so I could be taken to Bromley Magistrate's Court. As it was a Friday afternoon, we agreed that I would hand myself in first thing Monday morning when the court re-opened. If I was arrested or handed myself in over the weekend, I would have to be kept in custody until Monday morning anyway. We both agreed a plan of action and I terminated the call.

After having a lay-in on the Sunday morning, I got up and dragged myself to the boxing gym again. Then, in a canny re-run of recent events, I got another call from my mother to tell me that the police had turned up again to arrest me! Double-crossing bastards. I had agreed with the SO15 officer to hand myself in Monday morning, but they reneged on their promise not to arrest me before then and turned up on a Sunday morning to do precisely that. If they had caught me indoors, I would have spent all of Sunday daytime and night in a boring police cell.

Nervously, I went to bed on the Sunday night, fully expecting the police to make another visit, but they refrained from doing so, probably because I put the CCTV footage of them arriving at my mother's front door on our website and various third-party social media sites. I woke up and headed for Bromley police station for the second time. When I arrived, I announced myself to the desk officer and explained the situation. Then I was told that 'officers from London' were on their way down and I should wait for them. Everything I did from that point on was recorded.

I was waiting out in the sunshine when two officers in plain clothes approached me and introduced themselves, asking me to stay put until they came back out of the station. After about half an hour, they re-emerged and I realised that at least one of them was an officer who had picked me up from HMP Liverpool to take me to Ealing Probation Hostel. Both the officers were SO15 and had travelled down from London to escort me to court. I thought this was a strange way of dealing with things. I braced myself to be arrested and taken into custody.

After protesting about us filming them, one of the officers then said, 'Paul, there's a warrant out for your arrest, but what we're proposing to do is, not arrest you, but to take you up to Bromley Magistrates Court and do the business there.' Was this officer for real? I had a live arrest warrant in my name but he wouldn't arrest me? Instead, he was proposing for me to follow them *voluntarily* to the court for a hearing on the alleged breach of my PSS. They even allowed me to drive my own vehicle to the court, in convoy with them. This was a surreal and bizarre series of events! My life was, if anything, very 'abnormal' at the best of times but this was something new.

Please bear in mind that the arrest warrant was for an alleged breach of PSS, which carries perhaps the most lightweight punishments in British justice. The *maximum* I could receive if convicted is two weeks back in prison. That's less than shoplifting, but here were two of the country's top counter-terrorism officers wasting their time escorting me to a magistrates court. This during a time when the threat level for Islamist terrorism was at the highest level. If only I could communicate my situation to the entire British people there would be serious disorder and anger.

When we arrived at the court, I was babysat by the two officers for the rest of the day. Just before the hearing in front of the magistrates, I was handed a 'Breach Report', written by my probation officer which alleged that I had not informed him of my plans to travel to Northern Ireland! Unfortunately for him, I told the magistrates that I had incontrovertible evidence that this was total hogwash. The magistrates adjourned the hearing so that I could exhibit the evidence to the prosecutor. When the prosecutor examined the emails and text messages that I had printed out and arranged neatly in order, he was flabbergasted. 'Why on earth are you being breached?', he said. I told him I had absolutely no bloody idea. He immediately told me that he would withdraw the charges.

The hearing resumed and the prosecutor withdrew the charges and the magistrates told me I could leave, a free man. What an absolute farce. The prosecutor, to be fair, was quite embarrassed about the whole situation. After two separate arrest attempts at my mother's house, two visits to a police station to hand myself in, being escorted by anti-terrorism police, the whole debacle ended with the prosecutor and the magistrates throwing it out. I then realised why the two officers from SO15 had turned up and spent the day babysitting me. It's as simple as this: If I was convicted and sentenced to two weeks in prison, then they would be the ones who were on the spot to drive me back to HMP Liverpool! All of this happened within a week of my licence period ending and me resuming my political activities.

The Probation Extremism Unit would do everything within their power to frustrate my legitimate political activities. One of my main PSS conditions was that I had to seek their approval to reside at any address or hotel for a stay of one night or more. My probation officer was fond of approving addresses, then changing his mind and banning from staying there, then reversing his decision again and re-allowing me to stay there. There was no consistency in their treatment and decisions. Their approach was deliberately confusing and inconsistent so that I would make a mistake and then face prosecution. I would, at first, have to attend meetings at my local probation office, then later be forced to travel to South London for meetings.

When I moved temporarily to Belfast in the autumn of 2018, my probation officer tried to force me to return to Kent. It was only when I was arrested shortly after in Belfast for giving out anti-immigration leaflets in the town of Ballymena that they approved me to stay. It may have had something to do with the fact that the local police banned me from participating in any political activities while present in Northern Ireland. More on that arrest later.

A few months later, I asked permission to visit the European Parliament in Strasbourg to meet with elected patriot MEPs from numerous movements. As expected, I was refused permission and given no reason whatsoever for the refusal. All I wanted to do was visit elected democratic representatives, not engage in anything that could be construed as 'incendiary'. Nevertheless, I was refused out of hand. Then I applied to travel to Lanzarote again for a week's holiday. I explained that this break would be completely non-political but once again they refused point blank. It was clear to me that the Probation Extremism Unit would not permit me to leave the UK during the period of my PSS, for *any* reason. This is in stark contrast to the way they treat other offenders. I was different of course. They wanted to do everything they possible could to hinder and obstruct my legal activities.

In early November, I travelled from Belfast to the mainland for a day of action in the north of England. I emailed my probation officer my travel plans including my intention to stay at a guest house in Dartford. The day of action took place and I then headed south to Dartford and stayed for the weekend, as I outlined in my email. A few days later, I got a call from my probation officer to inform me that his superiors had taken the decision to prosecute me again for allegedly breaching my PSS.

I expressed my consternation at this latest round of nonsense, but he said it was out of his hands. I was being prosecuted for staying at the guest house in Dartford, even though it was approved as an address several times previously and they even had the temerity to approve it for me to stay in some time later! Talk about move the bloody goal posts. Apparently, the probation service did not believe my claim that my bail conditions in Northern Ireland allowed me to travel to the mainland. They wanted me to stay in Belfast where I could not carry out any political activities. How convenient.

Several months later, in early January 2019, I appeared once again in Bromley Magistrate's Court to plead 'not guilty' to the charges. The trial was then set for the 13th of March. When the day came, I attended court with all of my evidence once again superbly organised and ready to be used. My probation officer was in attendance, unlike last time, and the prosecutor began to present his case to the magistrates. Once again, the name of SO15 was flung around the court during the evidence. Experience has taught me never to expect victory when the case is being decided by magistrates, who are not proper judges.

My probation officer was called to the stand to give evidence, followed by me. After all of the evidence was given in court and the questioning by the respective solicitors and the magistrates, they retired to make a decision. I expected a guilty verdict because I had never won a case before a set of magistrates. Magistrates are usually solicitors or barristers who like taking a stab at being up on the bench playing the role of a real judge. They are far more likely to give politically biased decisions because their careers are not on the line.

When the three female magistrates reappeared, they began to explain the reasons for their decision and to my utter astonishment, dismissed the case against me! I was found 'not guilty'. This was an amazing and unexpected turn of events. The representatives from the Probation Extremism Unit were totally demoralised. For the second time the Probation Extremism Unit had tried to sabotage me and for the second time, I had managed to defeat them in court. I left the court and immediately posted a video to our limited social media. I was completely shocked at the result. This was my first and only victory in front of a group of magistrates. In fact, it was the first 'not guilty' verdict I had ever received.

This simple piece of good news grew legs around the patriot movement online and spirits were boosted across the board. For the first time, I had defeated the establishment in a fair legal contest. It also spelled the end for the Probation Extremism Unit's campaign of harassment and sabotage. After their second defeat, they backed off and pretty much left me to my own devices. In other words, they stopped subjecting me to blatant politically motivated harassment. Very shortly after, their period of oversight would be coming to an end and I would be glad to see the back of them.

35. Rebirth

After my prison licence expired, I was free to resume my political activities. The task in front of me was daunting, but I am not one to shirk a challenge. Britain First had ceased to exist, so I need to start from scratch and relaunch the entire organisation. I secured the use of entirely new IT systems and began to recruit new activists using our huge email list. I appointed new officers to key positions and set about rebuilding everything from the ground up. A new online payment system was secured, new bank accounts, new campaign systems, new administration databases, the full works.

Once the new infrastructure of the movement had been established, I set about organising activities around the nation. Over the next few months, in rapid succession, Britain first held a wave of protests, meetings and days of action across the country. This flurry of activity was indefatigable. In just a few months we had visited Huddersfield, Londonderry, Bradford, Bangor, Sunderland, Lisburn, Worcester, Durham, Halifax, Hertford, Dorset, Portrush, Belfast, Newtownards, Portadown, Carrickfergus, Newcastle, Ballymena, Manchester, Elland, Widnes, Nuneaton, Batley, Didsbury, Lurgan,

Worcester, Northampton, Dover, Maidstone, Poole, Stoke-On-Trent, Ware, Weymouth, Sandwell and so on. It was *relentless.*

Britain First started to gain publicity again, especially in Northern Ireland. Video reports of our activities criss-crossed social media once again. This was during a time when every other patriot individual, movement or party was sublimely inactive. Our support base started to receive letters and leaflets from HQ in the post. Membership started to increase steadily, as did donations and monthly payments. Email bulletins flowed into the inboxes of hundreds of thousands of our members and supporters. I relaunched an online merchandise shop. HQ was once again filled with boxes of envelopes, leaflets, bookmarks and letterheads. Organisers of new branches were being appointed nationwide. I set up an election department and we made plans to contest the local elections in May 2019. Everything was being rebuilt and relaunched. These organisational innovations - combined with incessant activities – put Britain First squarely back on the political landscape. Our national reboot was electrifying.

With the help of one of Northern Ireland's top QCs, I even took the unprecedented step of suing Facebook for political discrimination in Belfast high court. This was a plan I formulated in prison. Anti-discrimination legislation in Northern Ireland is very strict because of the legacy of the Troubles. Discrimination law in Northern Ireland covers 'political belief', unlike the mainland. So, we compiled a large bundle of evidence including dozens of screenshots and submitted the application. At the time of writing, the political discrimination case against Facebook is still rumbling on. Our case was simple, by closing our verified fan pages and cutting off nearly three million of our supporters, Facebook had committed political discrimination under the 'Fair Employment and Treatment (Northern Ireland) Order 1998', which made it illegal to discriminate on the grounds of political belief.

Facebook could waffle all it wanted to the media about so-called 'hate speech', but in a court of law the rules are different. They would have to provide real *evidence* to the judge, not just press releases. They would have to justify their actions before a senior and experienced high court judge.

Along with demanding evidence and examples of our transgressions, we also submitted a wealth of screenshots of pages and accounts on Facebook that were clearly hateful and offensive but which Facebook refused to take down. For example, we reported pages such as, 'Death to Israel', 'F*** Christianity' and 'Death to America'. In every instance, Facebook came back and were perfectly fine with them. We reported these accounts ourselves and when Facebook stated these pages did not breach their 'Community Standards', we screenshotted them and submitted them as evidence. We are hoping for a resolution to this landmark case in the summer of 2019.

One area where we had strong success was in the small loyalist town of Ballymena, just north of Belfast. Local residents from the town had contacted us and asked for a meeting. When we arrived, we were shocked by what we saw. The whole of the town was swamped by gypsy Roma migrants. I had only seen this level of Roma immigration once before, in Hexthorpe on the outskirts of Doncaster. Ballymena was being used almost exclusively as a dumping ground for busloads of these migrants. The locals were in uproar. I drove around the town filming a few short clips where I asked the migrants questions. They pretty much all confirmed that they received free houses and benefits. The video went viral on a third-party Facebook page, gaining half a million views in a few days.

I decided to launch an immediate Britain First campaign. We held a day of action in the town distributing localised leaflets and the response to our presence was overwhelmingly positive. Even republicans were talking to us in Celtic football shirts. Both sides of the Protestant/Catholic divide were livid at what was happening to their small town. The locals complained to us about anti-social behaviour and even attacks on residents. Obviously, I wanted to help these local people, to give them a political voice. The Old Gang parties of the DUP and Sinn Fein were completely ignoring all the complaints from locals. So, we felt we had to help these poor people who needed someone to make a stand for them.

After the day of action, we held a small meeting in a nearby pub and during the day we invited local residents to attend. I only expected about twenty or so of them to turn up. When 3pm arrived the pub and the immediate vicinity was bursting with locals, some two-hundred of them! We had to take the meeting outside onto the street due to the sheer number of attendees. This was a brilliant display of local anger and with hindsight I think it completely freaked out the police. To capitalise on the successful rally in Ballymena, we announced a second for two weeks' time. This time we began leafleting all the local estates with leaflets advertising the rally. We wanted a bigger crowd this time. Going by the sheer volume of leaflets that we distributed across the town, we were hoping for a huge increase in the number of locals.

Just a few days before the rally, I pulled up at an address in East Belfast. I was completely unaware of what was about to happen. Suddenly as I got out of the driver's door, my vehicle was surrounded by police officers and I was kept standing on the cold street for about half an hour while these officers made checks. Finally, I was arrested for a public order offence and taken to Musgrave Police Station where I was kept in custody for the next sixteen hours. I was interviewed by officers from Ballymena CID about the content of the leaflets we were distributing. I gave a silent interview and my solicitor was shocked that I would be arrested for such an innocuous anti-immigration leaflet.

Once again, the real object of the police operation was to tie me down with bail conditions. Upon release, I was given a list of restrictions which effectively banned me from political activities in the whole of Northern Ireland. I will reproduce them here:

1. Must not be within 500 metres of any public parade, protest or demonstration in Northern Ireland.

2. Must not enter the town of Ballymena as defined by the 30 mph speed limit, save to attend court.

3. Must not enter Dunsilly Carpark, Antrim on Saturdays between the hours of 5pm & 10 pm.

4. Not to be in possession of any material which is threatening, abusive or insulting or likely to stir up hatred or arouse fear.

5. Must not distribute any leaflet which is threatening, abusive or insulting or is likely to stir up hatred or arouse fear.

6. Must reside [redacted], Belfast & at no other address.

7. To sign bail at Musgrave Police Station on Tuesdays & Thursday at 3pm.

Banning me from being within five-hundred metres of any parade, protest or demonstration in Northern Ireland was designed to stop me organising and attending any legitimate political activities, plus any loyalist parades. Banning me from entering the town of Ballymena was clearly designed to sabotage the rally in the town that was due to take place several days later. Dunsilly carpark is a small parking facility on the outskirts of the town. It is here that the busloads of migrants are brought in. I was banned from going anywhere near it. The condition forcing me to 'sign on' at Musgrave Police Station - on Tuesdays and Thursdays - was specifically calculated to keep me in Northern Ireland and unable to travel to the mainland. If I was forced to stay in Northern Ireland, my bail conditions stopped me from engaging in political activities. These conditions were designed to neutralise me completely.

The news of my arrest was covered extensively across the media in Northern Ireland. This only increased local anger and frustration in Ballymena. When the rally took place on the following Saturday, around two-hundred locals still turned up, despite rumours in the town that everyone was going to be arrested on sight. These rumours obviously scared a lot of people off. This whole operation was a politically motivated stitch-up by the Sinn Fein run establishment to destroy our local campaign and silence Britain First in this part of the kingdom. I now had two lots of bail conditions which applied only to Northern Ireland. The first lot were from the arrest relating to giving a speech outside Belfast City Hall in August 2017. On top of these, I now had the Ballymena bail conditions. Because of this situation, I decided to move back to the mainland where all of these conditions and restrictions did not apply because Northern Ireland was a separate legal jurisdiction.

My trial for 'using insulting words in public' outside Belfast City Hall had been put on the back burner because of my incarceration in Elmley and Liverpool prisons during 2018. But now I was a free man once again, a trial date was set for 13th February 2019. We had a brilliant barrister and our solicitor too was a wily fox. The trial was wrapped up within a day and the judge was read all the interview statements by the prosecution, followed by the videos of the speeches. Both sides then gave closing statements and the trial was over. A pretty uneventful trial, all things considered.

The judge said at the end of the trial that he would adjourn to give a written judgement rather than make a decision on the spot. I did not like this development one little bit. I remember how judge Barron had adjourned for sentencing after the trial in Folkestone and was then leaned on by the Attorney General. I expected a re-run of this sequence of events. The judge did not even set a date for the verdict, he simply adjourned.

A few weeks later, I learned from my solicitor that the date for the verdict was set for 29th March. Once again, I made travel preparations and organised a security team. To be brutally honest, I expecting to be found guilty. The only question was whether or not I would be sentenced to prison again. Nevertheless, I made big preparations behind the scenes for this eventuality. Unlike when I was sent to Elmley and Britain First collapsed, this time I had people around me who I could trust and who I knew would keep the movement going in my absence. The new, reconstructed Britain First would not collapse like a house of cards if I was sent down again.

When I arrived at Laganside Courts in Belfast on 29th of March, I was understandably nervous. I had a big team of supporters with me and we headed to Court 7 to learn my fate. All four defendants were in the dock. A whole multitude of media outlets were there, including the BBC. The judge started reading from his pre-prepared judgement. He went into minute detail about the features of our case and talked about the unsuccessful prosecution of Pastor McConnell for a similar type of offence.

Then, to my complete stupefaction, he declared me 'not guilty' and dismissed me from the court! All but one of the defendants were found not guilty. This was the second 'not guilty' within two weeks, the first being with the probation service shortly before in Bromley. I was euphoric at this unexpected result. The Lord had smiled on our movement and had shielded us from the evil schemes of our enemies. My faith in the British judiciary had been restored. The police representatives in the court were visibly exasperated.

After a year and a half on bail, attending around a dozen court hearings and spending tens of thousands of pounds in legal fees for our defence, it all ended with a not guilty verdict. One by one the prosecutions hanging over my head were dropping like flies. My PSS period was about to expire and two of the three criminal prosecutions which threatened prison terms had been thrown out. Other civil cases which cannot be discussed were also being wound up. The legal pressure on our movement was subsiding fast.

Britain First as a movement had weathered the worst storm the establishment could throw at it. Starting when I was sent to HMP Elmley in March 2018, our movement had collapsed. Facebook had cut us off from three million of our supporters. Our administration and activities had ceased. Our movement was effectively bankrupt. Then, upon my release, I set about with furious energy to rebuild everything from scratch. Within six months, we had negotiated our way through several unsuccessful prosecutions, rebuilt our internal infrastructure, mobilised several hundred new activists, launched dozens of new branches and organised around seventy street activities.

Britain First participated for the first time in a local election campaign. Packs filled with letters, leaflets and bookmarks were flying out of HQ by the hundred. We took on new staff and moved into a new HQ office. In a thousand different ways, Britain First is booming and had successfully bounced back from the abyss. Britain First has proved itself to be a tough and unshakeable movement, able to overcome any act of sabotage from the British establishment. Our movement epitomises the fighting spirit and tenacity of the British people. The period between March 2018 and the not guilty verdict in March 2019 - when Britain First bounced back with maximum force - is nothing short of a miracle. The credit for this unexpected rebirth must be given to God, without whom *nothing* is possible.

36. Armageddon

Many times throughout history, what today we call 'Europe' - or 'the West' - has come close to extermination by barbarian hordes. In fact, it is a miracle that we have survived the invasions, conquests and genocide that our peoples have been subjected to. Modern generations know nothing about the debt they owe to ancient and medieval armies - and leaders - who halted the advance of Asian and Islamic intrusions.

In the 5th Century, an inexorable invasion of Europe began under Attila the Hun. His Asian hordes reached Central Europe, committing unspeakable atrocities against Europeans along the way. It was only when Attila died that the Huns withdrew from Europe. Had they pressed on into Western Europe, our entire civilisation would have perished, along with our people.

In the 6th Century, Islamic armies exterminated Christianity in the Levant and the Holy Land. The caliphs then pushed on into North Africa and finally crossed the Gibraltar Straights into modern-day Spain and Portugal. For centuries, the Iberian Peninsula was under brutal and sadistic rule by Islamic caliphates. These Islamic states forced the native Spaniards to hand over virgins as tribute to their rulers. The Islamic occupation of Spain was characterised by repression and genocide and lasted for 700 years, forever changing the ethnic and cultural landscape of the region.

During this era, a barbaric wave of Asians invaded Eastern Europe, called the Bulgars. These warrior tribes defeated the Roman armies and gave their name to the modern country, Bulgaria. During the same period, another brutal Asian people, the Magyars, invaded Eastern Europe and settled in modern-day Hungary, carrying out atrocities and massacres against Europeans. The Magyar language is still spoken to this day by modern Hungarians. To complete this wave of ethnic cleansing and genocide came the Avars, another Asian tribe that battled with the Eastern Roman Empire. Between them, these Asian tribes exterminated or displaced enormous numbers of native Europeans.

Shortly after conquering the Iberian Peninsula, the Muslim armies pushed across the Pyrenees into modern-day France, intent on destroying the powerful kingdom of the Franks. They reached an area just south of Paris and met the king of the Franks at the Battle of Tours. The fate of Europe hung in the balance. If the caliphs had succeeded in conquering the Franks, Christianity would have been exterminated and Europe would have become a Muslim continent. Everything depended on this single battle. Thankfully, Charles Martel - known as 'Charles the Hammer' - smashed the Muslim armies and saved Europe. Every person of European descent around the world owes their existence to Charles, King of the Franks.

A few centuries later, a feeble European and Christian attempt to hold back the Islamic hordes - known to history as the Crusades - was launched by Pope Urban. The Crusades ultimately failed to dislodge the Muslims from the Holy Land, although Jerusalem was taken by the Crusaders, but then lost again, to Islamic commander, Saladin. Richard the Lionheart, King of England, came close to recapturing Jerusalem from Saladin but he instead returned to Europe to secure his kingdom.

In 1453, the great Christian city of Constantinople fell to a huge Islamic army under the Ottomans, led by Mehmed II. The city was destroyed and the population enslaved or exterminated. The slaughter was unspeakable. The huge Christian church, the Hagia Sophia, was immediately converted to a mosque. The Ottomans - an Asian tribe also from the steppes - consolidated their grip on modern-day Turkey and renamed Constantinople, Istanbul. This campaign of conquest and extermination destroyed the Eastern Roman Empire and gave the Muslims a toehold in Eastern Europe.

In the 13th Century, a huge new invasion of Eastern Europe started. The Mongol invasion was even more terrible than the carnage wrought by Attila and the Huns. Slavic states, such as Rus and Kiev, were completely annihilated by the Mongol hordes. After subduing the states in Eastern Europe, the Mongols set their sights on Central Europe. Polish, Hungarian and Austrian armies were smashed in the relentless onslaught. Countless atrocities were inflicted on native Europeans by the Mongols. Huge numbers perished. Then, in 1242, for some unknown reason, the Mongols began to withdraw. If they had been determined, the Mongols could have conquered Europe and extinguished our entire civilisation.

After destroying Constantinople, the Ottoman Turks then turned their attention to Italy and Sicily, which they invaded, carrying out many massacres and crimes against the native inhabitants. When the Muslim forces reached the Italian city of Otranto, they gave the inhabitants a choice: Convert to Islam or die. Those who refused to convert to Islam were led to a hill outside the city and massacred. The execution site became known as the Hill of Martyrs. Sicily endured a much longer occupation by Islamic forces. This occupation changed the ethnic and cultural identity of Sicily forever, until the Muslims were expelled by the Knights Templar and the Normans.

With their new bridgehead in Southeast Europe after the fall of Constantinople, the Ottoman Muslims launched a full-scale invasion of Europe, conquering the Balkans and pushing into southern Russia. The Ottomans were utterly ruthless, massacring indigenous populations as they pushed further and further inland. Some European rulers desperately tried to halt the advance of the Ottomans. Resistance leaders, such as Vlad Dracula - also known as Vlad the Impaler - tried to match the brutal methods of the invading Turks. Vlad captured thousands of Ottomans and stuck them on spikes. When the Ottoman army approached, they were so horrified by the scene, they withdrew.

Despite the heroic resistance, all opposition to the Ottomans was crushed and they advanced to the gates of Vienna, in Austria. If the Ottomans could take Vienna, all Europe would fall to Islam. At the Battle of Vienna in 1683, the Ottoman army was defeated by a combined European force led by the Polish king Sobieski. After this failure, the Ottoman Turks started a slow withdrawal back towards Anatolia. Up to the late 1800s, the Ottomans continued to massacre local Europeans in the Balkans. This suppression was so brutal that a tower was constructed at Nis, Serbia, made entirely from the skulls of defeated Serbian resistance fighters. The tower still stands today and is an horrific reminder of the genocidal occupation of half of Europe by the Islamic Turks.

Since its inception in the 7th Century, Islam has been waging an unceasing war of jihad against the rest of the world. The pace of warfare has been frenetic and incessant. If you compare the number of Christian attacks against Islam with the number of jihad attacks against Europe, the situation is overwhelmingly lopsided. Islam is responsible for the clear majority of these wars and conflicts with Christendom over the last 1,400 years. Jihad is one of the most important topics in the Quran and for over a millennium, the passages urging Muslims to wage jihad have been followed to the letter. The assault on Christendom and Western civilisation has, at times, threatened to extinguish our existence. Thanks to a succession of European heroes, men such as Charles Martel, Prince Eugene of Savoy, Vlad Dracula, Sobieski, Richard the Lionheart, Queen Isabella and King Ferdinand and many others, our Christian, Western civilisation has avoided complete annihilation.

But knowledge of this epic and bloody struggle to survive - against Islam and Asia - has been completely censored in modern times. Modern generations are oblivious when it comes to these stupendous wars of survival. But the lives of billions of humans of European descent have only been made possible because of the heroic sacrifice and unparalleled resistance by the handful of armies and great commanders outlined above. The Western World is a fragile and delicate endeavour that needs defending with continuous and unrelenting vigilance. Judging purely by the history of the last two millennia, all the nation states, the peoples, the cultures and the traditions of our common Greco-Roman and Judeo-Christian heritage could be extirpated at a moment's notice if a single generation lowers its guard.

The West is more than a conglomeration of nations with a common heritage and culture. Birthed in the small but intellectually fertile states of ancient Greece, the concepts of liberty, law, democracy and individual rights that characterise the 'West' are history's greatest flowering of freedom. The innovations of Hellenic Greece were adopted, strengthened and codified by the awesome power and creativity of Rome. Building upon the legacy of these ancient cultural superpowers, Christianity weaved its magnificent moral framework into the bargain along with its ancient traditions. The result, after three thousand years of progress, is Western civilisation, the most enlightened and productive culture mankind has ever produced.

Western civilisation is an unparalleled achievement. From its very beginning, Western civilisation has led human development in literature, science, innovation, politics, architecture, philosophy and technology. While the rest of the world was hopelessly sunk in superstition and darkness, Western civilisation brought forth reason, justice, logic and free thinking. I do not agree with contemporary dogma that the 'Dark Ages' temporarily derailed progress and drafted in medieval stagnation. The so-called 'Dark Ages' produced some of the most enlightened advances in human history. Certainly, social immobility blights this period, as do the feudal hierarchies of most European societies. But generally speaking, the post-Roman period of the Middle Ages produced a flourishing of culture and technology, even if the social structure of Christendom was fossilised and static.

Both the Reformation and the Renaissance broke the death grip of the Inquisition and produced an awe-inspiring and breathtaking flourishing of progress such as the world has ever seen. What followed was the Enlightenment, the Age of Discovery, the Industrial Revolution and the European empires. The British Empire in particular, built roads, railways, canals, bridges, universities, schools, industry, agriculture, legal systems and law and order across what is known today as the Third World. Our empire, the largest in world history, lifted hundreds of millions of human beings from poverty and superstition and gave them civilisation. Democracy, technology, education, freedom, liberty and Christianity were spread to every corner of the earth. Our Greco-Roman and Judeo-Christian cultural heritage is the most beautiful, the most splendid, the most dazzling that has ever been conceived by humanity.

Britain is without doubt the most prodigious of all the nations of the West. This small kingdom led the field in many areas, including democracy, law, literature, inventions and the rights of the individual. Britain spread parliamentary democracy and our unique legal heritage across the globe. We are responsible for creating and building the nations of Australia, Canada, New Zealand and even the United States. The United States was founded by British colonists who took the innate yearning of our people for liberty, the rule of law and representative government to another level with the creation of the United States Constitution. Starting with the Magna Carta, through to the English Civil War, the Restoration, the Glorious Revolution and the development of constitutional monarchy, Britain has led the way in establishing the most benign systems of government known to man. When all of this is taken together, no other nation of the West can boast of such a mighty political, cultural, legal and democratic heritage. The English-speaking world that Churchill wrote about is the envy of all humanity.

In the late 1700s, left-wing thinking made its first appearance on the historical timeline with the French Revolution. The underlying ideology of the Revolution was republican and left-wing, pitting the 'people' against the monarchy and aristocracy. Even Christianity and the churches were vociferously attacked. Radical social change based on liberalism and other Enlightenment principles were imposed. The result was chaos and terror, similar in nature to the Bolshevik Revolution some 130 years later. Tens of thousands of innocent people were guillotined and hundreds of thousands arrested. Thankfully, this period of atrocity and chaos was eclipsed by the rise of Napoleon and his martial, imperial state.

A few decades later, a German Jew called Karl Mark and his associate Friedrich Engels published the Communist Manifesto and Das Kapital, which spawned the rise of socialism and communism. The short-lived Paris Commune of 1871 was the first socialist insurrection in history. However, the first major breakthrough for leftist ideology occurred in 1917, in the October Revolution which saw the dreaded Bolsheviks seize power in Russia. For the rest of the 20th Century, left-wing politics and ideology gradually gained in strength, augmented enormously with the victory of the Soviets in the Second World War. The so-called 'Cold War' was in fact a fraud. The socialist East and the capitalist West both pursued left-wing policies of multiculturalism, globalism, political correctness and social liberalism.

By the end of the 20th Century, the dominance of left-wing ideology was total and unchallenged across the media, education, politics and the social realm. While Sovict-style communism dominated in the East, in the West the 'Long march through the institutions' was taking place. This Marxist strategy - pioneered by the infamous 'Frankfurt School' - slowly but surely subjected the entire Western World to 'Cultural Marxism'. Cultural Marxism is otherwise known as 'political correctness', an insidious injection of communist policies, principles and thinking into all areas of society by left-wing activists. We are all familiar with the avenues of attack by Social Marxists: A never-ending witch-hunt against 'racism', the promotion of 'diversity', demonization of patriotism and national identity, LGBT advocacy, the sexualisation of the young, the unravelling of family values, the vilification of Christianity, the incessant character assassination of patriots and conservatives, media brainwashing and a continuous war on all aspects of our culture, customs, history and traditions. All of this was forcibly implemented in the Soviet Union and other communist tyrannies using the gun and the secret policeman. In the West, it is being implemented in the school, the college, the university, the newspaper, the radio and the TV.

The infestation of leftist thinking in all areas of life has been so successful that even political parties considered 'right-wing' pursue - or acquiesce to - left-wing political dogmas. Take, for example, the modern British Conservative Party. This supposedly right-wing and conservative - with a small 'c' - party is in fact a staunch champion of most of the major principles of left-wing ideology, such as open borders, political correctness, social liberalism, multiculturalism, big and intrusive government, high taxes, restrictions on free speech and much more. There is actually nothing 'conservative' about the modern Conservative Party. The modern Conservative Party in the UK is a toxic mixture of liberal and socialist policies. It is now innately a left-wing party. Every other major political party in the UK - Labour, the Liberal Democrats, the Green Party, the Scottish National Party, Plaid Cymru, the Respect Party and so on - are all left-wing when it comes to policy and ideology. There are no mainstream right-wing political parties in the UK, that's a fact.

The individuals and organisations that make up the 'political Right' in the modern era are demonised, subverted, censored, persecuted, harassed, attacked, mistreated, oppressed, victimised. This includes patriots, nationalists, conservatives and Christians. I am certain that if the establishment could get away with it, they would line us all up against a wall and shoot us in the back of the neck, or send us to the Gulags. At the moment, they don't have to, because oppression, demonization and harassment by the state is keeping all opposition to leftist policies firmly neutered in a box.

The political Right is only allowed to exist because of the total hegemony of left-wing policies. As soon as this hegemony is challenged or threatened, brutal repression will follow. This is what we are seeing in the modern era, starting with social media censorship and low-level persecution of the kind outlined in this book. Very soon the mask will completely slip and naked repression, internment and legislation will be imposed to stamp out dissent. Don't fool yourself with the lip-service paid to 'democracy' by modern politicians, we will soon be living in a communist police state. The Left will not allow itself to be usurped or supplanted by the Right. When they are forced to, they will suspend democracy and impose a police state. If you believe that the long traditions of democracy in our country are a safeguard against this prediction, you are a fool.

The death grip of the political Left on our civilisation is going to lead to its downfall. Starting immediately after the end of the Second World War, our leftist masters initiated a genocidal plan to open the borders of the West to mass immigration from the Third World. The political Left is internationalist and globalist in outlook and so it strives for the unification of mankind into a single sterile socialist culture and government. This is achieved with the eradication of individual cultures, nations, peoples and tribes and the creation, through enforced multiculturalism, of a universal society. This potty dream is, believe it or not, the driving force of the entire political Left.

Uncontrolled mass immigration has been proceeding for over seventy years now in the West and has led to the transformation of the ethnic, religious and cultural composition of dozens of ancient Western nations. The demographic trends are disturbing. Virtually all indigenous European peoples are due to become ethnic minorities within a few decades. These ancient indigenous peoples will largely disappear by the end of the century. Migrants are pouring into the West over porous borders by the millions. TV screens in the West have been saturated over the last few years with endless scenes of long columns of migrants heading towards the generous 'Soft Touch' welfare societies of Northern Europe.

Not assisting matters is the suicidally low birth rate among modern Europeans. From the Mediterranean to Scandinavia, fertility rates have hit rock-bottom, far below replacement levels. The promotion of feminism and liberal values among our youth has created a demographic crisis of apocalyptic proportions. Native populations in the West are declining rapidly. Family values, marriage and reproduction are being shunned in favour of hedonism, degeneracy, liberalism, abortion and sexual debauchery. In stark contrast, the birth rates among immigrant communities is sky-high, especially among Muslims. More than half of the babies being born in NHS wards are from immigrant communities. The population percentages in the West are shifting rapidly and inexorably towards the eradication of native populations.

Islam is now the fastest growing religion in Europe. Muslims now hold treacherous political elites across Europe to ransom, traitors who cosy up to Islamic communities in hope of attracting the bloc vote. Hundreds of thousands of young European girls are targeted by street-level Islamist grooming gangs. Scandals like Rotherham, Rochdale and Telford have shocked the nation. The West is subjected to never-ending Islamist terror attacks: Westminster Bridge, London Bridge, Manchester Arena, the Paris massacres, Charlie Hebdo, Nice, Berlin, Munich, Stockholm, St Petersburg Metro, 7/7, Madrid, Brussels Airport, Glasgow Airport, Lee Rigby, Sydney café siege, Orlando, San Bernardino, the Boston Marathon and on and on, endlessly. Over one hundred 'Sharia courts' operate with impunity in the UK alone. Mosques are sprouting up in every town and city across the West, funded by oil money from the Wahabi Gulf States.

In all Western nations, the influx of migrants and the transformation of our towns and cities into Islamist and immigrant ghettos is pushing native populations into the countryside, rural areas and coastal regions in a process the media describes as 'White Flight'. Christianity is in cataclysmic decline across Europe and many churches are being converted to mosques. Christianity has been sidelined in schools across Europe by the political Left. Engaging in celebrations of native culture, traditions and patriotism is strongly discouraged by the establishment and demonised by the media. British history is barely taught in the education system and young citizens leave school unaware of their own history and culture. Our national identity is suppressed and actively replaced by a rootless, globalist and socialist mindset which owes its allegiance to leftist dogmas such as 'diversity' and 'multiculturalism'.

Children across the West are being taught by leftist teachers that they can 'choose' their gender. LGBT indoctrination is being foisted on primary-age children. TV channels, celebrity gossip magazines and Hollywood films promote sexual promiscuity among our youth. Destructive feminism - which militates against marriage, family and childbirth - is being promoted relentlessly by the media. Family values are mocked and discouraged in favour of selfish liberalism. The social fabric of our ancient societies is being subverted by left-wing doctrines.

Politics is corrupt and filled to the brim with scoundrels who fiddle the taxpayer, break every promise they make and who ignore the will of the people on every front. Every winter, thousands of elderly pensioners freeze to death in their homes. Our treacherous government spends billions on foreign aid while thousands of veterans sleep rough. Our judiciary seems to care more about the rights of criminals than victims. Our Armed Forces are run down and cut to the bone, leaving our country dangerously exposed. Our public services are a national disgrace, barely keeping up with the standards found in Third World hellholes. Our people are taxed from every angle by greedy politicians to pay for a bloated and wasteful welfare state. Millions of our people are unemployed yet we allow a never-ending flood of cheap labour to pour into our country. The ever-increasing national debt we owe to the banks will shortly bankrupt our treasury.

Political correctness and the national obsession with 'racism' have consigned our people to being second-class citizens in our own land. Even the established Windrush Generation communities are deeply angry about the avalanche of migration and their own difficulties obtaining housing and jobs. Our prisons are dominated by aggressive and violent Islamist gangs who force inmates to convert. An estimated 23,000 wannabe jihadists and Islamic extremists walk the streets of our country, largely ignored by the police and intelligence services. Serious disparities are emerging between the constituent nations of the United Kingdom, leading to separatist sentiment. Scotland, Wales and Ulster have been given their own devolved parliaments yet England is denied its own representative governing body. Tuition fees and medical prescriptions are free in Scotland, Wales and Ulster, causing considerable resentment in England. After centuries of success, Unionism is crumbling and fading, thanks to this mismanagement.

It is hard to imagine how our country could be even more misgoverned than it is under the current regime. Our historic, ancient and prodigious nation is being deliberately dismantled. Do not think for one moment that this decline is accidental. It is the inevitable result of the failed left-wing policies pursued by successive waves of establishment politicians. What is facing our people and our nation is nothing short of total eradication from the face of the earth. If current trends continue, then Britain as we have always known it, will disappear, along with our people. It will be replaced by a vast concrete multicultural cesspit. Why anyone would want this is a mystery to me, but there is no shortage of left-wing activists and politicians spending their entire careers expending every ounce of strength they possess to achieve it. These zealots of the political Left are blinded and driven crazy by their globalist, multicultural vision of the future. They are more than happy to sacrifice the Western civilisation they hate to realise their ludicrous dream.

But, unfortunately for the Left, what lies before us is not a progressive and gradual march to a harmonious multicultural world society. The inevitable consequence of the present demographic trends is a bloody civil war which will claim the lives of countless millions. The rise of militant Islam, the proliferation of jihadi attacks, the never-ending influx of migrants, the expulsion of our people from our towns via 'White Flight', the persecution and oppression of patriotic Europeans, and so on, will very soon create a devastating and explosive conclusion to current leftist policies. In my humble opinion, what is brewing in Europe will soon spill over into violence and civil strife. It is inevitable and unstoppable. As Enoch Powell famously said, there will be 'Rivers of Blood'. It will be a ruinous and annihilative conflict that will devastate our continent from end to end.

I don't believe our people will walk gleefully towards dispossession and eradication without eventually putting up a huge fight to survive. At the present time, the vast majority of our people can go about their lives without too much inconvenience. As present trends accelerate, the consequences of current leftist policies will start to have a major impact on the daily lives of tens of millions of people. The problems will become too big to ignore. Then, and only then, will the Silent Majority swing into action. What will be needed when this 'critical mass' is reached is a robust, tough, uncompromising resistance movement. This movement will be the only refuge for our people as they confront their dark and terrible future. When looking back at the last decade of struggle, persecution, suffering and hardship, there cannot be any doubt that Britain First is the movement that will lead our people to freedom and save our country.

Our primary task over the next few decades is to survive all the establishment attempts to derail, infiltrate and destroy our movement. The worrying events described in this book are nothing but the tip of the iceberg. As the groundswell of patriotic discontent grows and swells during the upcoming election cycles, the left-wing police state I have predicted in this chapter will start to rear its ugly head with greater ferocity. What we have experienced so far will be a walk in the park compared to the horrors of the future. As leader of Britain First, I know I have an almost impossible job confronting me. I am fully aware that I will suffer greatly and be subjected to the most horrendous acts of sabotage and mistreatment. If you are shocked and disturbed by the details of my previous experiences at the hands of the establishment, then brace yourself for a major escalation in both the intensity and frequency of this persecution.

I am asked on a regular basis why I choose to shoulder this awful burden. The answer is brilliantly simple. I am an Englishman, born and bred, and I am conscious that there are millions of children in my country that deserve a future. Our children - and unborn future generations - are my encouragement and incentive for enduring the worst the establishment can throw at me. I consider it an honour and a privilege to be able to devote my life to the survival and future of my people. I am inspired by the example of my ancestors who displayed such heroic bravery in hundreds of conflicts to safeguard the inheritance that has been passed down to us. I would rather struggle and suffer as a patriot than live a prosperous life as a traitor. I would rather endure trials and tribulations than eke out an existence as a lemming who cares little for anything or anyone. I cannot remain silent while my country is raped and pillaged. If I must face adversity, heartache and misfortune by doing what is right, regardless of odds, then so be it. Doing the right thing is more important to me than living comfortably.

Many times throughout our long history, our civilisation has faced extermination. I have outlined most of these in this chapter. At the time of writing this book, we are already on our knees facing extinction. The West will soon disappear from the pages of history and the world will enter a new Dark Age. All the mighty achievements of Western civilisation I have mentioned above will be extinguished forever. There will be no coming back. Not only are we fighting for our children and grandchildren, we are fighting for the beautiful heritage of ten thousand years of tumultuous glory and progress. If we fail, all that we love and hold dear will perish for all eternity. We have a duty to a thousand generations of our people to honour and emulate their example, their sacrifice and their heroism. Likewise, a thousand unborn generations are depending on us to stand firm and fight for their futures.

We need staunch men and women who are willing to struggle and strive for the survival of our nation. There can be no place for cowardice, hesitation and faintheartedness in the years to come. We need a new breed of warrior to fight this battle, which is going to be terrible, on a scale never before witnessed by humanity. The Bible foretells the coming cataclysm, calling it Armageddon. Despite the horrendous persecution I have endured over the years, if there is to be a crusade to save our civilisation, I will be in the front line of the battle. May God and our Lord Jesus Christ strengthen our resolve and determination and grace us with victory against the evil that is engulfing our lives. Always remember, we are not alone. Watching over us are legions of mighty ancestors who are urging us to be worthy of their example. It is better to fight and to die than live on your knees as a slave and coward. 'Be strong, and let us fight bravely for our people and the cities of our God. The LORD will do what is good in his sight.'

Printed in Great Britain
by Amazon

87700378R00200